Papa

+

SUSAN

First published 2015 by
PALGRAVE

Palgrave in the UK is an imprint of Macmillan Publishers Limited, registered in England, company number 785998, of 4 Crinan Street, London, N1 9XW.

Palgrave Macmillan in the US is a division of St Martin's Press LLC, 175 Fifth Avenue, New York, NY 10010.

Palgrave is a global imprint of the above companies and is represented throughout the world.

Palgrave® and Macmillan® are registered trademarks in the United States, the United Kingdom, Europe and other countries.

ISBN: 978-1-137-54769-9 paperback

This book is printed on paper suitable for recycling and made from fully managed and sustained forest sources. Logging, pulping and manufacturing processes are expected to conform to the environmental regulations of the country of origin.

A catalogue record for this book is available from the British Library.

A catalog record for this book is available from the Library of Congress.

ZAGAT®

Seattle Restaurants 2012

LOCAL EDITOR
Alicia Comstock Arter

STAFF EDITOR
Carol Diuguid with Cynthia Kilian

Published and distributed by
Zagat Survey, LLC
4 Columbus Circle
New York, NY 10019
T: 212.977.6000
E: seattle@zagat.com
www.zagat.com

ACKNOWLEDGMENTS

We thank Geoff Litwin, Gail Miller, Nathan Myhrvold, Lei Ann Shiramizu and Mina Williams as well as the following members of our staff: Danielle Borovoy (assistant editor), Brian Albert, Sean Beachell, Maryanne Bertollo, Reni Chin, Larry Cohn, Nicole Diaz, Kelly Dobkin, Alison Flick, Jeff Freier, Matthew Hamm, Justin Hartung, Marc Henson, Ryutaro Ishikane, Rus Kehoe, Charles Koh, Natalie Lebert, Mike Liao, Mike Lima, Vivian Ma, James Mulcahy, Polina Paley, Amanda Spurlock, Chris Walsh, Jacqueline Wasilczyk, Sharon Yates, Anna Zappia and Kyle Zolner.

The reviews in this guide are based on public opinion surveys. The ratings reflect the average scores given by the survey participants who voted on each establishment. The text is based on quotes from, or paraphrasings of, the surveyors' comments. Phone numbers, addresses and other factual data were correct to the best of our knowledge when published in this guide.

Our guides are printed using environmentally preferable inks containing 20%, by weight, renewable resources on papers sourced from well-managed forests. Deluxe editions are covered with Skivertex Recover® Double containing a minimum of 30% post-consumer waste fiber.

ISBN-13: 978-1-60478-412-1
ISBN-10: 1-60478-412-1
Printed in the
United States of America

Contents

Ratings & Symbols

Zagat Top Spot	Name	Symbols	Cuisine	Zagat Ratings: FOOD	DECOR	SERVICE	COST
Z	Tim & Nina's	◐	*Pacific NW*	▽ 23	9	13	$150

Area, Address & Contact

Pike Place Market | 999 Pike Pl. (1st Ave.) | 206-555-6000 | www.zagat.com

Review, surveyor comments in quotes

Surveyors "keep the anoraks on" to dodge the drips at this "leaky" Pike Place Market fisherman's shack known for its "signature mix" of Southern Italian and Northwest cuisines (think hamachi antipasti) based on Captain T's catch of the day; prices are "pay-what-you-weigh" - even though you usually have to serve yourself while ducking to avoid the flying fish.

Ratings

Food, Decor & **Service** are rated on a 30-point scale.

- 0 - 9 poor to fair
- 10 - 15 fair to good
- 16 - 19 good to very good
- 20 - 25 very good to excellent
- 26 - 30 extraordinary to perfection
- ▽ low response | less reliable

Cost

The price of dinner with a drink and tip; lunch is usually 25% to 30% less. For unrated **newcomers** or **write-ins,** the price range is as follows:

- I $25 and below
- M $26 to $40
- E $41 to $65
- VE $66 or above

Symbols

- Z highest ratings, popularity and importance
- ◐ serves after 11 PM
- S closed Sunday
- M closed Monday
- no credit cards accepted

About This Survey

This **2012 Seattle Restaurants Survey** is an update reflecting significant developments since our last Survey was published. It covers 854 restaurants in the Seattle area, including 47 important additions. We've also indicated new addresses, phone numbers and other major changes, and we've added a foldout map to the back of the book. Like all our guides, this one is based on input from avid local consumers - 2,970 all told. Our editors have synopsized this feedback, highlighting representative comments (in quotation marks within each review). To read full surveyor comments - and share your own opinions - visit **ZAGAT.com,** where you will also find the latest restaurant news, special events, deals, reservations, menus, photos and more, **all for free.**

ABOUT ZAGAT: In 1979, we started asking friends to rate and review restaurants purely for fun. The term "user-generated content" had yet to be coined. That hobby grew into Zagat Survey; 33 years later, we have over 375,000 surveyors and cover airlines, bars, dining, fast food, entertaining, golf, hotels, movies, music, resorts, shopping, spas, theater and tourist attractions in over 100 countries. Along the way, we evolved from being a print publisher to a digital content provider, e.g. **ZAGAT.com** and **Zagat To Go** mobile apps (for iPad, iPhone, Android, BlackBerry, Windows Phone 7 and Palm webOS). We also produce marketing tools for a wide range of blue-chip corporate clients. And you can find us on Google+ and just about any other social media network.

UNDERLYING PREMISES: Three simple ideas underlie our ratings and reviews. First, we believe that the collective opinions of large numbers of consumers are more accurate than those of any single person. (Consider that our surveyors bring some 448,000 annual meals' worth of experience to this survey, visiting restaurants regularly year-round, anonymously - and on their own dime.) Second, food quality is only part of the equation when choosing a restaurant, thus we ask our surveyors to rate food, decor and service separately and then report on cost. Third, since people need reliable information in an easy-to-digest, curated format, we strive to be concise and we offer our content on every platform - print, online and mobile. Our Top Ratings lists (pages 8-15) and indexes (starting on page 134) are also designed to help you quickly choose the best place for any occasion, be it for business or pleasure.

THANKS: We're grateful to our local editor, Alicia Comstock Arter, an editor and blogger who covers the greater Seattle dining scene. Thank you. We also sincerely thank the thousands of people who participated in this survey - this guide is really "theirs."

JOIN IN: To improve our guides, we solicit your comments - positive or negative; it's vital that we hear your opinions. Just contact us at **nina-tim@zagat.com.** We also invite you to join our surveys at **ZAGAT.com.** Do so and you'll receive a choice of rewards in exchange.

New York, NY
December 21, 2011

Nina and Tim Zagat

What's New

Seattle restaurateurs are keeping their eyes on the economy this year, rolling out eateries mostly in the low-to-moderate price range, while continuing to lure wallet-conscious diners with budget-friendly happy hours, and relying on social media to create a stir and fill seats.

KEEPING IT COMFY: Perhaps also befitting the times, fancied-up American comfort food - often showcasing just-off-the-farm ingredients and a few taste twists - remains the leading cuisine trend. Among the latest are Belltown's **Coterie Room** and **Local 360, Hitchcock** on Bainbridge Island, Queene Anne's **Lloyd Martin** and Cormac Mahoney's **Madison Park Conservatory.** Meanwhile, breathing new life into the deli genre with their housemade charcuterie were **Dot's Delicatessen** in Fremont and Mercer Island's **Stopsky's Deli.**

NEXT-GENERATION ASIAN: Some arrivals don't mind getting crazy with flavor, including sushi innovators **Japonessa Cucina** in Pike Place and Capitol Hill's **Momiji,** Fremont's nouveau Korean **Revel,** ID's Chinese-Korean mashup **Red Lantern,** Capitol Hill Vietnamese street-fooder **Ba Bar** and Bellevue Chinese **Din Tai Fung.**

MOVING TARGET: The food truck craze rolls on with newcomers **Buns** (burgers) and **Molly Moon** (ice cream), while two vehicles have parlayed their popularity into brick and mortar: comfort-fooder **Skillet** and Korean-Hawaiian fave **Marination Mobile** have both begat Capitol Hill cafes. Pop-up eateries - open once a week, once a month or intermittently in an established restaurant's space - have also mushroomed, to wit **La Bête**'s Little Uncle, **Madison Park Conservatory**'s Tako Truk, **Mistral Kitchen**'s Arabesque, **Volunteer Park Cafe**'s Savage Street Cuisine, plus themed nights at **Rub with Love Shack** and **Sitka & Spruce.**

HOT ZONES: Capitol Hill continues to draw hip young things to hot spots like the upscale Italian **Altura,** Mexican **Poquitos,** Tamara Murphy's **Terra Plata**, a new branch of **Thai Curry Simple,** as well as Ba Bar and Momiji. Meanwhile, restaurateur Tom Douglas has been busy in South Lake Union, debuting four eateries aimed at the area's office workers: the burger bastion **Brave Horse Tavern,** pasta place **Cuoco,** Southerner **Serious Biscuit** and Tibetan **Ting Momo.**

UP NEXT: Powerhouse chef Ethan Stowell (**Anchovies & Olives, Tavolàta,** etc.) has five new quick-eats spots in the pipeline with single themes of fried chicken, burgers and hot dogs, fish 'n' chips, pizza and sandwiches. Charles Walpole (ex Anchovies & Olives) plans **Blind Pig Bistro** in Eastlake; Greg Atkinson (ex **Canlis**) will unveil the Bainbridge Islander **Marche**; the **Black Bottle** gang is at work on **Innkeeper** in Belltown; **Restaurant Zoe** plans its return on Capitol Hill; and chef Peter Birk (ex **Ray's Boathouse**) is headed for the upcoming **McCormick & Schmick's Harborside** on South Lake Union.

Seattle, WA
December 21, 2011

Alicia Comstock Arter

Most Popular

This list is plotted on the map at the back of the book.

1. Wild Ginger | *Pacific Rim*
2. Dahlia Lounge | *Pacific NW*
3. Canlis | *Pacific NW*
4. Cafe Juanita | *Italian*
5. Rover's | *French*
6. Metropolitan Grill | *Steak*
7. Cafe Campagne | *French*
8. Etta's | *Pacific NW/Seafood*
9. Ray's Boathouse | *Pac. NW/Sea.*
10. Serious Pie | *Pizza*
11. Bakery Nouveau | *Bakery/French*
12. Anthony's HomePort | *Pac. NW*
13. Il Terrazzo Carmine | *Italian*
14. Herbfarm | *Pacific NW*
15. Matt's in Market | *Pac. NW/Sea.*
16. El Gaucho | *Steak*
17. Seastar | *Seafood*
18. Tilth | *American*
19. Lola | *Greek*
20. Barking Frog | *Pacific NW*
21. Lark* | *American*
22. Jak's Grill | *Steak*
23. Salumi | *Italian/Sandwiches*
24. Daniel's Broiler | *Steak*
25. Elliott's Oyster Hse. | *Seafood*
26. Crush | *American*
27. Steelhead Diner | *Pacific NW*
28. Cactus | *Mexican/SW*
29. Purple Café/Wine | *Pacific NW*
30. Ruth's Chris | *Steak*
31. 13 Coins | *Italian*
32. Flying Fish | *Eclectic/Seafood*
33. Palace Kitchen | *American*
34. McCormick/Schmick | *Seafood*
35. Nishino* | *Japanese*
36. Le Pichet | *French*
37. Poppy | *American*
38. La Carta de Oaxaca | *Mexican*
39. Harvest Vine | *Spanish*
40. Monsoon | *Vietnamese*

Many of the above are among Seattle's most expensive eateries, but if popularity were calibrated to price, a number of others would surely join their ranks. To illustrate this, we list Best Buys starting on page 14.

Key Newcomers

Our editors' picks among this year's arrivals. See full list at p. 159.

Altura | *Italian* | Swank, up-to-the-minute Capitol Hiller feels old-school

Bar del Corso | *Italian* | Instant local hit in the old Beacon Hill Pub digs

Brave Horse Tavern | *American* | Playroom for the techie set

Coterie Room | *American* | Artfully reimagined classics in Belltown

Din Tai Fung | *Chinese* | Soup dumplings for Bellevue hipsters

Japonessa Cucina | *Japanese* | Billy Beach hot spot for glammed-up sushi

Lloyd Martin | *American* | Old-fashioned is new again in Queen Anne

Madison Park Conservatory | *American* | Clubby Cormac Mahoney venue

Momiji | *Japanese* | Sushi and kaiseki for Capitol Hill scenesters

Revel | *American/Korean* | Updated Korean comfort cooking in Fremont

Serious Biscuit | *Southern* | Biscuits get the Tom Douglas treatment

Terra Plata | *American* | Tamara Murphy does it again in Capitol Hill

* Indicates a tie with restaurant above

Top Food

28 Cafe Juanita | *Italian*
Paseo | *Caribbean*
Mashiko | *Japanese*
Spinasse | *Italian*
Herbfarm | *Pacific NW*
Rover's | *French*
Corson Building | *Eclectic*
Tilth | *American*

27 Nishino | *Japanese*
Kisaku Sushi | *Japanese*
Lark | *American*
Shiro's Sushi* | *Japanese*
La Carta/Mezcaleria | *Mex.*
Harvest Vine | *Spanish*
Il Terrazzo Carmine | *Italian*
Cantinetta | *Italian*
Boat St. Cafe | *French*
Salumi | *Italian/Sandwiches*
Nell's | *American*
Canlis | *Pacific NW*
Green Leaf | *Vietnamese*
La Medusa | *Italian/Med.*
Marination | *Hawaiian/Korean*

26 Mistral Kitchen | *American*
Bistro Turkuaz | *Turkish*
Tropea* | *Italian*
Pair | *American/Med.*
Tosoni's | *Continental*
Four Swallows | *Ital./Pac. NW*
Cafe Lago | *Italian*
Serious Pie | *Pizza*
Delancey | *Pizza*
Inn at Langley | *Pacific NW*
Le Gourmand | *French*
Olivar | *Spanish*
Metropolitan Grill | *Steak*
Dahlia Lounge | *Pacific NW*
Chez Shea/Lounge | *Fr./Pac. NW*
Señor Moose Café | *Mexican*
Med. Kitchen | *Lebanese/Med.*

BY CUISINE

AMERICAN (NEW)

28 Tilth
27 Lark
Nell's
26 Mistral Kitchen
Pair

AMERICAN (TRAD.)

25 Volunteer Park Cafe
Glo's
Dish
24 Geraldine's Counter
23 Ezell's

BBQ/SOUL

26 Pecos Pit BBQ
24 Kingfish
Pig Iron Bar-B-Q
22 Frontier Room
21 Jones BBQ

BURGERS

24 Red Mill Burgers
Lunchbox Lab
23 Zippy's
22 Elliott Bay
Two Bells B&G

CHINESE/TAIWANESE

26 Facing East
25 Bamboo Garden Szechuan
24 Shanghai Garden
Kau Kau BBQ
Fu Man Dumpling

DELIS/SANDWICHES

27 Salumi
24 Baguette Box
Three Girls Bakery
23 Smarty Pants
Bagel Oasis

DESSERTS

29 Cafe Besalu
Bakery Nouveau
27 Gelatiamo
25 Macrina
24 Le Panier

ECLECTIC

28 Corson Building
26 Sitka & Spruce
Joule
Elemental@Gasworks
25 Marjorie

Excludes places with low votes, unless otherwise indicated. Top Food excludes bakeries/dessert spots. For Tacoma Top Food, see page 11.

FRENCH

28 Rover's
27 Boat St. Cafe
26 Le Gourmand
Chez Shea/Lounge
Cafe Campagne

GREEK

25 Lola
22 Panos Kleftiko
Vios Cafe
18 Costa's
Costas Opa

ITALIAN

28 Cafe Juanita
Spinasse
27 Il Terrazzo Carmine
Cantinetta
26 Tropea

JAPANESE

28 Mashiko
27 Nishino
Kisaku Sushi
Shiro's Sushi
26 Toyoda Sushi

MEDITERRANEAN

27 La Medusa
26 Pair
Med. Kitchen
24 Andaluca
How To Cook A Wolf

MEXICAN

27 La Carta/Mezcaleria
26 Señor Moose Café
24 Ooba's Mexican Grill
Rancho Bravo
23 Agua Verde

PACIFIC NORTHWEST

28 Herbfarm
27 Canlis
26 Four Swallows
Inn at Langley
Dahlia Lounge

PAC. RIM/PAN-ASIAN

25 Wild Ginger
24 Lee's Asian
20 Chinoise
19 Dragonfish

PIZZA

26 Serious Pie
Delancey
25 Veraci Pizza
23 Flying Squirrel
Via Tribunali*

SEAFOOD

25 Matt's in Market
Oyster Bar/Chuckanut Dr.
Seastar
Aqua
Anchovies & Olives

STEAKHOUSES

26 Metropolitan Grill
25 Morton's
El Gaucho
John Howie Steak
24 Daniel's Broiler

THAI

26 Buddha Ruksa
25 Chantanee
Bahn Thai
Thai Tom*
Bai Pai Fine Thai

VEGETARIAN

25 Plum Vegan Bistro
24 Sutra∇
23 Cafe Flora
20 Bamboo Garden Vegetarian
19 Chaco Canyon Café∇

VIETNAMESE

27 Green Leaf
25 Tamarind Tree
Monsoon
22 Pho Thân Bros.
Pho Cyclo Café

BY SPECIAL FEATURE

BREAKFAST

26 Georgian
25 Macrina
Glo's
Dish
24 Geraldine's Counter

BRUNCH

28 Tilth
26 Señor Moose Café
Cafe Campagne
25 Macrina
Lola

HOTEL DINING

26 Inn at Langley
Georgian (Fairmont)
25 Lola (Andra)
Barking Frog (Willows)
Tulio (Vintage Park)

LATE DINING

26 Elemental@Gasworks
25 Umi Sake House
Lola
Aqua
Le Pichet

MEET FOR A DRINK

26 Mistral Kitchen
Four Swallows
Serious Pie
Olivar
Metropolitan Grill

OFFBEAT

28 Mashiko
23 Zippy's
22 Pink Door
21 'Ohana
Dixie's BBQ

PEOPLE-WATCHING

28 Spinasse
Corson Building
27 Il Terrazzo Carmine
26 Mistral Kitchen
Serious Pie

POWER SCENES

28 Rover's
27 Il Terrazzo Carmine
Canlis
26 Mistral Kitchen
Pacific Grill

RAW BARS

25 Seastar
Aqua
Monsoon East
24 Elliott's Oyster Hse.
Brooklyn Seafood

SINGLES SCENES

26 Metropolitan Grill
25 Lola
Wild Ginger
Le Pichet
Palace Kitchen

TRENDY

28 Corson Building
Tilth
27 La Carta/Mezcaleria
Salumi
Marination

WINNING WINE LISTS

28 Cafe Juanita
Herbfarm
Rover's
Corson Building
27 Harvest Vine

WORTH A TRIP

28 Herbfarm (Woodinville)
26 Four Swallows (Bainbridge Is)
Inn at Langley (Langley)
Pacific Grill (Tacoma)
25 Oyster Bar/Chuckanut (Bow)

BY LOCATION

BALLARD/SHILSHOLE

29 Cafe Besalu
28 Paseo
27 La Carta/Mezcaleria
26 Delancey
Le Gourmand

BELLEVUE

27 Cantinetta
26 Tosoni's
Med. Kitchen
Facing East
25 Flo

BELLTOWN

27 Shiro's Sushi
25 Umi Sake House
Macrina
Bisato
El Gaucho

CAPITOL HILL

28 Spinasse
27 Lark
26 Olivar
Sitka & Spruce
25 Marjorie

DOWNTOWN

27 Gelatiamo
26 Serious Pie
Metropolitan Grill
Dahlia Lounge
Georgian

EASTLAKE/LAKE UNION

- 27 Canlis
- 26 Elemental@Gasworks
- 25 Serafina
- 23 Cicchetti
- 21 Ivar's Salmon House

FREMONT/ WALLINGFORD

- 28 Paseo
- Tilth
- 27 Cantinetta
- 26 Joule
- 25 Art of the Table

GREEN LAKE/ GREENWOOD/ PHINNEY RIDGE

- 27 Kisaku Sushi
- Nell's
- 26 Eva
- 25 Carmelita
- 24 Red Mill Burgers

INTERNATIONAL DIST.

- 27 Green Leaf
- 25 Tamarind Tree
- Maneki
- 24 Shanghai Garden
- Kau Kau BBQ

KIRKLAND

- 28 Cafe Juanita
- 26 Med. Kitchen
- 25 Lynn's Bistro
- 24 Izumi
- 22 Trellis

MADISON PARK/ MADISON VALLEY

- 28 Rover's
- 27 Nishino
- Harvest Vine
- 25 Crush
- Luc

PIKE PLACE MARKET

- 26 Chez Shea/Lounge
- Cafe Campagne
- 25 Matt's in Market
- Beecher's Cheese
- Le Pichet

PIONEER SQ./SODO

- 27 Il Terrazzo Carmine
- Salumi
- 26 Pecos Pit BBQ
- 25 Macrina
- 24 Al Boccalino

QUEEN ANNE

- 27 Boat St. Cafe
- 25 Crow
- Macrina
- Bahn Thai
- Portage

REDMOND

- 26 Tropea
- 25 Pomegranate Bistro
- 24 Bai Tong
- Ooba's Mexican Grill
- 22 Typhoon!

SEATTLE WATERFRONT

- 25 Aqua
- 24 Elliott's Oyster Hse.
- 23 Bell St. Diner
- Six Seven
- 22 Anthony's Pier 66

SOUTH LAKE UNION

- 26 Mistral Kitchen
- 25 Seastar
- 24 Daniel's Broiler
- Flying Fish
- 23 Chandler's Crabhouse

TACOMA

- 26 Pacific Grill
- 25 Indochine Asian
- El Gaucho
- 23 Dash Pt./Lobster Shop
- 22 Pho Thân Brothers

WEST SEATTLE

- 29 Bakery Nouveau
- 28 Mashiko
- 26 Buddha Ruksa
- 25 Spring Hill
- 24 Jak's Grill

Top Decor

28 Georgian
Canlis

27 Palisade
SkyCity
Salish Lodge

26 Six Seven
Aqua
Herbfarm

25 Calcutta Grill
Olivar
Il Terrazzo Carmine
Moshi Moshi*
Rover's
Four Swallows
Place Pigalle
Art Restaurant
Inn at Langley
Hunt Club

24 Ray's Boathouse
Dahlia Lounge
Bastille Café & Bar
Thaiku
Oyster Bar/Chuckanut Dr.
El Gaucho
Barolo Ristorante
Cafe Juanita
Indochine Asian
Andaluca
Chandler's Crabhouse
John Howie Steak
Mistral Kitchen
Metropolitan Grill

23 Barking Frog
Corson Building
Umi Sake House
Seastar
Ponti Seafood Grill
Wild Ginger
Daniel's Broiler
Sip at the Wine Bar

OUTDOORS

Agua Verde
Bastille Café & Bar
El Camino
Flying Fish
Il Terrazzo Carmine
Nell's
Pink Door
Purple Café/Wine
Rist. Paradiso
Terra Plata

ROMANCE

Bis on Main
Boat St. Cafe
Book Bindery
Cafe Campagne
Cafe Juanita
Chez Shea/Lounge
Herbfarm
Pink Door
Portage
Rover's

ROOMS

Art Restaurant
Barolo
Canlis
Georgian
Herbfarm
John Howie Steak
Palisade
Salish Lodge
Six Seven
SkyCity

VIEWS

Aqua
Anthony's Pier 66
Beach Cafe
Canlis
Chandler's Crabhouse
Chinook's/Salmon Bay
Daniel's Broiler
Place Pigalle
Ray's Boathouse
Salty's
Six Seven
SkyCity

Top Service

28 Herbfarm

27 Canlis
Cafe Juanita
Rover's

26 Georgian
Il Terrazzo Carmine
Corson Building
Four Swallows

25 Bistro Turkuaz
Nell's
Metropolitan Grill
Morton's
Le Gourmand
Hunt Club
Bisato
Aqua
Palisade
Dahlia Lounge
Tilth
Nishino
Lark
Tropea

24 Chez Shea/Lounge
Capital Grille
El Gaucho
John Howie Steak
Art of the Table
Crow
Al Boccalino
Boat St. Cafe
Oyster Bar/Chuckanut Dr.
St. Clouds
Olivar
Mistral Kitchen
Perché No Pasta
Art Restaurant
Barking Frog
Crush
Place Pigalle
Daniel's Broiler

Best Buys

Everyone loves a bargain, and Seattle offers plenty of them. All-you-can-eat options are mostly for lunch and/or brunch. For prix fixe menus, call ahead for availability.

ALL YOU CAN EAT

23 India Bistro
Mayuri
22 Pabla
Habesha Ethiopian▽
21 Ivar's Salmon House
Roti Cuisine of India▽
Anthony's HomePort

CHEAP DATES

28 Paseo
27 Kisaku Sushi
La Carta/Mezcaleria
Green Leaf
26 Serious Pie
Delancey
Chez Shea/Lounge
Señor Moose Café
Med. Kitchen
Toyoda Sushi

CHILD-FRIENDLY

25 Plum Vegan Bistro
23 Pagliacci Pizza
22 Tutta Bella
Maltby Cafe
Vios Cafe
21 Gordito's
Chinook's/Salmon Bay
Original Pancake House
5 Spot
I Love NY Deli
Catfish Corner
Counter

EARLY-BIRD DINNER

24 Palisade
23 Bell St. Diner
Dash Pt./Lobster Shop
21 Ivar's Mukilteo
Anthony's HomePort
20 Salty's
Palomino

FAMILY-STYLE

28 Spinasse
Corson Building
25 Lola
Wild Ginger
Monsoon
23 Il Bistro
21 Jones BBQ
Alibi

HOT HAPPY HOURS

26 Serious Pie
25 Lola
John Howie Steak
24 Daniel's Broiler
23 Art Restaurant
Toulouse Petit
22 Pearl
Peso's Kitchen
20 Boka Kitchen
17 Joey

PUB FOOD

22 Elliott Bay
Brouwer's
Two Bells B&G
21 74th St. Ale House
20 Barking Dog
19 Columbia City Ale
Circa
17 Buckley's

PRIX FIXE DINNER (UNDER $40)

26 Cafe Campagne
23 Osteria La Spiga
21 Voilà! Bistrot
Queen City Grill
Marrakesh Moroccan▽
20 Purple Café/Wine
19 Chanterelle Specialty▽
Brasserie Margaux

QUICK BITES

29 Bakery Nouveau
28 Paseo
27 Salumi
Green Leaf
26 Serious Pie
Olivar
Pecos Pit BBQ
25 Crow

BEST BUYS: BANG FOR THE BUCK

In order of Bang for the Buck rating.

1. Gelatiamo
2. Uptown Espresso
3. Dick's Drive-In
4. Cafe Besalu
5. Bakery Nouveau
6. Crumpet Shop
7. Matt's Famous Chili Dogs
8. Marination Mobile
9. Piroshky Piroshky
10. Pecos Pit BBQ
11. Le Panier
12. Rancho Bravo
13. Three Girls Bakery
14. Pho Thân Bros.
15. Zippy's
16. Belle Pastry
17. Bakeman's
18. Paseo
19. Beecher's Cheese
20. Noah's Bagels
21. Red Mill Burgers
22. Ooba's Mexican Grill
23. Baguette Box
24. Macrina
25. Belle Epicurean
26. Alki Bakery
27. Kidd Valley
28. Mae Phim Thai
29. Essential Baking Co.
30. Jack's Fish Spot
31. Ezell's
32. Pho Cyclo Café
33. Gordito's
34. Honey Bear Bakery
35. Mike's Noodle House
36. Smarty Pants
37. Geraldine's Counter
38. Dish
39. Salumi
40. Bagel Oasis

BEST BUYS: OTHER GOOD VALUES

Agua Verde
Bahn Thai
Bamboo Garden Szechuan
Buns
Catfish Corner
Delfino's Pizza
Dilettante
Dixie's BBQ
Dot's Deli
El Camion
Elliott Bay Café
El Puerco Lloron
Facing East
5 Point Café
Fu Man Dumpling
Gilbert's/Bagel
Green Leaf
Hattie's Hat
Hi Spot Cafe
Hue Ky Mi Gia
Jalisco
Jones BBQ
Le Fournil
Lemongrass
Lockspot Cafe
Luisa's Mexican Grill
Luna Park Cafe
Malena's Taco Shop
Maltby Cafe
Monkey Bridge
Original Pancake House
Pagliacci Pizza
Plum Vegan Bistro
Rub With Love Shack
Serious Biscuit
611 Supreme
Skillet
Stellar Pizza
Stopsky's Deli
Tacos Guaymas
Thai Curry Simple
Thaiku
Thai Tom
3 Pigs BBQ
Uneeda Burger
Veraci Pizza
Wheeler Street Kitchen
Where Ya At Matt

RESTAURANT DIRECTORY

	FOOD	DECOR	SERVICE	COST

Abbondanza Pizzeria *Pizza* 19 | 14 | 21 | $21

West Seattle | 6503 California Ave. SW (Fauntleroy Way) | 206-935-8989
"You go for the pizza, not the decor" at this family-owned West Seattle "neighborhood Italian" where an amiable staff delivers "reasonably priced" "East Coast-style" pies, calzones and "basic pasta dishes"; locals "bring the kids", and homebodies like it "for takeout."

Adriatic Grill *Italian* - | - | - | M

Tacoma | 4201 S. Steele St. (Tacoma Mall Blvd.) | 253-475-6000 | www.adriaticgrill.com
This midpriced Italian near Tacoma Mall turns out fare made with "high-quality ingredients", including some "inventive options" and pizzas from a wood-fired oven; the big, bright room suits families and large parties, and the staff is "eager to please."

Agua Verde Cafe & Paddle Club ☒ *Mexican* 23 | 17 | 15 | $17

University District | 1303 NE Boat St. (Brooklyn Ave.) | 206-545-8570 | www.aguaverde.com
Located above a kayak rental store, this UD Baja-style Mexican offers "delicious fish tacos" and "killer margaritas" in a "low-budget", brightly painted spot with an "awesome view" of Portage Bay; though the "line down the sidewalk" can be "intimidating", the service is "fast and friendly", so the wait isn't too long - and the price "can't be beat."

Al Boccalino *Italian* 24 | 22 | 24 | $38

Pioneer Square | 1 Yesler Way (Western Ave.) | 206-622-7688
"Exuberant" chef-owner Luigi DeNunzio turns out Italian classics at this "unpretentious" ristorante located in an old brick Pioneer Square building; the "snug little corner" setting feels cozy and "romantic", and "reasonable" prices and a "low-key" staff add to the "welcoming" vibe.

Alibi Room *Pizza* 21 | 19 | 19 | $22

Pike Place Market | 85 Pike St. (1st Ave.) | 206-623-3180 | www.seattlealibi.com
One of the "secret spots" in Pike Place Market where hip locals dodge the tourist "hustle and bustle", this "hideaway" opposite the "gross-out" Gum Wall offers an affordable menu of "mostly pizzas" featuring "thin crusts" and a "wide variety" of classic and nontraditional toppings; a "friendly" staff and "sassy bartenders" keep the vibe "cool", and there are Friday and Saturday dance DJs in the lower-level lounge.

Alki Bakery ☒ *Bakery* 21 | 15 | 17 | $14

Georgetown | 5700 First Ave. S. (Orcas St.) | 206-762-5700
Kent | 20809 72nd Ave. S. (208th St.) | 253-867-5700
www.alkibakery.com
With a "thumbs-up" for their "fresh" sandwiches, pastries and "fantastic cookies", this affordable American bakery/cafe duo shines for breakfast and lunch; some call the service "lackluster", but they're good choices for their industrial park locations.

	FOOD	DECOR	SERVICE	COST

Allium *Pacific NW* | - | - | - | M |

Eastsound | 310 Main St. (bet. N. Beach Rd. & Prune Alley) | 360-376-4904 | www.alliumonorcas.com

Ferry riders make the relaxing trip to Orcas Island for chef Lisa Nakamura's sophisticated, well-priced Pacific NW plates crafted with urbane ingredients and skills she perfected at the French Laundry and The Herbfarm; located in the redone former Christina's space, it glows with antiques and happy conversations as diners gaze over the sea views of East Sound; P.S. the adjoining Lily offers soup, snacks and ice cream.

All-Purpose Pizza & Ale *Pizza* | ▽ 22 | 15 | 19 | $18 |

Leschi | 2901 S. Jackson St. (29th Ave.) | 206-324-8646 | www.allpurposepizza.com

This Leschi pizzeria is "set apart" from others by its "amazing sourdough crust" and other "zesty" fare including pasta, all at reasonable prices; parents give it "bonus points" for its "play-space for little ones" that's "complete with fresh dough", and everyone likes the "delivery" option in the underserved neighborhood.

NEW **Altura** S M *Italian* | - | - | - | E |

Capitol Hill | 617 Broadway E. (bet. Mercer & Roy Sts.) | 206-402-6749 | www.alturarestaurant.com

Capitol Hill's splurgy new Italian lures stylish diners with rich, up-to-the-minute dishes made from quality local ingredients, offered in prix fixe menus or à la carte; the fun, date-worthy space goes for a been-here-since-1800 look, with framed lace (albeit lace with reptilian figures), old-world furniture and an enormous plaster church angel overlooking the room - though the open kitchen with dining counter is a decidedly up-to-date touch.

Americana M *American* **(fka Table 219)** | ▽ 20 | 16 | 21 | $26 |

Capitol Hill | 219 Broadway E. (bet. John & Thomas Sts.) | 206-328-4604 | www.table219.com

Broadway diners think of this midpriced American bistro as an "old friend" with its comfort food such as chicken andouille sausage corndogs; brunch is served Friday-Sunday, and the cozy digs and "welcoming staff" make it easy to settle in for a chatty date or a get-together with friends; P.S. its name changed recently (post-Survey) when its chef became the new owner.

Anchovies & Olives *Italian/Seafood* | 25 | 20 | 21 | $43 |

Capitol Hill | 1550 15th Ave. (Pine St.) | 206-838-8080 | www.ethanstowellrestaurants.com

Ethan Stowell's Italian seafooder in Capitol Hill gets kudos for "amazing-quality fish, expertly prepared", including "raw small plates" like "standout" crudo and "oysters at their finest", dispensed by a "relaxed" crew; the budget-minded find it "a little expensive", but diehards swear they'd go "even if all they served was anchovies and olives."

	FOOD	DECOR	SERVICE	COST

Andaluca *Mediterranean* 24 | 24 | 24 | $41

Downtown | Mayflower Park Hotel | 407 Olive Way (4th Ave.) | 206-382-6999 | www.andaluca.com

Chef Wayne Johnson "really knows" how to inject "Spanish flair" into the tapas, paellas and dishes such as Cabrales-crusted beef tenderloin that "delight" with "subtle, unexpected" flavors at this Mediterranean in Downtown's Mayflower Park Hotel; the "charming, intimate" room filled with rich woods and murals and navigated by a "warm, efficient" staff is as much a "favorite" for a "shopper's stop" as for a "romantic dinner" - and even the "price points are on target."

Z **Anthony's HomePort** *Pacific NW/Seafood* 21 | 21 | 21 | $34

Shilshole | 6135 Seaview Ave. NW (near Shilshole Marina) | 206-783-0780
Kirkland | Moss Bay Marina | 135 Lake St. S. (Kirkland Ave.) | 425-822-0225
Des Moines | Des Moines Marina | 421 S. 227th St. (Marine View Dr.) | 206-824-1947
Edmonds | Edmonds Marina | 456 Admiral Way (Dayton St.) | 425-771-4400
Everett | Everett Marina Vill. | 1726 W. Marine View Dr. (18th St.) | 425-252-3333
Tacoma | 5910 N. Waterfront Dr. (bet. Pearl St. & Vashon Ferry Dock) | 253-752-9700
Gig Harbor | 8827 N. Harborview Dr. (Stinson Dr.) | 253-853-6353
Bellingham | Squalicum Harbor Marina | 25 Bellwether Way (Roeder Ave.) | 360-647-5588
Olympia | Marina | 704 Columbia St. NW (Market St.) | 360-357-9700
SeaTac | Sea-Tac Airport | 17801 Pacific Hwy. S. (bet. 176th & 180th Sts.) | 206-431-3000
www.anthonys.com
Additional locations throughout the Seattle area

These "quintessential Pacific Northwest" seafooders specialize in "fresh", wild fish and shellfish served in settings "on the water" so diners can "watch the passing boats"; though some say that the menu and "old-school" decor need "an update", service is mostly "prompt" and "personable" - and penny-pinchers reel in savings with "happy-hour" and "sunset specials."

Anthony's Pier 66 *Pacific NW/Seafood* 22 | 23 | 21 | $38

Seattle Waterfront | Pier 66 | 2201 Alaskan Way (Wall St.) | 206-448-6688 | www.anthonys.com

"Fresh, well-prepared" Pacific NW seafood is "first-class" and moderately priced at this "upscale" Waterfront link in the local Anthony's chain with a "beautiful harbor view" that just "oozes Seattle"; "relaxing" and "resort-y", it's a favorite for taking "out-of-town guests" where "tourists are treated like locals" by a "caring" staff.

Aoki Japanese Grill & Sushi Bar M *Japanese* 20 | 16 | 19 | $26

Capitol Hill | 621 Broadway E. (Roy St.) | 206-324-3633

"Fine-quality" sushi, sukiyaki and robata at relatively gentle prices are the signature of this Japanese "favorite" on Capitol Hill's trendy

Broadway; with Harvard Exit just around the corner, it's especially convenient for a "raw or cooked" meal for moviegoers, and "nice service" sweetens the deal.

Z Aqua by El Gaucho ◐ *Seafood* 25 | 26 | 25 | $59

(fka Waterfront Seafood Grill)

Seattle Waterfront | Pier 70 | 2801 Alaskan Way (Broad St.) | 206-956-9171 | www.waterfrontpier70.com

With "huge windows" overlooking Elliott Bay, this Seattle Waterfront seafooder from the El Gaucho folks offers "exceptional" fin fare and an "extensive, reasonably priced" wine list delivered with "impeccable" efficiency; the "stunning" room is "classy" enough for a special occasion or business dinner, and penny-pinchers sigh "if the view doesn't take your breath away, the bill will"; P.S. it changed names and underwent a minor face-lift post-Survey.

Art of the Table ⊠ *Pacific NW* 25 | 21 | 24 | $53

Wallingford | 1054 N. 39th St. (Woodland Park Ave.) | 206-282-0942 | www.artofthetable.net

"Beautiful" seasonal Pacific Northwest prix fixe menus are introduced course by course by chef Dustin Ronspies at this spendy Wallingford supper club "dining experience" offered on weekends in "tiny" rooms dressed in vintage furniture with a communal table where you "can't help but meet other diners"; P.S. on Monday nights, the scene changes to à la carte small plates (Sunday, Tuesday and Wednesday are reserved for private events).

Art Restaurant & Lounge *Pacific NW* 23 | 25 | 24 | $50

Downtown | Four Seasons Hotel | 99 Union St. (1st Ave.) | 206-749-7070 | www.artrestaurantseattle.com

"Light-filled and beautiful by day, moody and elegant by night", a modern setting is the backdrop for "delightful" Pacific Northwest fare from chef Kerry Sear at the Four Seasons Hotel Downtown, where local ingredients in "inventive" dishes and "excellent service" complete a package that's "pricey but worth it"; it's also popular for "pre-theater dining" and after work, when the lounge lures local business types with its "big-city feel" and "fabulous happy hour."

Asado *Argentinean* - | - | - | M

Tacoma | 2810 Sixth Ave. (bet. Anderson & Pine Sts.) | 253-272-7770 | www.asadotacoma.com

"Wonderful aromas" draw meat-lovers to this midpriced Argentine-style steakhouse in Tacoma, where the Angus beef and other fare is cooked on a mesquite-fired grill; the "lively bar" features a large selection of Argentine wines, and the candlelit gaucho setting includes wrought iron and booths with cowhide.

Assaggio Ristorante ⊠ *Italian* 24 | 21 | 24 | $39

Downtown | 2010 Fourth Ave. (Virginia St.) | 206-441-1399 | www.assaggioseattle.com

"Exceptional" Northern Italian dishes come with "interesting twists" at this "delightful" Downtowner known for "generous portions" at moderate prices; the dining room is painted with Italian murals à la Michelangelo and chef-owner Mauro "makes friends with everyone", making for an overall "superb experience."

Assimba Ethiopian Cuisine ☒ *Ethiopian* ∇ 24 | 11 | 19 | $20

Capitol Hill | 2722 E. Cherry St. (MLK Jr. Way) | 206-322-1019

This Capitol Hill Ethiopian is heralded for its "delicious" and inexpensive "doro wat" stews and curries made for both meat-eaters and vegetarians; the spot might be no-frills, but it's "friendly" and easy to find with its big sign and mint-green exterior.

Athenian *American/Seafood* 19 | 16 | 18 | $25

Pike Place Market | 1517 Pike Pl. (Pine St.) | 206-624-7166 | www.athenianinn.com

Pike Place Market insiders and tourists alike frequent this "funky" institution (which started as a bakery in 1909) for its "affordable", "genuine taste" of "old blue-collar Seattle" American breakfasts and seafood, served by "colorful" staffers in an "unmatched" spot to "watch the market wake up"; there's no dinner, but the second-floor booths have "wonderful views" of "ships and ferries coming and going" in Elliott Bay.

Ayutthaya *Thai* 20 | 11 | 20 | $20

Capitol Hill | 727 E. Pike St. (bet. Boylston & Harvard Aves.) | 206-324-8833

Locals look to this family-run Capitol Hill longtimer for "above-average" Thai favorites like coconut chicken and drunken noodles, served by a staff that "always has a smile"; it's "modestly decorated", but who cares when you can "easily eat and drink" for cheap?

Azteca *Mexican* 14 | 14 | 17 | $19

Ballard | 2319 NW Market St. (Ballard Ave.) | 206-782-7079
Eastlake | 1823 Eastlake Ave. E. (bet. Blaine St. & Yale Pl.) | 206-324-4941
Northgate | Northgate Mall | 401 NE Northgate Way (5th Ave.) | 206-362-0066
University Village | 5025 25th Ave. NE (Blakely St.) | 206-524-2987
Bellevue | 150 112th Ave. NE (bet. Main & 2nd Sts.) | 425-453-9087
Kirkland | 11431 NE 124th St. (116th Ave.) | 425-820-7997
Kent | 25633 102nd Pl. SE (256th St.) | 253-852-0210
Tacoma | 4801 Tacoma Mall Blvd. (48th St.) | 253-472-0246
Mill Creek | 15704 Mill Creek Blvd. (Bothell-Everett Hwy.) | 425-385-2209
Tukwila | 17555 Southcenter Pkwy. (south of Minkler Blvd.) | 206-575-0990
www.aztecamex.com
Additional locations throughout the Seattle area

"Americanized Mexican" favorites in "huge" portions are the draw at this chain where the "decent" fare comes from a "large" menu and the margaritas flow freely; the hacienda decor is "typical" and even if detractors dub it all "run-of-the-mill", the price is low and "service is friendly and prompt", making it an "alternative to fast food."

	FOOD	DECOR	SERVICE	COST

Azul ◐ *Pan-Latin* 22 | 18 | 19 | $25

Mill Creek | 15118 Main St. (bet. 151st & 153rd Sts.) | 425-357-5600 | www.azullounge.com

Affordable Pan-Latin fare draws Mill Creekers to this "boisterous" upscale spot offering "huge portions", "oh-my" margaritas and "friendly, quick" service; the "hip" quarters are especially "busy" on weekends, and regulars say "don't miss the happy-hour" deals.

NEW Ba Bar ◐ *Vietnamese* - | - | - | M

Capitol Hill | 550 12th Ave. (bet. E. Barclay & James Cts.) | 206-328-2030 | www.babarseattle.com

A flashback to chef-owner Eric Bahn's Saigon childhood, the sophisticated renditions of Vietnamese street favorites at this Capitol Hill arrival go down well with the bar's craft cocktails; though affordable, it's a bit pricier than many in the genre, but the industrial-chic decor with big windows and reclaimed-wood tables adds value - and is already attracting Seattle University students and profs, who can come for breakfast and hang out till the wee hours.

Bagel Oasis *Deli* 23 | 8 | 13 | $13

Ravenna | 2112 NE 65th St. (bet. Ravenna & 21st Aves.) | 206-526-0525 | www.seattlebageloasis.com

"Minimal" decor doesn't stop fans from "schlepping" to Ravenna for bagels, bialys and "interesting" sandwiches at this bakery/deli that some East Coast transplants call the "most authentic in town"; service can be "spacey", but it's "kid-friendly" with a small play area.

Baguette Box *Sandwiches* 24 | 13 | 16 | $13

Capitol Hill | 1203 Pine St. (Melrose Ave.) | 206-332-0220
Fremont | 626 N. 34th St. (bet. Evanston & Fremont Aves.) | 206-632-1511
www.baguettebox.com

"Awesome" "Vietnamese-inspired" sandwiches and "to-die-for" truffle fries keep this duo from Monsoon's Eric Bahn at the "top of the charts" for "urbanized" "cheap eats" say the Capitol Hillers and Fremont desk jockeys who "can't stop eating" them; the "hip", "casual" digs and "no-nonsense service" appeal to most, and impatient types can "call in an order for pickup."

Bahn Thai *Thai* 25 | 20 | 21 | $22

Queen Anne | 409 Roy St. (5th Ave.) | 206-283-0444 | www.bahnthaimenu.com

Around "for years", this budget-friendly Queen Anne Thai is still "satisfying" with "excellent" dishes including "awesome" pad Thai; the old house setting decorated with Asian touches makes for a "great date spot", and competent service helps when it gets busy before "theater, ballet or opera" at the nearby Seattle Center.

Bainbridge Island BBQ 🄼 *BBQ* ▽ 17 | 11 | 16 | $18

Bainbridge Island | 251 Winslow Way W. (bet. Hall Brothers Loop & Madison Ave.) | 206-842-7427 | www.bibbq.com

For day-trippers to Bainbridge Island, this "family-owned", gently priced barbecue joint is just the thing "when you have to have Q";

the menu variety and game-burgers add an edge, but "don't expect anything fancy" from decor that's pure Lone Star rumpus room, complete with longhorns over the fireplace - though there is a sports room with a big TV and it's kid-friendly too.

Bai Pai Fine Thai *Thai* 25 | 22 | 23 | $26

Ravenna | 2316 NE 65th St. (23rd Ave.) | 206-527-4800 | www.baipairestaurant.com

"O-o-oh, so good" say fans of this Ravenna Thai dishing out "delightfully flavorful" and "spicy" cuisine that's "innovative" to boot; the "upscale", "comfortable" room combines with the moderate prices and "responsive service" to make it "one of the better" in the category all-around.

Bai Tong *Thai* 24 | 18 | 22 | $24

Redmond | 14804 NE 24th St. (148th Ave.) | 425-747-8424
Tukwila | 16876 Southcenter Pkwy. (Wig Blvd.) | 206-575-3366
www.baitongrestaurant.com

Opened in 1989 by a flight attendant with her fellow Thai crew members and passengers in mind, the defunct SeaTac original spawned these "wildly popular" Siamese siblings considered "worth the drive" to Tukwila and Redmond for "standout" cuisine at "reasonable" prices; with soothing colors, upscale upholstery and "attentive but not intrusive" service, they're "always crowded, especially at lunch."

Bakeman's ⊠⇏ *Deli* 22 | 7 | 17 | $10

Downtown | 122 Cherry St. (2nd Ave.) | 206-622-3375 | www.bakemanscatering.com

"Bring your attitude" to this intentionally prickly Downtown basement luncheonette that's packed with a "devoted following" of hungry types snagging "fresh-baked" turkey sandwiches and "cheap", "hearty meals"; the owner is "famous for being rude", so find out "how to order before you go" - or "face a scolding."

Z Bakery Nouveau *Bakery/French* 29 | 18 | 20 | $13

West Seattle | 4737 California Ave. SW (Alaska St.) | 206-923-0534 | www.bakerynouveau.com

"Try anything and everything" urge surveyors "seduced" by the "heavenly smells" at this "sweet and savory" West Seattle French bakery turning out "beautiful", "delectable" pastries, artisan breads, cookies and sandwiches; the "tiny quarters" are "busy, busy" all day, resulting in sometimes "slow service", and frugal types find it "a little pricey", but the payoff's a "blissfully satisfied grin."

Bambino's Pizzeria *Pizza* - | - | - | I

Belltown | 401 Cedar St. (4th Ave.) | 206-269-2222 | www.getbambinos.com

"Clearly sent from the pizza gods", the affordable brick oven-baked pies at this Belltowner are "amazing" with NYC-style thin crusts and "flavorful" toppings so pleasing that fans even "break my diet" to indulge; service is "friendly" in the small, rustic setting, and there's beer and wine too.

	FOOD	DECOR	SERVICE	COST

Bamboo Garden Szechuan *Chinese* 25 | 16 | 17 | $20

Bellevue | 202 106th Pl. NE (2nd St.) | 425-688-7991 | www.bamboogardendining.com

Fiery, "real" Sichuan fare that "numbs your tongue" and even more "unusual things to eat" - such as sliced pork kidneys - draw "adventurous" diners to this Bellevue Chinese "hidden" in a strip mall just off the main drag; the "noisy dining room" is filled with foodies and expat "families", who dub it an "awesome experience" and a "great value."

Bamboo Garden Vegetarian *Chinese/Veg.* 20 | 11 | 17 | $18

Queen Anne | 364 Roy St. (bet. 3rd & 4th Aves.) | 206-282-6616 | www.bamboogarden.net

"Omnivores", vegans and those who keep kosher "love" the "mock meat", hot pots, noodles and such at this inexpensive vegetarian Queen Anne Chinese; a staff that "recognizes regulars" and a "great location" walking distance from the Seattle Center make it a convenient stop before the opera or ballet at McCaw Hall.

B&O Espresso ◐ *Coffeehouse* 20 | 18 | 18 | $19

Capitol Hill | 204 Belmont Ave. E. (Olive Way) | 206-322-5028 | www.b-oespresso.com

"Desserts to die for" fill the big cake case at this Capitol Hill coffeehouse and "gathering spot" where "affordable" "Middle Eastern specialties" and a "terrific brunch" are ferried by "relaxed" servers; "smoky-eyed waifs" and "brooding-student types" drink "endless rounds of black coffee" in the "funky, eclectic" setting.

NEW Bar del Corso ⊠ *Italian* - | - | - | M

Beacon Hill | 3057 Beacon Ave. S. (bet. Hanford & Stevens Sts.) | 206-395-2069 | www.bardelcorso.com

An instant neighborhood gathering place, this Beacon Hill Italian boîte offers imaginative pizzas and chic small plates starring local ingredients, ordered from a chalkboard menu by the bar; it resides in the former Beacon Hill Pub space, which has been given an urbane makeover adding a huge wood-burning oven, gleaming wooden floors and a gentrified mien.

Barking Dog Alehouse *Pub Food* 20 | 19 | 20 | $25

Ballard | 705 NW 70th St. (7th Ave.) | 206-782-2974 | www.thebarkingdogalehouse.com

Tucked into a side street in Ballard, this "boisterous neighborhood pub" serves "imaginative", affordable American fare and a selection of beers on weekly rotating taps; a "friendly staff" and a stylish interior that was one of Seattle's first remodeled with eco-conscious materials are additional draws.

Z Barking Frog *Pacific NW* 25 | 23 | 24 | $51

Woodinville | Willows Lodge | 14580 NE 145th St. (Woodinville-Redmond Rd.) | 425-424-2999 | www.willowslodge.com

"What's not to love?" bark backers of this Woodinville wine country "jewel" at the Willows Lodge that blends "rusticity and elegance" with its "fabulous", "creative" Pacific NW fare, "gracious hospitality" and "extensive" Northwest vino list in a "comfortable, welcoming setting" that includes an "indoor fire pit"; yes, it's "expensive" (though not as extravagant as the neighboring Herbfarm) but deemed definitely "worth the drive."

Barolo Ristorante *Italian* 24 | 24 | 22 | $44

Downtown | 1940 Westlake Ave. (bet. 6th & 7th Aves.) | 206-770-9000 | www.baroloseattle.com

"Excellent" Italian dishes with "modern twists" distinguish this "top-of-the-line" Downtowner as much as the "Ferraris outside" the front door; the "alluring" "contemporary" dining room features "elaborate candles, chandeliers" and "sexy" dining nooks, and the "hopping bar scene" feels like "New York"; service is "friendly", and while budget-watchers call it "a little pricey", "happy hour's a true bargain."

Bastille Café & Bar *French* 19 | 24 | 18 | $35

Ballard | 5307 Ballard Ave. NW (Vernon Pl.) | 206-453-5014 | www.bastilleseattle.com

"Friendly", "trendy" and "packed with beautiful people", this mid-priced Ballard French bistro is where steak frites "done right" meet salads and veggies from a "rooftop garden" that even has its own beehives; the "fabulous", "well-designed" setting features Parisian antiques and a 45-ft. zinc bar, and though it gets "noisy" and there are some "kinks to work out" with the "kitchen and staff", "Francophiles" agree it's a "winner."

Bayou on First *Cajun* - | - | - | I

Pike Place Market | 1523 First Ave. (bet. Pike & Pine Sts.) | 206-624-2598

Cajun seafood and "great gumbo and jambalaya" are a "nice change" from the typical Pike Place Market eatery options at this "unpretentious" diner on busy First Avenue; surveyors find the vibe "cool" and the staff "attentive", and wallet-pleasing prices seal the deal to make it "just right."

Beach Cafe *Eclectic/Seafood* 19 | 21 | 17 | $34

Kirkland | Woodmark Hotel | 1170 Carillon Pt. (Lake Washington Blvd.) | 425-889-0303 | www.beachcafekirkland.com

"Spectacular views" of Lake Washington are the highlight at this "popular" and "lively" Eclectic Kirkland seafooder with an "awesome patio" located at the Woodmark Hotel; though "gracious service" can get "overwhelmed", a "decent" menu with "something for everyone" plus "reasonable prices" and a "relaxed atmosphere" mean you can "even bring the kids."

Beecher's Handmade Cheese *Cheese* 25 | 15 | 18 | $14

Pike Place Market | 1600 Pike Pl. (Pine St.) | 206-956-1964 | www.beechershandmadecheese.com

"It's all about" the *fromage* at this Pike Place Market spot where locals and tourists go to "watch the cheese-making" and grab an affordable and "awesomely rich mac 'n' cheese" or "to-die-for grilled-cheese" sandwich to eat at the small counter or while "walking through the market"; the staff is "knowledgeable", but be aware of "crowds" when the "cruise ships are in town."

Belle Epicurean *Bakery/French* 23 | 17 | 19 | $15

Downtown | Fairmont Olympic Hotel | 1206 Fourth Ave. (bet. Seneca & University Sts.) | 206-262-9404

NEW **Madison Park** | 3109 E. Madison St. (Lake Washington Blvd. E.) | 206-466-1320

www.belleepicurean.com

"Scrumptious" brioche, croissants and affordable lunch sandwiches are among the offerings chef Carolyn Ferguson turns out at her "elegant" Downtown French bakery in the Fairmont Olympic, where locals and well-heeled tourists "grab a seat" in the "picture window" and "revel" in the "Parisian" ambiance while having a bit of a "splurge caloriewise"; P.S. the Madison Park branch opened post-Survey.

Belle Pastry *Bakery/Dessert* 24 | 14 | 16 | $12

Downtown | 77 Spring St. (bet. Post & Western Aves.) | 206-623-1983

Bellevue | 10246 Main St. (bet. 102nd & 103rd Aves.) | 425-289-0015

www.bellepastry.com

This "classy" Bellevue bakery provides "a little taste of France" thanks to baker-owner Jean Claude Ferre (who hails from Normandy and baked in Paris) and appeals to locals with its "accommodating" staff and affordable "quick bites"; the Downtown branch caters to the office crowd.

Bell Street Diner *Seafood* 23 | 21 | 22 | $28

Seattle Waterfront | Pier 66 | 2201 Alaskan Way (Bell St.) | 206-448-6688 | www.anthonys.com

"Excellent fish tacos" and crab cakes team up with a "fantastic" Elliott Bay view at this casual, midpriced Waterfront seafooder that's a popular link in the local Anthony's chain; tucked into a dockside building, it can be "hard to find" but it's "worth" seeking out, even if it gets packed when a "cruise ship" is docked nearby.

Belltown Pizza *Pizza* 20 | 13 | 18 | $20

Belltown | 2422 First Ave. (bet. Battery & Wall Sts.) | 206-441-2653 | www.belltownpizza.net

Belltowners chiming in on this "busy" New York-style pizzeria say its affordable pies with "thin", "delicious" crusts and "flavorful" toppings "smell so-o-o good from the street"; with an amiable staff, full bar and location central to the cocktail scene, it's also a "hot spot" "to start the night" or simply "watch the world go by."

Benihana *Japanese* 19 | 17 | 21 | $38

Downtown | 1200 Fifth Ave. (University St.) | 206-682-4686 | www.benihanaseattlewa.com

"The show is always on" at this midpriced Downtown branch of the "tasty" teppanyaki and sushi Japanese chain where steak, chicken and seafood are chopped, tossed and "cooked right in front of your eyes"; it's "festive for the family" (especially kids who are "entranced"), and even if critics cry "the same old, same old", it remains a "crowded" destination for "celebrating with a large party."

	FOOD	DECOR	SERVICE	COST

Bennett's Pure Food Bistro *American* 18 | 18 | 18 | $33

Mercer Island | 7650 SE 27th St. (bet. 76th & 77th Aves.) | 206-232-2759 | www.bennettsbistro.com

"Fresh, simple" fare based on ingredients from "local organic farmers" makes this midpriced American an "oasis" for Mercer Islanders seeking "generous" portions of natural foods like crab cakes and the "famous mac 'n' cheese" of its sibling, Beecher's; though some find the food and service "inconsistent", it's the "eat-and-be-seen" center of the upscale neighborhood.

Betty *American* 23 | 20 | 21 | $35

Queen Anne | 1507 Queen Anne Ave. N. (Galer St.) | 206-352-3773 | www.eatatbetty.com

"Home cooking with class" distinguishes this midpriced New American sibling to Crow offering "some of the best roast chicken" and steak frites and considered a "terrific" "standby" by Queen Anners; the "cozy" bistro setting is "cheerful and upbeat" and the staff's "pleasant", with a "seductive cocktail menu" and a new open-air deck sealing the deal.

Bick's Broadview Grill *American* 21 | 17 | 20 | $33

Greenwood | 10555 Greenwood Ave. N. (107th St.) | 206-367-8481

Known for its "hot sauce" selection and American "dishes that cause perspiration", this Greenwood habanero haunt turns out a "creative" menu with "amazing" flavors declare devotees; yes, the booths "are exceedingly uncomfortable" and it "can get loud", but "reasonable prices" and a "warm" staff tend to "make up for it."

Big Mario's Pizza ◐ *Pizza* - | - | - | I

Capitol Hill | 1009 E. Pike St. (bet. 10th & 11th Aves.) | 206-922-3875 | www.bigmariosnewyorkpizza.com

Late-risers and late-nighters chow down on inexpensive New York-style pizzas at this cool Capitol Hill sliceteria with ties to Via Tribunali and the 5 Point Café; there's a NYC-joint-in-the-'70s-and-'80s feel about the place, complete with a crowd that lingers until 4 AM on weekends.

Bing's Bar & Grill *American* 16 | 14 | 19 | $21

Madison Park | 4200 E. Madison St. (42nd Ave.) | 206-323-8623 | www.bingsbarandgrill.com

"Fantastic burgers" and a prime-rib dip some beef eaters call the "best in the West" draw Madison Park denizens to this unpretentious American "neighborhood staple"; with "Formica-topped diner decor" and red booths, it's a "step back in time" – with gentle prices to match.

Bin on the Lake *American* 20 | 22 | 20 | $42

Kirkland | Woodmark Hotel | 1270 Carillon Pt. (off SR-520) | 425-803-5595 | www.binonthelake.com

The view of Lake Washington makes a "beautiful" backdrop for dipping into a "fantastic by-the-glass wine selection" plus small and large plates at this Kirkland New American affiliated with the

Woodmark Hotel; surrounded by a business park, it's a bit pricey, but "elegant decor" and "warm" service are in the mix.

Bisato Ⓜ *Italian* 25 | 21 | 25 | $46

Belltown | 2400 First Ave. (Battery St.) | 206-443-3301 | www.bisato.com

Chef-owner Scott Carsberg offers "outstanding", "affordable" Venetian small plates at this Belltown haunt; the urbane setting has counter and table seating, and the staff "takes care of everyone."

Bis on Main *American* 24 | 22 | 23 | $44

Bellevue | 10213 Main St. (102nd Ave.) | 425-455-2033 | www.bisonmain.com

Even A-listers know reservations are "essential" at Joe Vilardi's "swank" New American in "old town" Bellevue, where "memorable" meals are built around a menu so appealing, diners have a "hard time deciding what to order"; the "chic" space features changing art and lends itself to "business" dining or a "quiet, romantic night out" enhanced by "experienced" staffers who "know their stuff."

Bistro Turkuaz Ⓢ Ⓜ *Turkish* 26 | 20 | 25 | $32

Madrona | 1114 34th Ave. (Spring St.) | 206-324-3039 | www.bistroturkuaz.com

Flying "under the radar", this "family-run" Madrona "gem" offers "delicious", "inventive" midpriced Turkish fare that locals say is "several notches above the usual"; the "lovely" old storefront lends itself to the antiques decorating the "cozy" room where a quiet ambiance encourages conversation.

Black Bottle ◐ *Eclectic* 22 | 20 | 19 | $28

Belltown | 2600 First Ave. (bet. Cedar & Vine Sts.) | 206-441-1500 | www.blackbottleseattle.com

NEW Black Bottle Postern ◐ *Eclectic*

Bellevue | 10349 NE 10th St. (Bellevue Way NE) | 425-223-5143 | www.blackbottlebellevue.com

"Delicious" small plates shine at this "hip" Belltown Eclectic where the "cool kids" gather for a "date" or a "late-night snack"; a "saucy" staff navigates the "trendy" "dark space" for an experience that's "more refined" than many stops on the area's cocktail trail, plus there's a bar menu until 2 AM; P.S. the Bellevue outpost opened post-Survey.

Black Pearl *Chinese* 17 | 9 | 16 | $21

Wedgwood | 7347 35th Ave. NE (75th St.) | 206-526-5115
Shoreline | 14602 15th Ave. NE (146th St.) | 206-365-8989

Mostly a "take-out" and delivery operation, this Chinese neighborhood duo is known for affordable Hunan and Sichuan cuisine including "hard-to-beat" housemade noodles and "homemade chow mein"; the decor is "nothing special", but the Wedgwood and Shoreline spots "beat a trek" to the ID when you're pinched for time.

Bleu Bistro Grotto ◐ *American* ∇ 21 | - | 18 | $26

Capitol Hill | 1801 E. Olive Way (E. John St.) | 206-322-3087

This "quirky" Capitol Hill hideaway recently (post-Survey) moved down the street into former-Quiznos digs redone with velvet-curtained booths and midpriced New American fare served in the glow of candles and Christmas lights; as ever, "it's not everyone's cup of tea", but hipsters warm to a "wasabi grilled cheese sandwich" plus an array of veggie choices; P.S. the "tiny little tables" are bigger now but still seem built for diners "under 100 pounds."

Blueacre *Seafood* 21 | 20 | 20 | $43

Downtown | 1700 Seventh Ave. (Olive Way) | 206-659-0737 | www.blueacreseafood.com

Kevin and Terresa Davis (Steelhead Diner) are behind this Downtown seafooder in the "old Oceanaire space" offering an "adventurous menu" of finny "comfort food"; the wood-paneled setting with nickel accents and high-backed booths is "cool", and though the "well-meaning" service "needs polishing" and the "tab rises rapidly", it's a "fair price" for what you get.

Blue C Sushi *Japanese* 16 | 16 | 16 | $23

Downtown | Grand Hyatt Hotel | 1510 Seventh Ave. (Pike St.) | 206-467-4022
Fremont | 3411 Fremont Ave. N. (34th St.) | 206-633-3411
University Village | University Vill. | 4601 26th Ave. NE (Montlake Blvd.) | 206-525-4601
Bellevue | Bellevue Sq. | 503 Bellevue Sq. (bet. Bellevue Way & 100th Ave.) | 425-454-8288
Lynnwood | Alderwood Mall | 3000 184th St. SW (Alderwood Mall Pkwy.) | 425-329-3596
Tukwila | Westfield Southcenter | 468 Southcenter Mall (bet. Andover Park & Southcenter Pkwy.) | 206-277-8744
www.bluecsushi.com

"Clever" kaiten "conveyor belt" sushi makes for a "fresh", "quick bite" - especially when kids are in tow - at this local Japanese sextet where where customers "grab" a dish as it passes by; the "trendy" chain (which also includes Boom Noodle) has Asian "hipster" decor and overhead TVs showing "amusing" videos, but wallet-watchers warn that since it's "pay by the plate", "costs can pile up."

Blue Star Cafe & Pub *American* 18 | 16 | 20 | $18
(fka Egg Cetera's Blue Star)

Wallingford | 4512 Stone Way N. (bet. 45th & 46th Sts.) | 206-548-0345 | www.bluestarcafeandpub.com

Whether for "great breakfasts" complete with "country fries" or pub food and "hard-to-pass-up" specials, this "reasonably priced" longtime Wallingford American specializing in eggs, burgers and beer gets "crowded" with locals; "super-friendly" service and 22 rotating microbrews on tap are other reasons it's a "neighborhood" "hang."

Bluff Restaurant, Bar & Terrace *Pacific NW* - | - | - | M

Friday Harbor | Friday Harbor House Inn | 130 West St. (1st St.) | 360-378-8455 | www.fridayharborhouse.com

"Beautiful" panoramic water views are a draw at this spot in the Friday Harbor House Inn where the "excellent" Pacific NW fare comes at "moderate" prices; the "cozy" decor features local artwork, and those in the know say happy hour is an "amazing" deal.

	FOOD	DECOR	SERVICE	COST

BluWater ◐ *American* | 16 | 18 | 17 | $27 |

Green Lake | 7900 E. Green Lake Dr. N. (Ashworth Ave.) | 206-524-3985
Leschi | 102 Lakeside Ave. S. (Lake Washington Pl.) | 206-328-2233
www.bluwaterbistro.com

A real "Seattle feel" and "views" of the water and sunsets are a lure at this lakeside duo of moderately priced Americans; the menus have "something for everyone" (even "grandma") though some find the food and service "decent but not special."

Z Boat Street Cafe *French* | 27 | 22 | 24 | $39 |

Queen Anne | 3131 Western Ave. (Denny Way) | 206-632-4602 | www.boatstreetcafe.com

Bon vivants feel like they're "escaping to France" at chef-owner Renee Erickson's "unpretentious" lower Queen Anne bistro, a sibling of the Walrus & the Carpenter, where the "fabulous" midpriced fare - including "killer housemade pickles" - comes via a "brilliant" staff; antique posters of Babar the Elephant add to the "delightful" dinner setting complete with slate tables and candlelight, while the more "sparse" adjacent area called the Boat Street Kitchen serves lunch and weekend brunch.

Boka Kitchen & Bar ◐ *Pacific NW* | 20 | 22 | 20 | $37 |

Downtown | Hotel 1000 | 1010 First Ave. (Madison St.) | 206-357-9000 | www.bokaseattle.com

The "happy hour" with its "younger" crowd trumps all at this "vibrant, hip" Downtown Pacific NWer in the Hotel 1000; the seasonal fare is "light" and "flavorful", and the "helpful" staff and "chic" vibe (the walls change color every 90 seconds) make it worth a bit of a "splurge."

Bonefish Grill *Seafood* | 21 | 20 | 21 | $34 |

Bothell | 22616 Bothell-Everett Hwy. (228th St.) | 425-485-0305 | www.bonefishgrill.com

"Excellent" fin fare including "the daily catch" is "simply presented" at this midpriced Bothell seafooder where surveyors agree the "Bang Bang Shrimp appetizer is a bang-up winner"; locals who pop in for "lunch or dinner" say even if it's not "fancy schmancy", it's "reliable" and "not bad for a chain."

Book Bindery ☒ *American* | - | - | - | M |

Queen Anne | 198 Nickerson St. (bet. 3rd & Warren Aves.) | 206-283-2665 | www.bookbinderyrestaurant.com

Posh New American eats from chef Shaun McCrain play with textures and flavors in this midpriced Queen Anne entry located alongside a tree-lined Lake Washington Ship Canal park; attached to the Almquist Family Vintners winery, the elegant room feels like a genteel library in an old-money mansion, with park and water views in the front, and, in back, the vintner's barrel room is visible through a windowed wall.

Boom Noodle *Japanese* | 17 | 18 | 16 | $21 |

Capitol Hill | 1121 E. Pike St. (11th Ave.) | 206-701-9130
University Village | 2675 NE Village Ln. (bet. 25th Ave. & 45th St.) | 206-525-2675

(continued)

FOOD | DECOR | SERVICE | COST

(continued)

Boom Noodle

Bellevue | 504 Bellevue Sq. (bet. 4th & 8th Sts.) | 425-453-6094
www.boomnoodle.com

This trio of "vibrant", "modern" ramen shops attracts a "cool clientele" with "distinctive", "affordable" Japanese "noodles served in every imaginable way"; the "hip, industrial" settings are "noisy" and "service varies", but even though they're trendy, they're also "family-friendly."

Brad's Swingside Cafe *Italian* 25 | 16 | 23 | $33

Fremont | 4212 Fremont Ave. N. (bet. 42nd St. & Motor Pl.) | 206-633-4057

Chef-owner Brad Inserra adds his own "style" to the "incredibly delicious" midpriced dishes at this Fremont Italian that's been a "buzzing" "neighborhood" "standby" for more than 20 years; locals say it's "like dining in a funky living room" - except with "attentive service" - and the "mom-and-pop feel" keeps the vibe "real."

Branzino *Italian/Seafood* 25 | 22 | 22 | $44

Belltown | 2429 Second Ave. (Battery St.) | 206-728-5181 | www.branzinoseattle.com

Boosters of this spendy Belltown Italian give it "bravos" for its "absolutely fabulous" fish and "exceptional" pastas; the "clubby" dining room is refreshingly "unpretentious" and the "helpful" staff makes diners "feel wanted", all adding up to a "terrific dining experience."

Brasserie Margaux *French/Pacific NW* 16 | 18 | 18 | $41

Downtown | Warwick Seattle Hotel | 401 Lenora St. (4th Ave.) | 206-777-1990 | www.margauxseattle.com

In the Warwick Hotel, this Downtowner proffers "tasty" French-Pacific NW dishes at "reasonable prices" - especially the daily "fixed price" deals; the traditionally decorated setting is "inviting", though a few opine that while "breakfasts are excellent, dinner's a step down."

NEW **Brave Horse Tavern** ◐ *American* - | - | - | I

South Lake Union | 310 Terry Ave. N. (bet. Harrison & Thomas Sts.) | 206-971-0717 | www.bravehorsetavern.com

Clearly the place to be, this South Lake Union playroom from Tom Douglas features value-priced burgers, brick-oven pretzels and other snacks that go down well with schooners of craft beer; tucked into the new Amazon.com HQ, it's full of cute geeks yakking it up at communal tables and trying their hand at shuffleboard and darts.

Brix 25° *American* - | - | - | E

Gig Harbor | 7707 Pioneer Way (Harborview Dr.) | 253-858-6626 | www.harborbrix.com

Fans say chef-owner Thad Lyman has "raised the bar" with his spendy New American in Gig Harbor and its "excellent" dishes complemented by a Pacific Northwest-focused wine list; an "intimate" dining room done up in earth tones completes the upscale-casual experience.

	FOOD	DECOR	SERVICE	COST

Brooklyn Seafood, Steak & Oyster House *Seafood* 24 | 21 | 23 | $42

Downtown | Brooklyn Bldg. | 1212 Second Ave. (University St.) | 206-224-7000 | www.thebrooklyn.com

Still creating "a lot of buzz", this Downtown "institution" offering an "incredible selection" of Northwest oysters and seafood reels in tourists and expense-accounters alike for its "spectacular" surf 'n' turf menu; service is "knowledgeable", and an 1890 building that "takes you back" is the setting for quite a "scene" when "crowded."

Brouwer's *Belgian* 22 | 22 | 16 | $23

Fremont | 400 N. 35th St. (Phinney Ave.) | 206-267-2437 | www.brouwerscafe.com

A "hip young crowd" "gets its Belgian on" at this Fremont pub where "delectable", affordable Brussels-inspired grub "goes down nicely" with an "outrageous" beer selection including "over 60 on tap"; if service is sometimes "slow", the former warehouse setting has an "awesome" "semi-medieval" look; P.S. 21-and-over only.

Buca di Beppo *Italian* 15 | 17 | 17 | $26

South Lake Union | 701 Ninth Ave. N. (Broad St.) | 206-244-2288
Lynnwood | 4301 Alderwood Mall Blvd. (44th Ave.) | 425-744-7272
www.bucadibeppo.com

"Boisterous" atmosphere, "kitschy decor" and moderate tabs are the draw at these South Lake Union and Lynnwood chain links where "big portions" of "Italian comfort food" mean "leftovers for days"; the "over-the-top" experience lends itself to a "family party" or "gang of hungry minors", and it's so popular, there's "always a wait."

Buckley's *American* 17 | 17 | 20 | $22

Belltown | 2331 Second Ave. (bet. Battery & Bell Sts.) | 206-588-8879
Seattle Center | 232 First Ave. W. (bet. John & Thomas Sts.) | 206-691-0232 ◐
www.buckleysseattle.com

"Casual pub grub" is "remarkably good" and relatively cheap at these "neighborhood" sports bars sporting the requisite "multiple TVs" plus booths, beer posters and "collegiate banners"; additional draws are weekend brunch and the Belltown branch's "Tuesday trivia nights."

Buddha Ruksa 🅼 *Thai* 26 | 19 | 21 | $24

West Seattle | 3520 SW Genesee St. (bet. 35th & 36th Aves.) | 206-937-7676 | www.buddharuksa.com

Followers promise "pure Thai bliss" at a "fair price" at this spot tucked into a side street in West Seattle, where "you haven't lived until you've had the crispy garlic chicken"; service is "pleasant" and the deep-red dining room strikes a "cosmopolitan" chord, but since it's "noisy" and "lines are long" to get in, some opt for "takeout."

Buenos Aires Grill *Argentinean* 21 | 18 | 19 | $45

Downtown | 220 Virginia St. (bet. 2nd & 3rd Aves.) | 206-441-7076 | www.buenosairescuisine.com

"Red-meat lovers rejoice" over the Argentinean mixed grills and "hearty" steaks with "authentic sauces" at this Downtown churrascaria; though service varies, on weekends "dancers tango up and down the aisles", making it all feel like "a quick trip to a sunnier locale."

Buffalo Deli ☒ *Deli* ▽ 27 | 10 | 18 | $15

Belltown | 2123 First Ave. (bet. Blanchard & Lenora Sts.) | 206-728-8759 | www.thebuffalodeli.com

Lunch East Coast-style is served at this "dependable" Belltown deli offering affordable "fresh, homemade" soups and sandwiches (including roast beef on a kimmelweck roll) inspired by the specialties of Buffalo, NY; fans assure "high-quality" standards, but busy locals sometimes call in or order online to "avoid the wait at the counter."

Buns *Burgers* - | - | - | I

Location varies; see website | No phone | www.bunsonwheels.com

Riding high with grass-fed beef and local ingredients, this snazzy truck dispenses hot-off-the-grill burgers on chubby brioche buns, or on a pile of poutine, at reasonable-for-the-quality prices; it's hard to miss, given its tricked-out paint job featuring burgers, the Space Needle and the city skyline.

Burrito Loco *Mexican* - | - | - | I

Crown Hill | 9211 Holman Rd. NW (13th Ave.) | 206-783-0719

"The world would be a sad place indeed" without this longtime Crown Hill Mexican assure fans of the "delicious" dishes at modest prices that are "not your beans-and-rice sort" of fare; one of the first local spots to freshen up south-of-the-border cuisine, it's "just as reliable as ever", though some hint it's time to "bring it up a notch."

Bush Garden *Japanese* ▽ 18 | 17 | 18 | $31

International District | 614 Maynard Ave. S. (bet. Lane & Weller Sts.) | 206-682-6830 | www.bushgarden.net

After nearly 60 years, this "old-style" Japanese in the ID continues to draw locals with its "traditional" menu of sushi and cooked dishes at "decent prices"; karaoke adds to the "interesting night out", and if some moan the "retro" decor "needs updating", others find the "classic" look and service "welcoming."

Z Cactus *Mexican/Southwestern* 22 | 20 | 20 | $26

Madison Park | 4220 E. Madison St. (bet. 42nd & 43rd Aves.) | 206-324-4140

West Seattle | 2820 Alki Ave. SW (63rd Ave.) | 206-933-6000

Kirkland | 121 Park Ln. (bet. Central Way & Lake St.) | 425-893-9799

www.cactusrestaurants.com

A "nuevo" Southwestern and Mexican menu includes "so many options" besides the "usual tacos and tamales" (e.g. "butternut squash enchiladas") at this "*muy* excellent" trio of "well-priced" cantinas; they're always "packed" with an "upbeat crowd", and the "bright", "upscale" decor and "friendly staff" stoke the "breezy" vibe.

Cafe Bengodi *Italian* - | - | - | M

Pioneer Square | 700 First Ave. (Cherry St.) | 206-381-0705

Acolytes attest this Pioneer Square cafe "hits the high notes" with its "fresh, simple" and "delicious" midpriced pizzas, pastas and other Italian fare from chef-owner (and neighborhood character) Luigi De Nunzio; service might be "a little slow", but no one minds when the "focus is the food."

Z Cafe Besalu M *Bakery/European* 29 | 17 | 22 | $12

Ballard | 5909 24th Ave. NW (bet. 59th & 60th Sts.) | 206-789-1463

The "line out the door" is a "testament" to the "flaky", "buttery" pastries, quiche and other "heavenly" bites at this casual European bakery/cafe that's like "Paris in Ballard"; it's "cozy" (if a "hole-in-the-wall" with "tight" seating) and "service is pleasant", all leaving devotees deeming it "worth the wait" for "something steaming from the oven" - but "it's too bad they close at 3 PM."

Z Cafe Campagne *French* 26 | 22 | 23 | $38

Pike Place Market | 1600 Post Alley (bet. 1st Ave. & Pine St.) | 206-728-2233 | www.campagnerestaurant.com

This midpriced Pike Place Market "favorite" elicits "ooh-la-la's" for "fine" bistro fare including "addictive" lamb burgers and frites delivered by a "pleasant", "professional" staff; the "cozy" quarters hung with vintage posters channel "St.-Germain" for patrons who praise it as a "great bargain" for the genre.

Cafe Flora *Vegetarian* 23 | 21 | 21 | $30

Madison Park | 2901 E. Madison St. (29th St.) | 206-325-9100 | www.cafeflora.com

"Fantastic", "inventive" fare made from "locally sourced ingredients" "doesn't need meat" to "satisfy" at this moderately priced "old vegetarian standby" in Madison Park; it's "staffed by shining examples of healthy people", and while the "leafy atrium" is a favorite seating area, the entire place is "airy and light-filled."

Z Cafe Juanita M *Italian* 28 | 24 | 27 | $62

Kirkland | 9702 NE 120th Pl. (97th Ave.) | 425-823-1505 | www.cafejuanita.com

"Dazzled" fans "can't say enough" about the "superbly prepared" "creative" dishes chef-owner Holly Smith turns out at her "charming" Northern Italian "hidden" in Kirkland and rated No. 1 for Food in the Seattle Survey; set in a midcentury house with a "cozy fireplace", the simple dining room has a "warm", "romantic" feel and the "top-notch" staff is "congenial" and "knowledgeable", making for an experience that's "expensive" but "all-around outstanding."

Cafe Lago *Italian* 26 | 19 | 22 | $35

Montlake | 2305 24th Ave. E. (Lynn St.) | 206-329-8005 | www.cafelago.com

This Montlake Italian "gem" is the "real deal" for "unbeatable" handmade pastas including "delicate, delicious lasagna" and "outstanding" applewood-baked pizzas with "thin crusts"; the stylish spot with an open kitchen and "friendly service" "never seems to have an off night", and though a few find it "rather pricey", it's "always packed."

	FOOD	DECOR	SERVICE	COST

Cafe Nola *American* 21 | 20 | 19 | $36

Bainbridge Island | 101 Winslow Way E. (Madison Ave.) | 206-842-3822 | www.cafenola.com

"Close to the ferry terminal" and drawing day-trippers and locals alike, this "delightful little place" on Bainbridge Island feels "ever-young" with its "interesting" midpriced New American menu and "assertive flavors"; while service might be "hit-and-miss", the "outside dining" on the seasonal patio is always "a plus for sunny days."

Café Ori ⇏ *Chinese* ∇ 18 | 7 | 12 | $17

Bellevue | 14339 NE 20th St. (bet. 140th & 148th Aves.) | 425-747-8822 | www.cafeoribellevue.com

Bellevue locals "don't have to drive to the ID" with this nearby strip-mall Chinese offering "huge portions" of "Hong Kong–style" and Taiwanese "must-haves" for "inexpensive" tabs; even if it's cash-only and the service has its ups and downs, it's good for groups.

Café Presse ◐ *French* 23 | 18 | 19 | $24

Capitol Hill | 1117 12th Ave. (bet. Madison & Spring Sts.) | 206-709-7674 | www.cafepresseseattle.com

"Really French" and "really reasonable", Le Pichet's Capitol Hill sibling (with the "same smart service") is a "favorite" for its "delicious" fare that's "prepared with care"; the front room is more "popular" than seating in back, and some 80 newspapers and magazines encourage the "intellectual" and "hip crowd" to "hang out" from 7 AM to 2 AM.

Cafe Veloce *Italian* ∇ 21 | 20 | 18 | $20

Kirkland | 12514 120th Ave. NE (Totem Lake Blvd., opp. Totem Lake Mall) | 425-814-2972 | www.cafeveloce.com

Gearheads gather at this motorcycle-themed Italian in Kirkland where the inexpensive pizzas and other chow comes with some unexpected Cajun influences and is served in "large portions"; decorated with vintage bikes and manned by a "young staff" that fits the vibe, it's also "fun for kids."

Café Vignole ☒Ⓜ *Italian* - | - | - | M

South Seattle | 9252 57th Ave. (Rainier Ave.) | 206-721-2267 | www.cafevignole.biz

Locals appreciate this moderately priced family-run Italian just off South Seattle's old Lake Washington driving route; the "small, cozy" European-style room is presided over by a "personable owner-chef", and there's live music on alternate Saturdays.

Café Yarmarka *Russian* - | - | - | I

Pike Place Market | 1530 Post Alley (bet. Pike Pl. & Pine St.) | 206-521-9054

"For the borscht to taste any better" it would have to be mom's "homemade" cheer champions of this hidden find inside the Pike Place Market offering pierogi, pelmeni and other "authentic Russian food"; it sweetens the pot by adding complimentary side dishes to each order, and there are dessert pastries and cakes too.

	FOOD	DECOR	SERVICE	COST

Z Calcutta Grill *American* — 21 | 25 | 23 | $45

Newcastle | Golf Club at Newcastle | 15500 Six Penny Ln. (New Castle Coal Creek Rd.) | 425-793-4646 | www.newcastlegolf.com

"Amazing" "180-degree views" of the lake and mountains are "worth the trip" to this New American at the Golf Club at Newcastle set at the "top of a high hill" and named for a golfers' betting game (not the city); some find the bill "a bit expensive", but the "bagpiper at sunset" is an extra treat May-September.

Z Canlis *Pacific NW* — 27 | 28 | 27 | $80

Lake Union | 2576 Aurora Ave. N. (Westlake Ave.) | 206-283-3313 | www.canlis.com

"Opulent" cuisine and "exceptionally polished" service with a backdrop of "stunning Lake Union views" have put this "longtime favorite" of Seattle's "who's who" in a "class of one" since it opened in 1950 - only now chef Jason Franey adds his "own spin" to a "very contemporary" Pacific NW menu; the overall package of "civilized fine dining" and "wonderful ambiance" in a "perfect midcentury modern room" means "you'll pay dearly", but "they do it so well."

Z Cantinetta M *Italian* — 27 | 22 | 23 | $39

Wallingford | 3650 Wallingford Ave. N. (bet. 36th & 37th Sts.) | 206-632-1000

Bellevue | 10038 Main St. (bet. 100th & 101st Aves.) | 425-233-6040

www.cantinettaseattle.com

Handmade pastas that "melt in your mouth" are a highlight of the "fabulous" Italian menu drawing locals to this pricey yet "unassuming" Tuscan-themed "gem" in Wallingford (with a Bellevue offshoot that opened post-Survey); the "lively crowd" keeps the "cozy" room "packed" and "noisy", but a "pleasant staff that tries hard" lets you "forgive a little."

Capital Grille *Steak* — 23 | 23 | 24 | $56

Downtown | The Cobb | 1301 Fourth Ave. (University St.) | 206-382-0900 | www.thecapitalgrille.com

A "capital idea" for a "lawyers' lunch", "expense-account" meal or "before-theater" dinner, this "meat-eater's paradise" Downtown has "clubby" steakhouse decor and is decked out with paintings of famous Seattleites; add in "professional" service and 400 wine labels, and regulars say "it may be a chain" but it's "doing everything right" - including using local ingredients.

Capitol Club *Mediterranean* — ▽ 19 | 21 | 20 | $30

Capitol Hill | 414 E. Pine St. (bet. Bellevue & Summit Aves.) | 206-325-2149 | www.thecapitolclub.net

Part of Capitol Hill's "thriving bar scene", this Pine Streeter turns out "inventive" midpriced Mediterranean tapas amid "sexy" Moroccan decor that lends itself to a "romantic outing"; the upstairs balcony is a popular perch for "people-watching" the action below, while weekend DJs and Tuesday flamenco dancing round out the entertainment.

FOOD	DECOR	SERVICE	COST

Carmelita Ⓜ *European/Vegetarian* 25 | 22 | 23 | $35

Greenwood | 7314 Greenwood Ave. N. (bet. 73rd & 74th Sts.) | 206-706-7703 | www.carmelita.net

"Gourmet" fare with a "creative" "melding" of Mediterranean, Italian and other Modern European flavors has long been luring herbivores to this "upscale" Greenwood spot that's one of the few "totally vegetarian" places in Seattle; a "warm, inviting setting" including a garden patio and "amazing cocktails" ferried by a "helpful staff" add to the "pleasant surprise."

Carolina Smoke *BBQ* - | - | - | I

Bothell | 23806 Bothell Everett Hwy., Ste. A (238th St. SE) | 425-949-8672 | www.carolinasmoke.com

This Bothell joint jumps with happy vibes, and its Carolina-style slow-smoked barbecue is offered alongside lots of housemade sides, not to mention the four kinds of BBQ sauce on the table; situated in a house right next to the highway, its comfortable dining room is packed with fans of resident pit master David Hayward, who hails from Charleston, SC.

Caspian Grill Persian Ⓜ *Persian* - | - | - | M

University District | 5517 University Way NE (bet. 55th & 56th Sts.) | 206-524-3434 | www.caspiangrill.com

"Solid, simple" fare "and lots of it" can be found at this University District Persian with homestyle versions of the cuisine on its moderately priced menu; weekend belly dancers add to the Middle Eastern mix in a setting with low lighting and Persian rugs.

Catfish Corner *Southern* 21 | 10 | 15 | $15

Capitol Hill | 2726 E. Cherry St. (MLK Jr. Way) | 206-323-4330
Kent | 25445 104th Ave. SE (256th St.) | 253-859-4333 Ⓢ
www.mo-catfish.com

Fin fanciers say "forget your diet and enjoy" the Creole-spiced catfish at these budget-friendly Southern cafes in Capitol Hill and Kent that provide a "soul-food" "pick me up"; the decor and service are no-frills, and regulars know to "arrive early" or be "in for a long wait."

Chaco Canyon Organic Café *Vegan* ∇ 19 | 16 | 15 | $18

University District | 4757 12th Ave. NE (50th St.) | 206-522-6966
NEW **West Seattle** | 3770 SW Alaska St. (38th St.) | 206-937-8732
www.chacocanyoncafe.com

"Earth-friendly service" and fare (both cooked and raw) draws the "tie-dye crowd" and UW students to this affordable University District vegan; fans say they "feel healthier just walking in the door" of the "cute little cafe", and it even has a "happy hour" complete with organic booze; P.S. the West Seattle offshoot opened post-Survey.

Chandler's Crabhouse *Seafood* 23 | 24 | 23 | $46

South Lake Union | 901 Fairview Ave. N. (Valley St.) | 206-223-2722 | www.schwartzbros.com

"Fresh, well-prepared" seafood is the lure at this South Lake Union "high-ender" where a variety of crabs comes complete with the "ever-changing view" of seaplanes and "other people's yachts"; it's located "on the water" but also near the streetcar line, and while twice-daily happy hours soothe frugal types, "attentive, professional service" completes a "luxurious experience."

Chantanee *Thai* 25 | 22 | 20 | $25

Bellevue | Key Ctr. | 601 108th Ave. NE (bet. 4th & 8th Sts.) | 425-455-3226 | www.chantanee.com

"Extraordinary Thai cuisine" with "lots of nontraditional" choices (think Siamese sushi) and "refreshingly authentic spice levels" makes this gently priced spot with "efficient service" a Bellevue "favorite"; while the move from its former strip-mall setting to the "glitzier" Key Center building rattles some, that's nothing a craft cocktail at its acclaimed lounge, Naga, can't cure.

Chanterelle *Eclectic* ∇ 19 | 16 | 19 | $25

Edmonds | 316 Main St. (bet. 3rd & 4th Sts.) | 425-774-0650 | www.chanterellewa.com

Regulars keep returning to this "cozy", "quirky" Edmonds "standby" for its moderately priced Eclectic fare including daily "breakfasts to die for" and "iconic tomato soup"; located on the ground floor of a century-old building "near the ferry", the "pleasant" setting affords "beautiful views of the Sound" from some tables.

Cheesecake Factory ◐ *American* 17 | 16 | 17 | $28

Downtown | 700 Pike St. (7th Ave.) | 206-652-5400
Bellevue | 401 Bellevue Sq. (4th St.) | 425-450-6000
Tukwila | Westfield Mall | 205 Strander Blvd. (Southcenter Pkwy.) | 206-246-7300
www.thecheesecakefactory.com

Backers bellow the American grub "rocks" at these affordable chain links offering a "vast menu" capped off by an "unbelievably enormous" selection of cheesecakes; the "huge portions" make "doggy bags" de rigueur, and though some call service "a little slow" and doubters dis it's "overrated", "the long wait" attests to its popularity.

Chez Shea Ⓜ *French/Pacific NW* 26 | 22 | 24 | $55

Pike Place Market | 94 Pike St. (1st Ave.) | 206-467-9990

Shea's Lounge Ⓜ *French/Pacific NW*

Pike Place Market | 94 Pike St. (1st Ave.) | 206-467-9990
www.chezshea.com

"Innovative" but not "over-the-top" cuisine makes for "romantic" candlelit dinners at this Pacific NW-French "hidden" in Pike Place Market, where arched windows open for summer breezes while looking out on Elliott Bay and "caring" service completes an "unforgettable experience"; P.S. those seeking something "considerably less expensive" head for snacks at the adjacent Shea's Lounge.

Chiang's Gourmet *Chinese* 23 | 12 | 16 | $19

Lake City | 7845 Lake City Way NE (80th St.) | 206-527-8888
Renton | 17650 140th Ave. SE (Petrovitsky Rd.) | 425-235-8877 Ⓜ
www.chiangsgourmet.com

In an area with few Asian restaurants, this Lake City "gem" with a Renton sibling offers multiple menus (Chinese, Chinese-American,

FOOD | DECOR | SERVICE | COST

Sichuan, vegetarian plus dim sum) and features "authentic" fare like "homemade noodles" and "stinky tofu", all at "affordable" tabs; there's "not much service or decor", but expect a "wait."

Chinoise Café *Asian* 20 | 16 | 20 | $27

Queen Anne | 12 Boston St. (Queen Anne Ave.) | 206-284-6671 | www.chinoisecafe.com

Boosters applauding this "comfortable" Queen Anne fixture for its "imaginative sushi rolls" and "range" of items from various "Asian cuisines" say they'd be "happy to order anything on the menu"; adding to the attraction, service is "friendly" and the simple setting features some colorful art - plus it won't burn a hole in your wallet.

Chinook's at Salmon Bay *Seafood* 21 | 19 | 21 | $30

Magnolia | Fishermen's Terminal | 1900 W. Nickerson St. (18th Ave.) | 206-283-4665 | www.anthonys.com

Where "real Seattleites dine" on "well-priced seafood", this "lively", "family-friendly" Magnolia eatery on a "working dock" at Fishermen's Terminal "can't be beat" for "quality" fin fare; its "helpful" service, "boathouse decor" and "outstanding view" of the "fishing fleet" also make it a "favorite" when "taking out out-of-town friends."

Chiso *Japanese* 24 | 20 | 20 | $38

Fremont | 3520 Fremont Ave. N. (36th St.) | 206-632-3430 | www.chisofremont.com

For Japanese "hot dishes" and sushi "par excellence", Fremonters swear by this "casual, friendly" midpriced spot offering "high-quality" local produce and fish from around the world; situated mere steps off the main drag, the "sleek, modern" hideaway is navigated by an "attentive staff", and insiders say "a seat at the sushi bar is a must."

Chloé Bistrot 🅼 *French/Seafood* - | - | - | M

Laurelhurst | 3515 NE 45th St. (36th Ave.) | 206-257-0286 | www.chloebistrot.com

Still a best-kept secret, this moderately priced "Paris in Laurelhurst" from Laurent Gabrel (Voilà! Bistrot) focuses on bistro classics, seafood and "good-value French wines"; red banquettes and mirrors provide a warm, cheery ambiance - with a little romance tossed in.

Chuck's Hole In the Wall BBQ 🅂 *BBQ* - | - | - | I

Pioneer Square | 215 James St. (bet. 2nd & 3rd Aves.) | 206-622-8717 | www.holeinthewallbbq.blogspot.com

This weekday-lunch-only Pioneer Square BBQ joint flies under the radar despite its inexpensive, crave-worthy brisket, hot links and pork ribs from a noted pit master; the nuthin'-much digs in an old hillside building feature counter seats that fill up with local office types enjoying the smoky, tangy goods washed down with sweet tea.

Ciao Bella *Italian* 23 | 19 | 21 | $33

University Village | 3626 NE 45th St. (bet. 35th & 40th Aves.) | 206-524-6989

Pizza and other Italian "standards" that "taste like excellent home cooking" come at "reasonable" prices at this "neighborhood"

University Village ristorante; the intimate, romantic little room makes for "a relaxing evening", and the staff is "friendly and professional."

Cicchetti *Mediterranean* 23 | 23 | 23 | $33

Eastlake | 121 E. Boston St. (bet. 1st & Warren Aves.) | 206-859-4155 | www.serafinaseattle.com

A wood-fired oven turns out "unusual, delicious" Med small plates and handmade pizzas plus "terrific" cocktails and Italian wines at this midpriced Eastlaker named for Venetian bar snacks; the "unpretentious" "little cousin to Serafina" next door, it has a "gracious staff" and is set in a stylish midcentury architect's former office, with an upstairs dining room that looks out on "all of lit-up Seattle."

Circa Neighborhood Grill & Ale House *Eclectic* 19 | 14 | 18 | $24

West Seattle | 2605 California Ave. SW (Admiral Way) | 206-923-1102 | www.circawestseattle.com

West Seattle locals fill this relaxed eatery serving affordable and "creative" Eclectic pub grub plus "weekend breakfasts" that are "fresh and beautifully made"; the "upbeat, cozy" ambiance with antique lights and service from a "friendly" staff make it "worth the seemingly unavoidable wait."

CJ's Eatery *Diner* 18 | 12 | 20 | $18

Belltown | 2619 First Ave. (bet. Cedar & Vine Sts.) | 206-728-1648

Cheap, quick and "well-prepared" diner breakfasts and lunches in "generous" servings are the ticket at this "cheery" Belltown cafe that also draws the weekend brunch brigade for pancakes and eggs dispensed "fast"; it gets "packed", but no one minds much given the "decent eats and friendly, diverse crowd"; P.S. a post-Survey renovation may outdate the above Decor score.

Coastal Kitchen *American/Eclectic* 20 | 17 | 19 | $27

Capitol Hill | 429 15th Ave. E. (bet. Harrison & Republican Sts.) | 206-322-1145 | www.seattle-eats.com

Wild finfish and all-day breakfast are always on the Eclectic-American menu at this Capitol Hiller where an additional "quirky" "international" coastal bill of fare (e.g. Greek, Peruvian, Tunisian) changes with the seasons; "hipsters crowd the joint" and regulars "bring the kids" as the "rotating" lineup of gently priced "fresh" fare delivered with "friendly service" "keeps offering reasons to go back."

Coho Cafe *Pacific NW/Seafood* 18 | 17 | 17 | $28

Issaquah | 6130 E. Lake Sammamish Pkwy. SE (62nd St.) | 425-391-4040
Redmond | 8976 161st Ave. NE (Redmond-Woodinville Rd.) | 425-885-2646
www.cohocafe.com

"Creative", "well-priced" Pacific Northwest seafood is a specialty on the "diverse" menu at this Issaquah-Redmond pair that fills the bill for both "business lunches" and "everyday dining" with the "family"; service is "reliable", and the decor's "just the right side of kitschy", and though some note it could use a touch of "freshening", others are "never disappointed" with the experience.

	FOOD	DECOR	SERVICE	COST

Coliman Mexican Restaurant & Taqueria *Mexican* — | - | - | - | I |

Georgetown | 6932 Carleton Ave. S. (Marginal Way) | 206-767-3187 | colimanrestaurant.freehostia.com

Mexican breakfasts and other inexpensive favorites including tacos de carne asada keep locals coming all day to this "family-run" cantina in Georgetown; the low-key, "unpretentious" setting and service also make it a natural for "getting a beer" and watching south-of-the-border soccer matches on the TV.

Columbia City Ale House *Pub Food* — | 19 | 18 | 18 | $24 |

Columbia City | 4914 Rainier Ave. S. (bet. Ferdinand & Hudson Sts.) | 206-723-5123 | www.seattlealehouses.com

Wallet-friendly American pub grub such as fish tacos in beer batter is made with "high-quality ingredients" at this Columbia City spot and cousin to the Hilltop and 74th Street Ale Houses; "rotating taps" featuring "local microbrews" and the pub ambiance contribute to an experience that's "better than you'd expect"; P.S. 21 and over only.

Copacabana Cafe *S American* — | - | - | - | I |

Pike Place Market | 1520½ Pike Pl. (Pine St.) | 206-622-6359

Since 1964 this family-run Bolivian in the heart of the Pike Place Market has sated patrons with "terrific" paella and *sopa de camarones* at small tabs; while the "second-story" setting is "narrow", it's a fine perch for "watching the shoppers" and taking in a view of Elliott Bay.

Copperleaf *Pacific NW* — | - | - | - | E |

SeaTac | Cedarbrook Lodge | 18525 36th Ave. S. (bet. 184th & 186th Sts.) | 206-901-9268 | www.cedarbrooklodge.com

Tucked near SeaTac Airport, this romantic, upscale Cedarbrook Lodge dining room proffers farm-to-table Pacific Northwest fare from a French Laundry alum, Mark Bodinet; the modern room has a dressed-up Northwest feel with light wood and a huge stone fireplace, and looks out over the patio and tree-lined gardens.

Z Corson Building M *Eclectic* — | 28 | 23 | 26 | $87 |

Georgetown | 5609 Corson Ave. S. (Airport Way) | 206-762-3330 | www.thecorsonbuilding.com

"Incredible" locavore prix fixe meals served "family-style" at "communal tables" draw "in-the-know diners" to Matt Dillon's Georgetown Eclectic "food mecca", where a kitchen garden and a "cool" old building conjure up the feeling of a "provincial home"; courses start with an "unpretentious introduction" from the chef and proceed with "pro" service, so acolytes assess it's "worth every pretty penny"; P.S. closed Monday–Wednesday, à la carte Thursday and Friday.

Costa's *American/Greek* — | 18 | 13 | 18 | $21 |

University District | 4559 University Way NE (47th St.) | 206-633-2751 | www.costasontheave.com

U of W students and faculty have been frequenting this University District vet since 1975 for its "homey", budget-friendly Greek fare

FOOD | DECOR | SERVICE | COST

(plus pastas and other American options) in a setting that provides a "touch of the Aegean"; "decent service" also helps make it a pleasant choice just "for snacks" or even all-day breakfast.

Costas Opa *Greek* 18 | 15 | 18 | $25

Fremont | 3400 Fremont Ave. N. (34th St.) | 206-633-4141 | www.costasopa.com

"Plentiful", wallet-pleasing fare helps make this Greek stalwart a "favorite stop" for a Fremont "night out"; the interior with its hanging plates and Hellenic decor gets "points for atmosphere", though critics hint it's best when you "don't expect much."

NEW Coterie Room *American* - | - | - | M

Belltown | 2137 Second Ave. (Blanchard St.) | 206-956-8000 | www.thecoterieroom.com

Unlike any other food in town, the midpriced American cooking reaches for oohs and ahhs at this Belltown Spur sibling serving lush, reimagined classics like foie gras shaved over toast and buttermilk-fried chicken with bacon hash; its tony space features a bar wall covered with live plants and pretty old windows looking out on the sidewalk trees; P.S. you can opt to add $10 to the final bill to buy beer for the crew at evening's end.

Counter, The *Burgers* 21 | 12 | 17 | $18

Ballard | 4609 14th Ave. NW (46th St.) | 206-706-0311 | www.thecounterburger.com

With a "mind-bending" (over 300,000, they say) possible burger combinations, this Ballard link in the national chain gets the "love" for "high-quality" natural beef and sides including "crazy-good sweet potato fries"; the stylish industrial-looking spot further "ensures even the pickiest eater's happiness" as long as budget-minded members are prepared for a little "sticker shock" when the bill shows up.

Crash Landing Pizza *Pizza* - | - | - | I

Ballard | 702 NW 65th St. (7th Ave.) | 206-706-1480 | www.crashlandingpizza.blogspot.com

East Coast expats go for the "fine", Philly-style pizzas made with thin crusts at this "no-frills" Ballard storefront; there's a "laid-back atmosphere" but "few tables", so some just "get it to go."

Crepe de France *French* ▽ 23 | 14 | 13 | $26

Pike Place Market | 93 Pike St. (1st Ave.) | 206-624-2196

"Savory and sweet" French crêpes made with "fresh produce" "satisfy your craving" at this midpriced spot with red walls in the Pike Place Market; diners order at the counter and are "served on paper plates", but at least there's seating (a rarity in the market).

Crow Restaurant & Bar *American* 25 | 21 | 24 | $41

Queen Anne | 823 Fifth Ave. N. (bet. Aloha & Valley Sts.) | 206-283-8800 | www.eatatcrow.com

For "date nights" and "pre-theater", this "great little spot on lower Queen Anne" (and "hip" sibling of Betty) gets kudos for its midpriced "creative" American dishes including pan-roasted chicken and house lasagna that please "the foodie and the traditionalist alike"; the staff is "welcoming" and "efficient", but keep in mind that the brightly painted "warehouse-esque setting" gets "loud" on "busy nights."

Crumpet Shop *Bakery* 24 | 12 | 19 | $11

Pike Place Market | 1503 First Ave. (Pike St.) | 206-682-1598 | www.thecrumpetshop.com

"So addictive it ought to be criminal" trumpet fans of the "fresh, real crumpets" at this "wee little shop" on the First Avenue side of the Pike Place Market that's "unique" while being priced for a "tight budget"; there are "tons of toppings" to crown the toasted namesake, and it's worth a "special trip", even though it gets "crowded and touristy."

Z **Crush** M *American* 25 | 22 | 24 | $64

Madison Valley | 2319 E. Madison St. (23rd Ave.) | 206-302-7874 | www.crushonmadison.com

Fans find chef Jason Wilson's New American in Madison Valley "awesome in every way", from the "inventive" menus to the setting in a 100-plus-year-old Victorian house to the interior's "elegant" white "mod" decor; an "outstanding staff" "happily guides you" through the "feast", adding up to a "class act" with a bill to match.

NEW **Cuoco** *Italian* - | - | - | M

South Lake Union | 310 Terry Ave. N. (bet. Harrison & Thomas Sts.) | 206-971-0710 | www.cuoco-seattle.com

Those craving up-to-the-minute Italian fare in South Lake Union find it at Tom Douglas' posh new hideaway specializing in handmade pastas; the rustic, spacious room is relaxed yet spiffy enough for a business dinner or a date; P.S. there's a family-style Sunday Night Supper for $25 per person, as well as Monday afternoon bocce ball (in season) with drinks and snacks out on the 'piazza.'

Cutters Bayhouse *Pacific NW/Seafood* 22 | 23 | 21 | $40

Pike Place Market | 2001 Western Ave. (Virginia St.) | 206-448-4884 | www.cuttersbayhouse.com

"Unobstructed" views of Elliott Bay help keep this moderately priced Pacific NW seafooder "busy", as does its "deliciously fresh and tasty" local fish from a menu that "appeals to the widest set of palates"; just be aware that service is "hit-and-miss" and that it also can get "touristy" during the high season – but that's understandable given the location near Pike Place Market.

Cyclops *Eclectic* ∇ 19 | 19 | 19 | $19

Belltown | 2421 First Ave. (Wall St.) | 206-441-1677 | www.cyclopsseattle.com

Artists and hipsters fill this "funky" Belltowner known for its "outrageous" decor and Cyclops eye sign as much as its Eclectic menu, complete with an "addictive" veggie burger; offbeat art fills the interior, and though the service might "need attention", the "prices are low."

	FOOD	DECOR	SERVICE	COST

Dahlak Eritrean *Eritrean* - | - | - | M

South Seattle | 2007 S. State St. (20th Ave.) | 206-860-0400

Fans of Eritrean cuisine swear by this South Seattle eatery for its "exceedingly well-prepared" *kitfo* (a spicy version of beef tartare) and lamb stews; the experience is "funky" - in a good way - with moderate prices rounding out the endorsement.

Z Dahlia Lounge *Pacific NW* 26 | 24 | 25 | $48

Downtown | 2001 Fourth Ave. (Virginia St.) | 206-682-4142 | www.tomdouglas.com

Local flavor wiz Tom Douglas' founding Downtown restaurant is "still buzz-worthy" after more than two decades, dishing out Pacific Northwest fare including "fabulous crab cakes" and "beyond heavenly" coconut cream pie; the "sultry" red dining room has "arty" touches like papier-mâché fish lamps and the staff is "first-class", so it's understandably "busy" - be sure to "reserve a table."

Z Daniel's Broiler *Steak* 24 | 23 | 24 | $59

Leschi | Leschi Marina | 200 Lake Washington Blvd. (Alder St.) | 206-329-4191
South Lake Union | 809 Fairview Pl. N. (Valley St.) | 206-621-8262
Bellevue | Bellevue Pl. | 10500 NE Eighth St., 21st fl. (Bellevue Way) | 425-462-4662
www.schwartzbros.com

"Breathtaking views" and "outstanding" prime meat combine with "top-notch service" to make dining at these classic "high-end" steakhouses a "memorable" experience, whether for a "perfect date" or business dinner; the "dark, secluded" settings are often filled with a "slightly older" crowd that's most likely on an "expense account."

Dante's Inferno Dogs *Hot Dogs* ∇ 21 | 11 | 20 | $9

Location varies; see website | 206-283-3647 | www.dantesinfernodogs.com

Catering to "night owls who forgot to eat" and farmer's-market-goers, these five sausage-centric food carts "fix a hot-dog craving", offering "excellent" franks with "plenty of style" for little money; their locations change regularly, so check the website.

Da Pino $ *Italian* - | - | - | I

Ravenna | 2207 NE 65th St. (Ravenna Ave.) | 206-725-1772 | www.cafedapino.com

Situated in the front of what's basically a sausage-making deli, this Ravenna Italian may be "easy to drive right by" but gets props from locals as a "great little" place for a wallet-friendly sandwich or early dinner; though regulars warn that chef-owner Pino Rogano can be "easily distracted", no one denies "the guy can cook."

Dash Point Lobster Shop *Seafood* 23 | 22 | 22 | $38

Tacoma | 6912 Soundview Dr. NE (Markham Ave.) | 253-927-1513

Lobster Shop *Seafood*

Tacoma | 4015 Ruston Way (McCarver St.) | 253-759-2165
www.lobstershop.com

These "cozy, inviting" Tacoma seafooders have been "special-occasion" spots for years, with an "accommodating" staff serving "excellent" lobster plus a variety of "fresh-quality" Northwest fish at moderate prices; both have "lovely views" of Commencement Bay and offer $15 two-course twilight meals from 4:30–6 PM.

Delancey Ⓜ *Pizza* 26 | 18 | 20 | $28

Ballard | 1415 NW 70th St. (bet. Alonzo & Mary Aves.) | 206-838-1960 | www.delanceyseattle.com

At this midpriced "hip pizzeria" in Ballard, husband-and-wife team Brandon Pettit and Molly Wizenberg offer wood-fired pies with "perfectly cooked, slightly charred" crusts and "well-thought-out" artisanal toppings like housemade sausage; service with "attitude" goes with the terrain, and since the simple setting is small, it's "crowded" with sometimes "long waits."

Delfino's Chicago Style Pizza *Pizza* 23 | 13 | 17 | $17

University Village | University Vill. | 2631 NE University Village St. (25th Ave.) | 206-522-3466 | www.delfinospizza.com

"Rich, spicy and delicious" deep-dish and stuffed-crust pizzas make Windy City émigrés "feel at home" at this University Village corner spot with wood paneling and booths; if the "service seems slow", regulars remind that it takes 25–35 minutes to bake these more-substantial pies and the "bit higher prices" reflect both the "quality" and the amount of ingredients going into them.

DeLuxe Bar & Grill *Burgers* 17 | 15 | 18 | $20

Capitol Hill | 625 Broadway E. (Roy St.) | 206-324-9697 | www.deluxebarandgrill.com

After half a century, this Capitol Hill "old favorite" is "still going strong" dishing out "tasty" burgers and American comfort food at gentle prices; the "neighborhood" feel and "conviviality" hasn't changed "over the years", keeping it "popular" as ever for a "late-night meal."

Dick's Drive-In ◐ *Burgers* 19 | 9 | 18 | $7

Capitol Hill | 115 Broadway E. (bet. Denny Way & John St.) | 206-323-1300

Crown Hill | 9208 Holman Rd. NW (13th Ave.) | 206-783-5233

Wallingford | 111 NE 45th St. (bet. 1st & 2nd Aves.) | 206-632-5125

Lake City | 12325 30th Ave. NE (Lake City Way) | 206-363-7777

Queen Anne | 500 Queen Anne Ave. N. (Republican St.) | 206-285-5155

NEW **Edmonds** | 21910 Hwy. 99 (220th St. SW) | 425-775-4243

www.ddir.com

These "iconic" Seattle drive-ins (first opened in 1954) are "always a guilty pleasure" for their "tasty" fresh beef burgers, "hand-cut fries" and old-fashioned "handmade" ice-cream shakes that "satisfy" whether it's "2 PM or 2 AM", all at a "can't-beat" price; they're "always packed" with everyone from hungry "students to CEOs", but service is "speedy" – just be sure to "bring cash."

Die BierStube *German* ▽ 21 | 22 | 18 | $25

Roosevelt | 6106 Roosevelt Way NE (bet. 61st & 62nd Sts.) | 206-527-7019 | www.diebierstube.com

One of the first German-themed pubs around, this affordable Roosevelt sibling of Feierabend slings "authentic" bratwurst sausages and Bavarian pretzels and offers 16 imported lagers, weisses and dopplebocks on tap; a "helpful staff" and brauhaus decor enhance the mood of a crowd that includes soccer-watching fans.

Diggity Dog's Hot Dogs & Sausages *Hot Dogs* ∇ 20 | 15 | 18 | $10

Wallingford | 5421 Meridian Ave. N. (55th St.) | 206-633-1966

Twenty-four kinds of "good, cheap" franks and sausages plus a condiment bar that's "the doggy bomb" satisfy surveyors at this "friendly" Wallingford "hangout" with cooked-to-order service; dessert cravers can finish with froyo, and moms and pops confirm that "kids love" the whole package - complete with a kiddie play-space in back.

Dilettante Mocha Café *Dessert* 23 | 17 | 17 | $18

Downtown | Rainier Sq. | 1300 Fifth Ave. (University St.) | 206-223-1644 ☒

Downtown | Westlake Ctr. | 400 Pine St. (4th Ave.) | 206-903-8595

Downtown | 818 Stewart St. (8th Ave.) | 206-682-2929 ☒

Kent | Kent Station | 514 Ramsay Way (4th Ave.) | 253-852-3555

Dilettante Mocha Café & Martini Bar *Dessert*

Capitol Hill | Brix Bldg. | 538 Broadway E. (bet. Mercer & Republican Sts.) | 206-329-6463

www.dilettante.com

Chocolate brings "happiness" at these affordable "home-grown" cafes serving "decadent" hot chocolate, shakes and housemade pastries; surveyors seek them out for dessert "dates" or "relaxing" with friends, and though some note that the "service needs work", the sleek Capitol Hill flagship ups the ante with Austro-Hungarian dinners plus a "surprisingly vibrant scene" at the martini bar.

Dinette ☒ M *European* 25 | 22 | 21 | $36

Capitol Hill | 1514 E. Olive Way (bet. Denny Way & Howell St.) | 206-328-2282 | www.dinetteseattle.com

"Fantastic toasts" with varied toppings are a highlight at this sometimes "overlooked" Capitol Hill rustic European also proffering "fantastic" entrees and specials "handmade with love and care", all at moderate prices; "courteous" service and "charming" decor that includes Florentine serving trays hung as art add to the appeal.

NEW Din Tai Fung *Chinese* - | - | - | M

Bellevue | Lincoln Sq. | 700 Bellevue Way NE (bet. 7th & 8th Sts.) | 425-698-1095 | www.dintaifungusa.com

This Bellevue link of a Taiwan-based chain plies the Shanghai-style soup dumplings that hipsters hanker for, plus lots of noodle options, all well priced for such a trendy new place; big windows at the entrance allow a view of the dumpling-makers at work, a welcome diversion for those waiting for seats in the sleek dining room.

Dish, The M ⊄ *American* 25 | 15 | 23 | $18

Fremont | 4358 Leary Way NW (8th Ave.) | 206-782-9985

"Classic hearty breakfasts" shine at this affordable Fremont "hot spot" that's loved for its "homestyle" American food; "lines can be long" but there's "free coffee" for those "waiting" and a "helpful" staff moving things along; P.S. lunch is also served on weekdays.

Dixie's BBQ *BBQ* — 21 | 9 | 12 | $15

Bellevue | 11522 Northup Way (116th Ave.) | 425-828-2460 | www.porters-place.com

There's "fire and brimstone" in the hot sauce named "the man" at Bellevue's well-known, budget-minded barbecue joint; housed next to an old auto-repair business, the family-run operation serves up "lotsa attitude" with a side of "down-home" cornbread, though fans lament "it's not the same" since the passing of beloved owner Gene Porter.

NEW **Dot's Delicatessen** *Deli* — - | - | - | I

Fremont | 4262 Fremont Ave. N (bet. 43rd St. & Motor Pl.) | 206-687-7446 | www.dotsdelicatessen.com

At this new deli specializing in charcuterie made in-house with local meats, Freemonters drop in for affordable lunches (hot dog and a beer, anyone?) and early dinners of, say, cassoulet or sausage platters; an old mercantile storefront, its bright space is dotted with taxidermy and a set of antlers, with a case offering its meats, sausages and pâtés to go.

Dragonfish Asian Cafe *Asian* — 19 | 19 | 19 | $29

Downtown | Paramount Hotel | 722 Pine St. (8th Ave.) | 206-467-7777 | www.dragonfishcafe.com

Located Downtown in the Paramount Hotel, this "go-to" for "theatergoers" and conventioneers offers "reliable" Pan-Asian dishes and "unusual", "delicious" sushi at moderate tabs; the staff can "get you in and out quickly" if need be, and the "awesome happy hour" is known for its bargain small plates - plus it's "open late."

Duke's *Seafood* — 19 | 18 | 20 | $27

Green Lake | 7850 E. Green Lake Dr. N. (bet. Ashworth & Densmore Aves.) | 206-522-4908

South Lake Union | 901 Fairview Ave. N. (south shore of Lake Union) | 206-382-9963

West Seattle | 2516 Alki Ave. SW (58th St.) | 206-937-6100

Kent | 240 W. Kent Station St. (1st Ave.) | 253-850-6333

Tacoma | 3327 Ruston Way (bet. Alder & 40th Sts.) | 253-752-5444

Tukwila | Westfield Southcenter | 757 Southcenter Mall (Strander Blvd.) | 206-243-5200

www.dukeschowderhouse.com

"Excellent" clam chowder and sustainable Alaskan seafood (think salmon and halibut) are the lure at this local mini-chain where fish-lovers and families "get together"; service is "friendly", and if some of the dishes are "a bit pricey", that's tempered by the "beautiful" water views at most of the branches.

Earth & Ocean *American* — 22 | 22 | 21 | $56

Downtown | W Hotel | 1112 Fourth Ave. (Seneca St.) | 206-264-6060 | www.earthocean.net

"Chic" New American cuisine featuring "fine" "housemade charcuterie" and direct-from-the-farm produce draws Downtown denizens to this pricey respite in the W Hotel; the "minimalist modern" room adds to the "sophisticated" vibe; P.S. a post-Survey chef change may outdate the above ratings.

Eats Market Café Ⓜ *American* 20 | 14 | 17 | $19

West Seattle | Westwood Vill. | 2600 SW Barton St. (26th Ave.) | 206-933-1200 | www.eatsmarket.com

This wallet-friendly West Seattle "neighborhood haunt" is "just right" say fans of its deli selections, "interesting" American entrees and housemade items such as home-cured corned beef for the signature Reuben; though service varies and it's located in the out-of-the-way Westwood Mall, fans insist it's "worth the drive", and the proof is it's "always packed" on the weekends.

El Camino *Mexican* 22 | 21 | 21 | $26

Fremont | 607 N. 35th St. (Evanston Ave.) | 206-632-7303 | www.elcaminorestaurant.com

Tucked into a side street in Fremont, this modern, midpriced Mexican is a "treasured find" say surveyors who find the sliced steak with cheese enchiladas and other "unique" dishes so "superb", they "want to steal the recipes"; imbibers dub the made-from-scratch margaritas "awesome", and the service and patio in the colorful quarters also get a thumbs-up.

El Camion *Mexican* ∇ 28 | 5 | 10 | $10

Ballard | 5314 15th Ave. NW (bet. 53rd & 54th Sts.) | 206-297-1124
North Seattle | 11728 Aurora Ave. N. (bet. 115th & 125th Sts.) | 206-367-2777
SODO | 1021 Occidental Ave. (bet. King St. & Royal Brougham Way) | 206-659-0236 Ⓢ
www.elcamionseattle.com

At the front of the food-truck craze, this trio of cheap Mexican joints-on-wheels has lines at breakfast and lunch for their "awesome tamales" and "delicious street tacos" deemed more authentic than many restaurant renditions; the brainchild of owner-chef Scott McGinnis, the shiny black trucks with red lettering are hard to miss.

El Chupacabra *Mexican* ∇ 16 | 14 | 16 | $19

Greenwood | 6711 Greenwood Ave. N. (bet. 67th & 68th Sts.) | 206-706-4889 | www.myspace.com/seattlechupacabra

"Cheap, plentiful" Mission-style Mexican fare is set off by "delicious sauces on the table" at this Greenwood "neighborhood hangout" named after a legendary "blood-sucking creature"; the old house decorated with Day of the Dead art draws its share of "tattooed and pierced" diners, and the "too cool for school" staff gives "surprisingly good service", plus you can "sit on the deck on sunny days."

Elemental@Gasworks ◐ Ⓢ Ⓜ *Eclectic* 26 | 20 | 21 | $56

Lake Union | 3309 Wallingford Ave. N. (34th St.) | 206-547-2317 | www.elementalatgasworks.com

There's no menu or wine list at this "epicurean experience" in Lake Union, where chef Laurie Riedeman and sommelier-host Phred Westfall serve a spendy Eclectic prix fixe paired with pours; though they may or may not reveal "what you're eating and drinking", fans assure it's all "outstanding" and say bring "an open mind and a designated driver"; P.S. since it's no rez and gets "crowded", it's good to note the wine bar Elemental Next Door.

El Gallito *Mexican* ∇ 19 | 14 | 20 | $19

Capitol Hill | 1700 20th Ave. (Madison St.) | 206-329-8088

Every little Mexican joint has its fans, and the rooster's rooters crow about the chiles rellenos and "excellent" enchiladas at this humble, wallet-friendly Capitol Hill cafe; not much to look at, the decor is pure cantina and the location is a bit sketchy, but mole is notable among the "excellent sauces."

Z El Gaucho *Steak* 25 | 24 | 24 | $69

Belltown | 2505 First Ave. (Wall St.) | 206-728-1337

Bellevue | City Center Plaza | 450 108th Ave. NE (bet. 4th & 6th Sts.) | 425-455-2715

Tacoma | 2119 Pacific Ave. (21st St.) | 253-272-1510

www.elgaucho.com

Made for a "swanky" night out, these "old-school" steakhouses turn out meat "without peer" that surveyors praise as "beefy, rich and tender"; though the dining rooms are "dark", they've thought of everything - "flashlights" and even "reading glasses" are supplied by waiters in tuxedos - and those who find the bill a bit "breathtaking" can still "get a decent deal" at happy hour in the bar.

Elliott Bay ◐ *Pub Food* 22 | 17 | 21 | $25

West Seattle | 4720 California Ave. SW (bet. Alaska & Edmunds Sts.) | 206-932-8695

Burien | 255 SW 152nd St. (4th Ave.) | 206-246-4211

www.elliottbaybrewing.com

These "feel-good" twins dish out "surprisingly good", well-priced pub "staples" made with mostly local ingredients, including burgers, "fresh, simple seafood" and onion rings "worth writing home about"; "excellent" service adds to the "enjoyable" atmosphere, not to mention the "top-quality" suds on tap that are brewed on-site.

Elliott Bay Café *American* 18 | 16 | 17 | $17

Capitol Hill | Elliott Bay Bookstore | 1521 10th Ave. (bet. Pike & Pine Sts.) | 206-436-8482

Pioneer Square | 103 S. Main St. (1st Ave.) | 206-682-6664

www.elliottbaycafe.com

"Cozy up with a book or laptop" at these Pioneer Square and Capitol Hill siblings where owner Tamara Murphy focuses on "tasty" New American dishes, including creative options for vegans and veggies; the Pioneer Square branch is underground, while the Capitol Hill branch is in Elliot Bay Bookstore.

Z Elliott's Oyster House *Seafood* 24 | 21 | 22 | $42

Seattle Waterfront | 1201 Alaskan Way (Seneca St.) | 206-623-4340 | www.elliottsoysterhouse.com

"Go for the oysters and stay for everything else on the menu" say afishionados who "forget the prices and feast" at this "outstanding"

Seattle Waterfront seafood "heaven"; the "seafaring" decor hardly competes with the "amazing" views of Elliott Bay, which, along with the "great vibe", make it a "must-visit" for locals and tourists alike, plus there's much-appreciated valet service after 5 PM.

El Mestizo *Mexican* ∇ 24 | 15 | 17 | $22

Capitol Hill | 526 Broadway (James St.) | 206-324-2445 | www.elmestizorestaurant.com

This cheery Mexican enlivens Capitol Hill's dining options with its affordable, "authentic" tacos, mole and chicken tortilla soup plus more unusual dishes such as the chile en nogada; the "nice ambiance" includes traditional art and nighttime candles, and it's also popular "for a quick lunch" with Seattle University students and visitors and the staff at Swedish Hospital across the street.

El Puerco Lloron *Mexican* 21 | 10 | 12 | $15

Pike Place Market | 1501 Western Ave. (Pike Place Hillclimb) | 206-624-0541 | www.elpuercolloron.com

"Cheap, tasty" Mexican fare "about as authentic" as any around makes this Pike Place Market cantina on the Hillclimb a longtime favorite; though it's "not the best decor", it feels like "Tijuana" to regulars, who tend to prefer it for lunch.

El Ranchon Family Mexican *Mexican* ∇ 22 | 20 | 25 | $25

Magnolia | 3416 W. McGraw St. (34th Ave.) | 206-281-9233

Magnolians are "greeted by name" at this Mexican cantina where "complimentary chips and salsa" precede "large portions" of "stick-to-your-ribs" "Americanized" fare; the "family-owned" spot is also family-friendly and affordable, so locals agree "you can't beat it."

Emmer & Rye *American* 22 | 16 | 19 | $37

Queen Anne | 1825 Queen Anne Ave. N. (Howe St.) | 206-282-0680 | www.emmerandrye.com

An old Queen Anne Victorian house is the setting for this New American from chef Seth Caswell, whose "artful" midpriced dishes are made from "locally grown", "sustainable" products that are often sourced from the farmer's market a few blocks away; service is "helpful" but not "hovering", and though the decor reminds some of "grandma's family room", early reports say it looks "promising."

Emmett Watson's Oyster Bar *Seafood* 22 | 13 | 18 | $22

Pike Place Market | 1916 Pike Pl. (bet. Stewart & Virginia Sts.) | 206-448-7721

Hidden in the "tourist-laden" Pike Place Market, this "funky" "little dive" gets "love" for its "simple, super-fresh oysters" and "spectacular" chowders at "bargain" prices; don't expect to be coddled by "quirky" staffers, who have "just the right amount of attitude."

Endolyne Joe's *American* 18 | 19 | 19 | $24

West Seattle | 9261 45th Ave. SW (Wildwood Pl.) | 206-937-5637

Located in "deep West Seattle", this New American "hangout" near the Fauntleroy ferry dock dishes out "hearty" fare with "ever-changing" themed menus and decor that "keep one's interest piqued" (though it's also known for its classic burgers); a sibling of Hi-Life and 5 Spot, it offers "good value" and leaves diners with the "happy" feeling of a "home-cooked meal."

Enza Cucina Siciliana *Italian* | - | - | - | M |

Queen Anne | 2128 Queen Anne Ave. N. (Boston St.) | 206-694-0055 | www.enzaseattle.com

Mamma Enza Sorrentino turns out "authentic" Sicilian-Italian fare including "excellent" housemade lasagna and gelato at this sibling of Mondello that's located on Queen Anne's Restaurant Row; the "charming" decor in warm orange-and-brown tones lends itself to an "intimate dinner", and a "play corner for kids" is appreciated by parents; though prices are reasonable, frugal types will especially like the $23 three-course dinner menu offered Sunday through Thursday.

Essential Baking Co. *Bakery* | 22 | 16 | 15 | $13 |

Wallingford | 1604 N. 34th St. (Woodlawn Ave.) | 206-545-0444
Georgetown | 5601 First Ave. S. (Orcas St.) | 206-876-3746 ☒
Madison Valley | 2719 E. Madison St. (bet. 27th & 28th Aves.) | 206-328-0078
www.essentialbaking.com

"Imaginative" pastries, "salads and sandwiches" make for "fresh, tasty" and affordable breakfasts and lunches at this trio of "organic" bakeries; the cozy vibe means they're ideal hideaways on "a rainy day" even when they're "crowded", though nitpickers note "it can take a while for your order to appear."

Z Etta's *Pacific NW/Seafood* | 25 | 20 | 23 | $41 |

Pike Place Market | 2020 Western Ave. (bet. Lenora & Virginia Sts.) | 206-443-6000 | www.tomdouglas.com

Tom Douglas' "addictive" seafood haunt in the Pike Place Market offers his take on lots of Pacific NW "favorites" like crab cakes, salmon and coconut cream pie that are made with "fresh, local products" and served by a "terrific" staff; even with its popularity, it's still "down-to-earth" (if "a bit pricey"), and though it gets "a tad crowded", fans urge just "hang in there."

Eva *American* | 26 | 22 | 23 | $42 |

Green Lake | 2227 N. 56th St. (Kirkwood Pl.) | 206-633-3538 | www.evarestaurant.com

Locally grown produce puts the "fresh" in the fare at Amy McCray's Green Lake American bistro that's a "foodie oasis" offering "generous portions" plus a wine list that includes a "great selection of half bottles", all at prices considered "outstanding for the quality"; "relaxed" service in a simple "country French" setting makes for a "classy" but "never stuffy" experience.

Ezell's Famous Chicken *American* | 23 | 6 | 16 | $12 |

Capitol Hill | 501 23rd Ave. (Jefferson St.) | 206-324-4141
South Seattle | 11805 Renton Ave. S. (72nd Ave.) | 206-772-1925
NEW **Kent** | 25616 102nd Pl. SE (Kent Kangley Rd.) | 253-854-4535
NEW **Renton** | 17620 140th St. SE (Petrovitsky Rd.) | 425-255-0460
Renton | 4575 NE Fourth St. (Duvall Ave.) | 425-228-9008

(continued)

Ezell's Famous Chicken

Woodinville | 17323 140th Ave. NE (Woodinville-Duvall Rd.) | 425-485-8960
www.ezellschicken.com

"Soulful, spicy" "Southern-style chicken" is "fried to perfection" at this "famous" no-frills take-out chainlet where gizzards and sweet potato pie are also on the "inexpensive", "authentic" American menu; service is "fast" and fans who crow about "artery-clogging goodness" overlook the lack of decor, while photos of its "celebrity clientele" remind everyone it was "Oprah's pick."

Facing East M *Taiwanese* — 26 | 15 | 20 | $19

Bellevue | Belgate Plaza | 1075 Bellevue Way NE (bet. 10th & 12th Sts.) | 425-688-2986

"Prepare to stand in line" with the expat and local following of this Bellevue strip-maller that's "worth the wait" for its "mouthwatering", "modern" Taiwanese dishes at wallet-friendly prices; "friendly" service and a sleek decor scheme are two more reasons it's so "popular."

Fadó Irish Pub *Irish* — 17 | 19 | 16 | $21

Pioneer Square | 801 First Ave. (Columbia St.) | 206-264-2700 | www.fadoirishpub.com

Burgers and "well-pulled pints" meet "boxty, pasties and bangers" on the menu at this Pioneer Square "traditional Irish pub" where Sounders and Seahawks fans head post-game to join the resident young crowd; a "build-your-own" Bloody Mary bar on game days adds to the draw, as do wallet-friendly tabs.

FareStart ☒ *Pacific NW* — 23 | 19 | 22 | $27

Downtown | 700 Virginia St. (Westlake Ave.) | 206-267-7601 | www.farestart.org

Pacific Northwest meals come at an "excellent price" while aiding a "great cause" - training the homeless for restaurant jobs - at this Downtowner that offers weekday lunches and "fabulous" weekly "guest chef" fund-raiser dinners; surveyors overlook service that's "not perfect" as they "love the concept", and the "bright and airy" venue makes for an overall "joyous experience."

FareStart Café @ 2100 ☒ *Deli* — - | - | - | I

South Seattle | 2100 Bldg. | 2100 24th Ave. S. (Walker St.) | 206-407-2195 | www.farestart.org

South Seattleites "love the sandwiches" at this cafe branch of the "worthy" Fare Start organization that trains disadvantaged youth then helps them find jobs in the food industry; surveyors call the inexpensive meals a "wonderful way to support" the cause.

Feierabend *German* — 18 | 19 | 17 | $21

South Lake Union | 422 Yale Ave. N. (bet. Harrison & Republican Sts.) | 206-340-2528 | www.feierabendseattle.com

The German pub "comfort food" at this South Lake Union sibling of Die BierStube is "solid, filling and tasty" - the better to "slow down the absorption" of the 18 Teutonic brews on tap; local office jockeys come for an "affordable" lunch or dinner, while game-day fans say it's "great for watching sports events" on the TV; P.S. you must be 21 to enter.

Firenze Ristorante Italiano *Italian* 22 | 16 | 21 | $35

Bellevue | Crossroads Mall | 15600 NE Eighth St. (156th Ave.) | 425-957-1077 | www.firenzerestaurant.com

"Terrific" "old-world" Italian dishes at agreeable prices have surveyors calling this Bellevue Florentine a "best-kept secret"; stucco walls and crisp white linens set a romantic mood, so backers urge "don't be deterred" that it's located "in a strip mall", plus the "friendly owner" is "often there to chat" and the staff "makes you feel like family."

5 Point Café ◐ *American* 18 | 14 | 18 | $17

Belltown | 415 Cedar St. (bet. 4th & 5th Aves.) | 206-448-9993 | www.the5pointcafe.com

Seattle's "historic greasy spoon" (opened 1929), this Belltown American "total dive" where the "jukebox rocks" dishes out "above-par" "greasy, fatty" and "cheap" diner fare "24/7"; it's "perfect after a concert or a show", with "friendly servers" and a "lively crowd" including "characters" nursing "hangovers" with "all-day breakfasts" and "strong drink."

5 Spot ◐ *American* 21 | 19 | 21 | $23

Queen Anne | 1502 Queen Anne Ave. N. (Galer St.) | 206-285-7768 | www.chowfoods.com

This Queen Anne "quirky" American "hot spot" mixes it up "for locals and visitors alike" offering "rotating" regional theme menus and decor (e.g. Bourbon Street, Florida Gulf Rim) plus other "satisfying" comfort food at budget-friendly tabs; a "cheerful staff" adds to the "charm", but on weekend mornings, advocates advise "arrive at the opening" to "avoid the wait."

Flo *Japanese* 25 | 21 | 22 | $43

Bellevue | 1150 106th Ave. NE (12th St.) | 425-453-4005 | www.florestaurant.com

Beautifully presented "rolls really rock" at this Bellevue Japanese proffering "insanely delicious" cuisine including "dishes rarely available anywhere else"; the "tasteful", "higher-end" decor and an "extremely friendly staff" impress, even if the fare is a bit on the "pricey" side.

Flying Fish *Eclectic/Seafood* 24 | 21 | 22 | $45

South Lake Union | 300 Westlake Ave. N. (Thomas St.) | 206-728-8595 | www.flyingfishseattle.com

Chef-owner Christine Keff's "out-of-the-box" thinking produces "some of the best fish dishes" in town say fans of this Eclectic seafooder in South Lake Union; the bright, "lively" quarters make a "fine" setting for business lunches, happy hour or a dinner that's "everything you look for in a night out"; P.S. takeout is next door at On the Fly.

	FOOD	DECOR	SERVICE	COST

Flying Squirrel Pizza *Pizza* 23 | 17 | 19 | $21

Ballard | Sunset Tavern | 5433 Ballard Ave. NW (bet. Market St. & 22nd Ave.) | 206-784-4880
Seward Park | 4920 S. Genesee St. (50th Ave.) | 206-721-7620
NEW **Maple Leaf** | 8310 Fifth Ave. NE (83rd St.) | 206-524-6345
www.flyingsquirrelpizza.com

This "friendly", affordable Seward Park "haunt" gets "love" from fans who "crave" its thin-crust pizza topped with "flavorful" and "unusual ingredients" (e.g. garlic-roasted pulled pork) with some usually hard-to-find local "Molly Moon ice cream to top it off"; clearly the "out-of-the-way location" is no deterrent, as it's "packed" and "loud" - but now there are branches in Ballard and Maple Leaf too.

Fonte Roaster & Wine Bar *European* ∇ 20 | 22 | 19 | $25

Downtown | 1321 First Ave. (Union St.) | 206-777-6193 | www.cafefonte.com

Serving "excellent" artisanal omelets, pizzas and hot baked sandwiches, this affordable Euro cafe caters to Downtown power-diners with flourishes like a beer giraffe (a glass tower that keeps six pints of brew cold right on your table), specialty wine and cocktail lists and house-roasted coffee; a "friendly staff" and a stylish modern space that looks out at the Seattle Art Museum also fuel an upbeat mood.

Fort St. George *Japanese* ∇ 18 | 10 | 15 | $15

International District | 601 S. King St. (6th Ave.) | 206-382-0662

You'll "feel like you're in Tokyo" when you climb the stairs to this ID joint with "Japanese takes on American dishes" such as "chicken-katsu spaghetti"; neophytes might find the menu "confusing", but devotees declare the wallet-friendly "fusion" fare is "delicious" enough to "keep going back."

Four Swallows S M *Italian/Pacific NW* 26 | 25 | 26 | $45

Bainbridge Island | 481 Madison Ave. N. (Wyatt Way) | 206-842-3397 | www.fourswallows.com

It's "worth the ferry ride" from Seattle for "some of the best" cuisine at this Bainbridge Island Pacific NW-Italian where "seasonal ingredients prepared perfectly" assure "everything on the menu is a winner"; the "charming historic house" features a "bar with cozy booths" and "light-filled front rooms", all attended by an "excellent" staff.

14 Carrot Cafe *American* 20 | 13 | 18 | $19

Eastlake | 2305 Eastlake Ave. E. (Lynn St.) | 206-324-1442 | www.14carrotcafe.com

Known for its tahini-stuffed French toast, this "funky" Eastlake "hangout" also lures locals with its "interesting chalkboard specials"; the American fare makes for a "hearty", healthy and "inexpensive" breakfast or lunch (but no dinner), just "get there early on Sunday."

Frankie's Pizza & Pasta *Italian* 20 | 15 | 18 | $21

Redmond | 16630 Redmond Way (166th Ave.) | 425-883-8407 | www.frankiesredmond.com

"Well-made" pizza and pastas such as spaghetti and meatballs have made this wallet-friendly Redmond Italian a "favorite" local "hangout"; "great values" on wine fuel the "warm", "casual" vibe in the "family-run and family-oriented" brick-walled digs.

Frank's Oyster House ⓢ Ⓜ *American* 20 | 17 | 19 | $34

Ravenna | 2616 NE 55th St. (26th Ave.) | 206-525-0220 | www.franksoysterhouse.com

Denizens of Ravenna head to this New American for "excellent" oysters, "fine" steak and gussied-up comfort food "without shelling out too many" clams; the dark room has an old supper club feel, which makes for a "great happy hour" and a "bar scene."

Frontier Room ⓢ Ⓜ *BBQ* 22 | 16 | 19 | $25

Belltown | 2203 First Ave. (Blanchard St.) | 206-956-7427 | www.frontierroom.com

A "lively young" crowd chows down at this Belltown BBQ where the "rib-sticking" smoked meats, "divine" mac 'n' cheese and other offerings come at "good prices"; a "cool cowpoke" decor adds appeal.

Fuji Sushi *Japanese* 22 | 16 | 19 | $26

International District | 520 S. Main St. (bet. 5th & 6th Aves.) | 206-624-1201

This "simple" IDer rolls out "definite value" with its sushi, sashimi and traditional cooked dishes that give raters a "reliable" Japanese fix; it's always "busy", but the modern setting leaves a few cold, so some opt for "carryout."

Fu Man Dumpling House Ⓜ *Chinese* 24 | 9 | 18 | $16

Greenwood | 14314 Greenwood Ave. N. (bet. 143rd & 144th Sts.) | 206-364-0681

"Run, don't walk" to this hole-in-the-wall Chinese in Greenwood say fans of its "homemade noodles and dumplings" "made to order" and served with an "addictive" "spicy, rich garlic sauce"; it's "always crowded for a reason", and low prices add to the "delight."

F.X. McRory's *Seafood/Steak* 18 | 19 | 18 | $31

Pioneer Square | 419 Occidental Ave. S. (King St.) | 206-623-4800 | www.fxmcrorys.com

"Beef and more beef" gets dished out at this "New York–style steak and oyster house" in Pioneer Square where specialties such as the Roasting Box prime rib are backed up by a bar with a "formidable" whiskey collection and bartenders with "know-how"; located next to CenturyLink Field (Seahawks and Sounders) and Safeco Field (Mariners), it's "packed" on game days thanks to moderate prices, plus locals know "it's the place to go" to root for the home team.

Galanga Thai Cuisine ⓢ *Thai* - | - | - | I

Tacoma | 1129 Broadway (bet 11th & 13th Sts.) | 253-272-3393 | www.galangathai.com

"Consistent", "authentic" Thai cuisine is ferried by a "friendly" staff at this inexpensive cafe in Tacoma's financial district; the colorful setting adds to an "unpretentious" vibe that makes it a local "favorite."

	FOOD	DECOR	SERVICE	COST

Galerias *Mexican* | 22 | 21 | 19 | $26 |

Capitol Hill | 611 Broadway E. (Mercer St.) | 206-322-5757 | www.galeriasgourmet.com

"Delicious sauces and entrees" go "beyond standard Mexican" with "innovative" spins at this "upscale" Capitol Hill cantina; decor featuring handmade chairs and wispy curtains adds to the "unique experience", as does a display of "hundreds of tequila bottles", and the staff makes sure you "leave happy."

Gallery Café at the Frye Ⓜ *American/European* | - | - | - | I |

Capitol Hill | Frye Art Museum | 704 Terry Ave. (Cherry St.) | 206-622-9250 | www.fryemuseum.org

After touring the free exhibits at the Frye Art Museum in Capitol Hill, surveyors head to its "quiet", inexpensive cafe for "an informal lunch" of "fresh", seasonal New American-European fare; the contemporary architecture makes a stylish backdrop, and there's also happy hour on Thursdays, when the gallery is open later.

Gaudi *Spanish* | - | - | - | M |

Ravenna | 3410 NE 55th St. (bet. 34th & 35th Aves.) | 206-527-3400 | www.gaudiseattle.com

"Authentic" cuisine leans to "comparatively pricey" paellas and tapas at this "cute and cozy" Ravenna Spaniard just north of the U of W; owners who hail from Spain, artwork, stained glass and a wine list focusing on Spanish wines contribute to the Iberian flair.

Z Gelatiamo *Dessert* | 27 | 14 | 18 | $8 |

Downtown | 1400 Third Ave. (Union St.) | 206-467-9563 | www.gelatiamo.com

A "local cafe setting" draws hungry office workers to Seattle's No. 1 Bang for the Buck - this Downtown parlor for affordable lunchtime sandwiches, Italian pastries and especially "fantastic gelato" that's "taken to new levels" with flavors such as rice or salted caramel; "giant windows" lend themselves to "people-watching" in the small space.

Z Georgian, The *French/Pacific NW* | 26 | 28 | 26 | $66 |

Downtown | Fairmont Olympic Hotel | 411 University St. (bet. 4th & 5th Aves.) | 206-621-7889 | www.fairmont.com

Again voted No. 1 for Decor in Seattle, this "ornate" creamy-yellow dining room with 30-ft. ceilings in the "grand setting" of the 1924 Fairmont Olympic Hotel is a "classic" Downtown destination for special occasions with its "amazing" French-Pacific NW cuisine and "elegant" "service to match"; it's "ideal for business dining" and for "afternoon tea", and while prices are high, a $49 prix fixe is a treat before a performance at Benaroya Hall or the 5th Avenue Theatre.

Geraldine's Counter Ⓜ *American* | 24 | 18 | 20 | $17 |

Columbia City | 4872 Rainier Ave. S. (Ferdinand St.) | 206-723-2080 | www.geraldinescounter.com

What early birds call "one of the best breakfasts in Seattle" can be had at this budget-minded Columbia City "mainstay" serving

American "home cooking" such as coffeecakes, "Southern biscuits" and French toast - plus lunch and dinner too; the "super-cute" diner-like spot draws a "diverse crowd", and somehow "they manage to keep everyone happy."

Gilbert's Main Street Bagel Deli *Deli* 21 | 14 | 15 | $18
(aka Gilbert's on Main)

Bellevue | 10024 Main St. (bet. 100th & 102nd Aves.) | 425-455-5650
Bellevue locals find "a taste of home" at this "popular" breakfast and lunch deli located on Old Main Street where "Gilbert himself is a total kick" when he serves the "generous portions" of walletwise "chow"; the "relatively small" setting with bistro tables "gets packed at prime times", but you can also "sit outside" on the patio.

Glo's *American* 25 | 8 | 17 | $17

Capitol Hill | 1621 E. Olive Way (bet. Belmont & Summit Aves.) | 206-324-2577
Breakfast seems "like your mom made it" at this Capitol Hill "hole-in-the-wall" that "can't be beat" for eggs Benedict and other budget-minded American eats; the place is "old and beaten up", but no one cares - just remember to "bring your copy of *War and Peace*" for the "long waits on weekends."

Goldbergs' Famous Delicatessen *Deli* 18 | 13 | 16 | $20

Bellevue | Marketplace at Factoria | 3924 Factoria Blvd. SE (40th Ct.) | 425-641-6622 | www.goldbergsdeli.com
West Coasters and "displaced" NYers alike dig into fare that's "as deli as it gets" at this Bellevue eatery where "delicious" Reuben and pastrami sandwiches reign and even come with a "tray of housemade pickles"; "huge" portions and reasonable prices keep 'em coming.

NEW **Golden Beetle** *Mediterranean* - | - | - | M

Ballard | 1744 NW Market St. (bet. 17th & 20th Aves.) | 206-706-2977 | www.golden-beetle.com
Maria Hines (Tilth) draws the Ballard intellectual crowd to her new eatery riffing on spicy Eastern Mediterranean favorites from kibbeh to b'steeya, made with estimable local, organic ingredients, hand-ground spices and sometimes a bit of whimsy; the space has a calming feel, featuring pale walls hung with striking black-and-white photos from Turkey and Egypt and a lengthy bar mixing seasonal cocktails; P.S. there's also weekend brunch.

Gordito's Healthy Mexican Food *Mexican* 21 | 12 | 18 | $14

Greenwood | 213 N. 85th St. (Greenwood Ave.) | 206-706-9352
Everett | 1909 Hewitt Ave. (Oakes Ave.) | 425-252-4641
www.gorditoshealthymexicanfood.com
Burritos as "wide as your leg" are "fresh" and come at "budget prices" at this Greenwood-Everett Mexican duo where the "healthy" in the name refers to grilled meat, no-lard beans and fresh salsas; if the decor's "nothing to write home about" the "efficiency of the staff is a thing of wonder."

	FOOD	DECOR	SERVICE	COST

Gordon Biersch *Pub Food* 15 15 17 $28

Downtown | Pacific Pl. | 600 Pine St. (6th Ave.) | 206-405-4205 | www.gordonbiersch.com

It's a "delicious" "combination of plasma TVs, food and beer" - with a cheer for the "garlic fries" from fans who frequent this midpriced Downtown brewhouse for a "quick bite" of American pub grub when "out shopping" or going to the Pacific Place Cinemas; the "cavernous" setting is "comfortable", and even if it's a chain link, its staffers "know their stuff."

Gorgeous George's Mediterranean Kitchen *Mediterranean* ▽ 25 16 25 $26

Phinney Ridge | 7719 Greenwood Ave. N. (78th St.) | 206-783-0116 | www.gorgeousgeorges.com

"Full-flavored" Mediterranean dishes and Grandma's Chicken that "makes a humble bird taste luxurious" are "served with a gorgeous smile" at this affordable Phinney Ridge favorite; the place is "small" and filled with "regulars", and when "ebullient" chef-owner George Rashed "occasionally bursts into song", it adds to the "good humor."

Grazie Ristorante Italiano *Italian* 22 19 24 $30

Bothell | 23207 Bothell-Everett Hwy. (232nd St.) | 425-402-9600
Tukwila | 16943 Southcenter Pkwy. (Strander Blvd.) | 206-575-1606
www.grazierestaurant.com

This duo offers "some of the best" Italian dishes in the area, including specialties such as fettuccine di mare and veal Marsala; both branches are decorated in a casual-modern style and have "unassuming" service and moderate prices, and Southcenter's strip-mall location also works to "top off a day of shopping."

Greenlake Bar & Grill *American* 17 15 17 $23

Green Lake | 7200 E. Green Lake Dr. N. (72nd St.) | 206-729-6179 | www.greenlakebarandgrill.com

"Interesting twists on classics" are among the "wide variety" of American dishes that lure locals to this bar and grill right across the street from Green Lake; additional incentives are two "fabulous" happy hours daily and a sidewalk patio that's a natural "hangout."

Z Green Leaf *Vietnamese* 27 13 19 $20

International District | 418 Eighth Ave. S. (Jackson St.) | 206-340-1388 | www.greenleaftaste.com

At this "always busy" spot in the ID, "servers rush through the tight spaces" bearing "delicious" Vietnamese dishes filled with flavors "that are always balanced perfectly"; the opening of a second dining level added more seats, so there's "lots to like for the money."

Grill on Broadway *American* 15 15 16 $26
(aka Broadway Grill)

Capitol Hill | 314 Broadway E. (bet. Harrison & Thomas Sts.) | 206-328-7000 | www.thegrillonbroadway.com

"It's the scene, not the food" that draws a "diverse crowd" to this "popular" Capitol Hill American dishing out "affordable" meals including a "weekend brunch buffet" in a setting with garage-style doors that roll open in summer; if the service is "hit-or-miss", who cares? - the "main attraction is drinking and people-watching."

Guanaco's Tacos Pupuseria *Salvadoran* ∇ 22 | 8 | 15 | $13

Capitol Hill | 219 Broadway Ave. E. (John St.) | 206-328-6288
University District | 4106 Brooklyn Ave. NE (41st St.) | 206-547-2369
www.guanacostacos.webs.com

"Starving students" are among the frugalistas at this duo that keeps it "cheap, good and simple" with hearty Salvadoran specialties including *pupusas* (handmade corn or rice-flour tortillas with fillings); Capitol Hill works for a "quick bite", and the UD location is "always packed" and has a "flexible" staff willing to combine items "however you'd like."

Guaymas Cantina *Mexican* 19 | 10 | 17 | $14

Downtown | Harbor Steps | 1303 First Ave. (University St.) | 206-624-5062
Green Lake | 6808 E. Green Lake Way N. (2nd Ave.) | 206-729-6563

Tacos Guaymas *Mexican*

Capitol Hill | 1415 Broadway E. (bet. Pike & Union Sts.) | 206-860-3871
Fremont | 106 N. 36th St. (1st Ave.) | 206-547-5110
West Seattle | 4719 California Ave. SW (Alaska St.) | 206-935-8970
White Center | 1622 SW Roxbury St. (bet. 16th & 17th Aves.) | 206-767-4026
Everett | 1814 112th St. SE (19th Ave.) | 425-338-7998
Tacoma | 2630 S. 38th St. (Pine St.) | 253-471-2224
Lynnwood | 5919 196th St. SW (58th Pl.) | 425-670-3580
www.tacosguaymas.com

A "good alternative" to the big chains, these "low-cost" local taquerias offer "Mexican truck food" (a real compliment in these parts) with the "bricks-and-mortar" bonus: beer; the "handmade salsas" are "tasty" and the horchata drinks "refreshing", plus it's all served "quickly."

Habesha Ethiopian *Ethiopian* ∇ 22 | 20 | 19 | $22

Downtown | 1809 Minor Ave. (Howell St.) | 206-624-0801 | www.habeshaseattle.com

Raters "rave" about the "terrific", affordable Ethiopian food at this Downtowner in the Denny Triangle district; "warm" service and "arty" touches make it an "attractive" choice "before a theater performance", and there's also an "excellent" all-you-can-eat lunch.

Hale's Ales Brewery & Pub *Pub Food* 15 | 17 | 19 | $20

Fremont | 4301 Leary Way NW (bet. 7th & 8th Aves.) | 206-782-0737 | www.halesbrewery.com

Fans of this Fremonter call it "a cut above" the usual pub with its leather couches, "efficient" staff and wallet-friendly menu sporting a "killer burger" plus "a few unusual items" to mix it up; less-enthusiastic eaters find it merely "ok", but all hail it for "the real star - the beer."

Harbor City Barbeque *Chinese* - | - | - | I

International District | 707 S. King St. (bet. Canton Alley & 7th Ave.) | 206-621-2228

"Luscious", "huge *har gow*" are among the "excellent" dim sum making this Chinese "gem" a go-to for ID dumpling fans, but there's also "surprisingly great BBQ duck" (it's hanging right in the window); while the dining room is large, it fills up on weekends - so go early.

Z Harvest Vine *Spanish* 27 | 21 | 23 | $49

Madison Valley | 2701 E. Madison St. (27th Ave.) | 206-320-9771 | www.harvestvine.com

Cognoscenti congregate at the copper bar to "watch the magic" as chefs prepare "fabulous" Basque tapas to "mix and match" with a "broad selection of Spanish wines" at this "romantic" Madison Valley casa; service is "knowledgeable" and the place is "always packed" (reservations are recommended) - just "watch what you're ordering because those small plates can add up."

Hattie's Hat ◐ *Diner* 17 | 16 | 17 | $16

Ballard | 5231 Ballard Ave. NW (Vernon Pl.) | 206-784-0175 | www.hatties-hat.com

Whether for a "lowbrow" weekend breakfast or a "funky night" out, the bases are covered at this Ballard institution where the beloved "dive" decor recalls "old Seattle" (the hand-carved wood bar's over 100 years old) and the menu is filled with "über-comfort food"; it all comes at agreeable prices, just "watch out for those drinks - they kick butt."

Henry's Taiwan *Chinese* - | - | - | I

International District | 502 S. King St. (5th Ave.) | 206-624-2611
Bellevue | 549 156th Ave. SE (Lake Hills Blvd.) | 425-213-5392

Sought out for beef noodle soup and "stinky tofu", Taiwan expat Henry Ku's inexpensive International District and Bellevue Chinese offer unique dishes such as hand-shaved noodles - plus fruit smoothies; when the yellow-walled 24-seat cafe gets "cramped" full of locals and office workers, cognoscenti suggest "takeout is the way to go."

Z Herbfarm, The M *Pacific NW* 28 | 26 | 28 | $215

Woodinville | 14590 NE 145th St. (Woodinville-Redmond Rd.) | 425-485-5300 | www.theherbfarm.com

"Atop the bucket list" of sybaritic surveyors is the "amazing" evening of "serious dining" at this Woodinville wine country "destination" where "you're never sure what will come next" during the nine-course Pacific NW "extravaganza" of "pure perfection", complete with wines and "unparalleled service" that's rated No. 1 in Seattle; it all begins with a tour of the garden and afterward some "stay the night" in the suites, but be aware that you might need to "get a second job" to foot the bill.

Hi-Life *American* 21 | 22 | 21 | $25

Ballard | 5425 Russell Ave. NW (Market St.) | 206-784-7272 | www.chowfoods.com

"The menu changes" to reflect the seasons so "there's always something new" to try at this affordable Ballard New American that's a "winner for all generations"; the staff's "esprit de corps" and the "relaxed" mood in the "historic firehouse" setting make it a local "favorite" - especially for Sunday's family-style "fried-chicken supper" with all the fixin's.

	FOOD	DECOR	SERVICE	COST

Hill's Food & Wine *Pacific NW* ▽ 20 | 20 | 20 | $28

Shoreline | 1843 NW Richmond Beach Rd. (bet. 15th & 20th Aves.) | 206-542-6353 | www.hillsneighborhoodrestaurant.com

There's a "cozy community feel" at this Shoreline Pacific Northwester offering an "inventive, delicious" menu and wine list "at a fair price"; it's so "comfortable" some say it's "like the dining room of a house", plus there's a "friendly staff" and a "lovely little patio in the summer" to make it even more "pleasant."

Hilltop Ale House *Pub Food* 20 | 15 | 19 | $21

Queen Anne | 2129 Queen Anne Ave. N. (Boston St.) | 206-285-3877 | www.seattlealehouses.com

"Simple" soups and sandwiches - including a Reuben that's "so juicy and g-o-o-o-d" - come at a "fair price" and are washed down with a "rotating selection" of "tasty microbrews on tap" and "cask beer" at this "lively" American Queen Anne sibling of 74th Street and Columbia City Ale Houses; the Old English setting features a sports bar and dining up front plus "quieter" quarters "in the back", all making it especially popular "after work and on the weekends."

Hi Spot Cafe *American* 23 | 19 | 21 | $19

Madrona | 1410 34th Ave. (Union St.) | 206-325-7905 | www.hispotcafe.com

"Light, flavorful" pancakes and waffles, "rich, distinctive" coffee and eggs in just about "every manner" imaginable make this budget-friendly American in Madrona a breakfast-and-lunch "go-to" that's a "high spot in anyone's day"; a "perky" staff navigates the "funky, eclectic" setting in an "old house", for an overall "cheery ambiance", and weekend brunch is "to die for", so it's naturally "tough to get in sometimes."

Hitchcock M *American/Pacific NW* - | - | - | M

Bainbridge Island | 133 Winslow Way E. (bet. Madison Ave. S. & Madrone Ln. N.) | 206-201-3789 | www.hitchcockrestaurant.com

A food haven for locals as well as day-trippers from Seattle, chef-owner Brendan McGill's Bainbridge Islander brings a fun sensibility to its up-to-the-minute, European-inspired Pacific NW cuisine, which showcases locally sourced and house-cured ingredients; factor in moderate prices and a tasteful, cozy dining room, and no surprise, it's a hit, and has already expanded into the space next door, adding a takeaway deli counter and an adjacent year-round outdoor seating area.

Ho Ho Seafood ◐ *Chinese/Seafood* 20 | 11 | 17 | $23

International District | 653 S. Weller St. (bet. Maynard & 7th Aves.) | 206-382-9671

"Daily specials" are always "a great deal" at this large, airy Chinese IDer where seafood comes from live tanks so everything's "cooked fresh" and portions are big enough to share; since it's open until 3 AM on weekends, the club kids concur there's "no better place to continue the party after the bars close."

	FOOD	DECOR	SERVICE	COST

Honey Bear Bakery *American* — 19 | 12 | 17 | $13

Lake Forest Park | Third Place Books | 17171 Bothell Way NE (Ballinger Way) | 206-366-3330 | www.honeybearbakery.com

The "aromatic smell" lures surveyors to this American cafe located in Lake Forest Park's Third Place Books, where "tantalizing" pastries and bread for sandwiches come from the on-site bakery; a natural for lunch, it's just as popular for "grabbing a cuppa joe", having a "committee meeting" or hosting a "gathering of friends."

Honey Court ◐ *Chinese* — 19 | 7 | 12 | $19

International District | 516 Maynard Ave. S. (bet. King & Weller Sts.) | 206-292-8828

After more than 20 years, this ID standby is still a "solid" and economical choice for "real" Chinese dishes including "delicious" dim sum; large round tables with lazy Susans are good for groups, and partyers come for "late-night eats" available until 3:30 AM on the weekend.

Hosoonyi *Korean* — ▽ 23 | 13 | 14 | $19

Edmonds | 23830 Hwy. 99 (bet. 238th & 240th Sts.) | 425-775-8196

"Soft tofu soup" is "the tastiest" at this "authentic" Edmonds Korean say fans who also praise the kimchee and "seafood pancakes"; the decor is bright if not fancy and the price is right, so despite service that "can be a little brisk", it "gets crowded."

How To Cook A Wolf *Italian/Mediterranean* — 24 | 20 | 20 | $42

Queen Anne | 2208 Queen Anne Ave. N. (bet. Boston & McGraw Sts.) | 206-838-8090 | www.howtocookawolf.com

"Sassy", spendy and "boisterous", this Italian-Mediterranean Queen Anne "hot spot" from celebrity chef Ethan Stowell (Anchovies & Olives, Staple & Fancy, Tavolàta) keeps foodies "coming back" for its "delicious" fresh pastas, crudos and other "seasonal", "unique dishes"; the staff exudes "easygoing charm", but the "speakeasy-meets-space-diner" setting is "tight" and "teeny", leaving most "wishing they took reservations."

Hudson *American* — ▽ 19 | 16 | 22 | $26

Georgetown | 5000 E. Marginal Way S. (Hudson St.) | 206-767-4777 | www.hudsonseattle.com

"It's all pretty tasty" from breakfast through dinner at this "solid" Georgetown American cafe - especially if you order the house specialty shrimp 'n' grits; the "comfortable" retro room has a horseshoe bar and a "diner" feel, and it draws a crowd on weekend mornings.

Hue Ky Mi Gia *Chinese/Vietnamese* — - | - | - | I

International District | Ding How | 1207 S. Jackson St. (12th Ave.) | 206-568-1268

NEW **Kent** | 18230 E. Valley Hwy. (S. 180th St.) | 425-282-1268

"Fresh, delicious" Chinese and Viet cuisine comes with low tabs at this family-owned ID cafe that's known for its braised duck noodle soup made from the grandfather's recipe; a large picture of their noodle cart in Vietnam adorns the quarters as a "fast, attentive" staff tends to the local crowd; P.S. a second branch opened recently in Kent.

FOOD | DECOR | SERVICE | COST

Hunt Club *Pacific NW* 22 | 25 | 25 | $51

First Hill | Sorrento Hotel | 900 Madison St. (Terry St.) | 206-343-6156 | www.hotelsorrento.com

In the "historic" 1909 Sorrento Hotel on First Hill, this Seattle classic turns out "well-prepared" Pacific NW cuisine with Italian touches in an "elegant English hunting club" setting; tabs are pricey, but service is "dignified", making it ideal for "special occasions" and "romantic" evenings - especially given the large list of after-dinner spirits.

Icon Grill *American* 20 | 22 | 20 | $33

Downtown | 1933 Fifth Ave. (Virginia St.) | 206-441-6330 | www.icongrill.net

The "tricked-out", "quirky" blown-glass-and-knickknack-filled setting at this Downtown American comfort-fooder reads "beautiful" to some and "over-the-top" to others, but fans agree the "mac 'n' cheese is better than mom's"; service is "pleasant" and the bar offers "friendly encounters", so in the end it's "well worth the price."

Il Bistro ◐ *Italian* 23 | 23 | 22 | $40

Pike Place Market | 93A Pike St. (1st Ave.) | 206-682-3049 | www.ilbistro.net

This Pike Place Market trattoria "hideaway" "has been around forever" for a "good reason" - its "dependable" pastas and other "satisfying" midpriced Italian fare; fanning "romance", the "candlelit respite" is nestled in a grottolike "underground" space "away from the insanity" of the market, and looks out onto a cobblestone street.

NEW Il Corvo *Italian* - | - | - | I

Pike Place Market | 1501 Western Ave. (Pike Pl. Hillclimb) | 206-622-4280 | www.ilcorvopasta.wordpress.com

Tender housemade pastas, sauces and charcuterie are among the artisanal Italian specialties on offer at this rustic Pike Place Market niche that shares space with Procopio Gelateria on the Hillclimb; with just a counter and a few tables, it feels like a private lunch club, as the chef chats with diners while cooking each dish to order, bringing it to table and making everyone feel cosseted; P.S. closes at 3 PM.

Il Fornaio *Italian* 20 | 21 | 21 | $35

Downtown | Pacific Place | 600 Pine St. (6th Ave.) | 206-264-0994 | www.ilfornaio.com

Sure, it's a chain link, but this Downtown Italian in Pacific Place Mall doesn't "taste like it" with its "varied" midpriced menu and "regional specials"; a staff that "steers you in the right direction" and three seating options - the "white-tablecloth" dining room, bakery/cafe or risotteria - add to the appeal before a movie or after shopping.

I Love New York Deli *Deli* 21 | 11 | 15 | $18

Pike Place Market | 93 Pike St. (1st Ave.) | 206-381-3354

University District | 5200 Roosevelt Way NE (52nd St.) | 206-523-0606

www.ilovenewyorkdeli.net

This deli duo is "the place to go" for NY-style noshes like a "hand-cut" Reuben on "the freshest bread" and other "pricey" but "huge sandwiches"; the Pike Place Market location is just a stand, but the UD shop has seats, and even if "it ain't Katz's" it's "3,000 miles closer."

I Love Sushi *Japanese* 22 | 15 | 20 | $36

South Lake Union | 1001 Fairview Ave. N. (Ward St.) | 206-625-9604
Bellevue | 11818 NE Eighth St. (118th Ave.) | 425-454-5706
Bellevue | 23 Lake Bellevue Dr. (118th Ave.) | 425-455-9090
www.ilovesushi.com

"Fresh" fin fare is "expertly presented" in classic and "innovative" versions for "reasonable prices" at this trio where sushi and cooked seafood is served by a "kind staff"; the modern decor varies from location to location, but at all the chefs are likely to merrily "yell in Japanese at you every time you go in and out."

Il Terrazzo Carmine *Italian* 27 | 25 | 26 | $51

Pioneer Square | 411 First Ave. S. (bet. Jackson & King Sts.) | 206-467-7797 | www.ilterrazzocarmine.com

Carmine Smeraldo makes everyone "feel like a regular" at his "suave" Pioneer Square Italian where the "stellar" fare is "sinfully delicious" and the "exceptional" staff is "warm and friendly"; the Florentine country setting "breathes power and elegance" and it's always full of "movers and shakers", so just remember to "bring the moolah" and "you will be happy."

India Bistro *Indian* 23 | 15 | 18 | $25

Ballard | 2301 NW Market St. (Ballard Ave.) | 206-783-5080
Roosevelt | 6417 Roosevelt Way NE (bet. 64th & 65th Sts.) | 206-517-4444
www.seattleindiabistro.com

They "really rock the tandoor" at these separately owned Northern Indians serving "hot, fresh and flavorful" dishes with "spice", all at "fair prices"; the Roosevelt interior is modern while Ballard is "simple" and "comfortable", and at lunchtime both offer a buffet of "well-made dishes", making them a "regular stop" for bargain-biters.

Indochine Asian Dining Lounge *Asian* 25 | 24 | 21 | $31

Tacoma | 1924 Pacific Ave. (bet. 19th & 21st Sts.) | 253-272-8200 | www.indochinedowntown.com

"Simple but elegant" Asian fusion cuisine from an "extensive, inventive" menu that includes "tasty curries" and "honey-walnut prawns" makes this "upscale" yet "reasonably priced" Tacoma spot "worth a detour"; located near the University of Washington-Tacoma and the Museum District, it boasts a "gorgeous" interior with tables surrounding a pond that's a fine place to "share portions with others" or have a business meeting.

Inn at Langley *Pacific NW* 26 | 25 | 24 | $124

Langley | Inn at Langley | 400 First St. (Anthes Ave.) | 360-221-3033 | www.innatlangley.com

Travelers attest it's "worth a trip" to dine on the "bounty of Whidbey Island" at the six-course Pacific NW prix fixe dinners from chef Matt Costello proffered at this "weekend drop-out spot" in Langley; the experience is "expensive", but service is "excellent" and a double-sided river rock fireplace adds to the "romantic" feeling - if possible, get a "table near the open kitchen" to watch the chef cook and talk about the "ingredients"; Friday-Sunday only; reservations essential.

Inn at Ship Bay ☒ⓜ *American* - | - | - | M

Eastsound | 326 Olga Rd. (bet. Ship Bay Ln. & Yellow Brick Rd.) | 877-276-7296 | www.innatshipbay.com

Thoughtfully prepared New American dishes, many made from local Orcas Island produce, seafood and meats, are the focus at this picturesque Eastsound inn; ensconced in an 1869 farmhouse in the middle of an old seaside orchard, it makes use of a bank of porch windows to let in the moonlight and a view of twinkling stars over the waters of Ship Bay.

Island Soul Caribbean ☒ *Caribbean/Soul Food* - | - | - | I

Columbia City | 4869 Rainier Ave. S. (bet. Edmunds & Ferdinand Sts.) | 206-329-1202 | www.islandsoulrestaurant.net

"Succulent smoked" jerk chicken, curried goat and "coconut corn muffins that are a highlight" keep fans coming to this affordable Columbia City Caribbean, which also cooks up some soul food favorites; the space feels like a "big family living room" and is tended by "casual service", plus there's live calypso, reggae or jazz on weekends.

Ivar's Acres of Clams *Seafood* 21 | 18 | 19 | $27

Seattle Waterfront | Pier 54 | 1001 Alaskan Way (Madison St.) | 206-624-6852 | www.ivars.com

A local "favorite for generations", this historic Waterfront fish house offers "reasonably priced" Pacific Northwest "fruits of the sea" and is known for its "very rich" chowder with "chunks of clams"; the "Old Seattle" setting on a wharf has a "retro-glam vibe" with a "great Elliott Bay view", and service is "polite"; P.S. Sunday brunch is "a steal", and there's also a seafood bar by the sidewalk for takeout.

Ivar's Mukilteo Landing *Seafood* 21 | 21 | 21 | $27

Mukilteo | Mukilteo Ferry Dock | 710 Front St. (Mukilteo Spdwy.) | 425-742-6180 | www.ivars.net

Situated on the Mukilteo Dock with a "glorious" view "from nearly every table" of Whidbey Island and the ferries loading and unloading, this seafooder draws locals and tourists alike for "fresh" chowder and salmon; the midpriced menu is buoyed by an "early-bird" Beat-the-Tide dinner and early and late happy hours; there's also the outdoor Fish Bar for to-go orders.

Ivar's Salmon House *Pacific NW/Seafood* 21 | 22 | 20 | $31

Lake Union | 401 NE Northlake Way (north shore of Lake Union) | 206-632-0767 | www.ivars.com

Views of Lake Union are a scenic backdrop at this Pacific NW seafooder decorated in a Native American cedar longhouse theme complete with carved totems; there's an open pit for alder-smoked and grilled dishes - including "probably the best salmon in town" - and a skilled staff "answers any questions" about the midpriced fin fare; happy-hour specials and the Seafood Bar up front offer particular bargains.

Izumi Ⓜ *Japanese* 24 | 15 | 20 | $30

Kirkland | Totem Lake West Ctr. | 12539 116th Ave. NE (124th St.) | 425-821-1959 | www.izumikirkland.com

Fin fans agree it's "worth the drive" to Kirkland's Totem Lake neighborhood for the "outstanding" sushi plus tempura, teriyaki and other Japanese fare offered at "reasonable prices" at this stalwart; the "classy" interior (for a "strip-mall" shop anyway) has Asian accents, and the pleasant vibe is underscored by a "very personable staff."

Jack's Fish Spot *Seafood* 22 | 10 | 19 | $13

Pike Place Market | 1514 Pike Pl. (Post Alley) | 206-467-0514 | www.jacksfishspot.com

Pike Place Market shoppers drop in for "insanely delicious" Northwest seafood that's an "incredible deal" at this "funky" stall where the "fresh" fish on ice makes its way into lunches including fish 'n' chips and cioppino; counter seating behind the live crab and shellfish tanks provides a prime perch for watching passersby.

Jade Garden ◐ *Chinese* 22 | 10 | 14 | $19

International District | 424 Seventh Ave. S. (King St.) | 206-622-8181

Look for the brick facade, big red awning and a line of fans waiting for "authentic, hot and wonderful" dim sum at this "rockin'", "cheap" Chinese ID cafe; those who know say "don't go for the service or decor" but for the goods from the carts that continually roll through the "crowded", "noisy" rooms - and brace for "hour-long waits."

Z Jak's Grill *Steak* 24 | 18 | 22 | $43

Laurelhurst | 3701 NE 45th St. (37th Ave.) | 206-985-8545

West Seattle | 4548 California Ave. SW (bet. Alaska & Oregon Sts.) | 206-937-7809

Issaquah | 14 Front St. N. (Sunset Way) | 425-837-8834

www.jaksgrill.com

Meat mavens tout "the quintessential steak" experience complete with "huge portions" as the prime incentive at this trio of "reasonably priced" bastions of beef; the "casual", low-lit modern setting and "friendly staff" add to the "neighborhood atmosphere", and while the "no-reservations" policy means "expect a long wait" for a table, most think the "payoff's worth it."

Jalisco *Mexican* 19 | 14 | 19 | $18

Georgetown | 8517 14th Ave. S. (Cloverdale St.) | 206-767-1943

Lake City | 12336 31st Ave. NE (Lake City Way) | 206-364-3978

Queen Anne | 129 First Ave. N. (bet. Denny Way & John St.) | 206-282-1175 ◐

"Delicious" Mexican fare comes at a "just-right" price at this local chain where the enchiladas, tacos and "crazy-good salsa" "taste better than the hole-in-the-wall decor might suggest"; "quick service" keeps things moving for an "office lunch" or a group.

	FOOD	DECOR	SERVICE	COST

NEW Japonessa Cucina *Japanese* | - | - | - | M |

Pike Place Market | 1400 First Ave. (Union St.) | 206-971-7979 | www.japonessa.com

This Pike Place contemporary Japanese from Billy Beach (ex Umi Sake House) rocks young urbanites with mammoth sushi rolls glammed up with big flavors and cantina ingredients and offered at won't-break-the-bank prices; the sleek digs are date-worthy and the staff moves swiftly to keep everybody happy - and the fact that it's always happy hour doesn't hurt either - but just be sure to make a reservation.

Jhanjay Vegetarian Thai *Thai/Vegetarian* | 25 | 16 | 21 | $23 |

Ballard | 5313 Ballard Ave. NW (22nd Ave.) | 206-588-1469
Wallingford | 1718 N. 45th St. (Densmore Ave.) | 206-632-1484
www.jhanjay.com

The "chefs tease-out every delicious morsel" of flavor from the ingredients used at this Ballard-Wallingford Thai vegetarian duo offering a "ridiculously extensive" menu filled with "attractively presented" "fresh, vibrant" fare; simple, modern decor and pleasing service complete the experience that's wallet-friendly to boot.

Joey ◐ *Eclectic* | 17 | 21 | 18 | $32 |

South Lake Union | 901 Fairview Ave. N. (Aloha St.) | 206-749-5639
Bellevue | 800 Bellevue Way NE (8th St.) | 425-637-1177
Tukwila | Westfield Southcenter | 758 Southcenter Mall (bet. Andover Park & Southcenter Pkwy.) | 206-835-6397
www.joeyrestaurants.com

Though the midpriced Eclectic menu is "reliable", "most people don't go here for the food" say those familiar with these "sleek", "hip" links in a Canadian chain where the attractions include "hot waitresses" and "eye-candy" clientele; anyone wishing to avoid the "loud singles scene" is best advised to "eat on weeknights" or "early on the weekends."

John Howie Steak *Steak* | 25 | 24 | 24 | $72 |

Bellevue | The Bravern | 11111 NE Eighth St. (bet. 110th & 112th Aves.) | 425-440-0880 | www.johnhowiesteak.com

From "prime cuts" to "Japanese Wagyu", the steaks are "phenomenal" at chef-owner John Howie's namesake in Bellevue's Shops at the Bravern mall; the "stylish" dining room offers "white-linen dining" and "top-notch service", just "bring a small bank loan" to cover the bill - or go for "deals" at lunch and at happy hour in the "chic, modern bar."

Jones Barbeque *BBQ* | 21 | 8 | 15 | $16 |

Columbia City | 3810 S. Ferdinand St. (Rainier Ave.) | 206-722-4414 M
SODO | 2454 Occidental Ave. (Lander St.) | 206-625-1339
West Seattle | 4417 Fauntelroy Way (Avalon Way) | 206-257-4946
www.jonesbarbeque.com

"All the world is love" for ribs and brisket fans smitten by the "old-fashioned barbecue" on the "sweet side" that's served at this smoky trio; "decor? - not really", but the "well-priced" fare comes in "large portions" and is deemed "worth the week's intake of cholesterol and salt."

	FOOD	DECOR	SERVICE	COST

Joule Ⓜ *Eclectic* 26 | 20 | 23 | $41

Wallingford | 1913 N. 45th St. (Burke Ave.) | 206-632-1913 | www.joulerestaurant.com

"Wonderfully thought-out" combinations of ingredients define the "super-creative" offerings with French, Korean and American influences at this "intriguing" Wallingford Eclectic from chefs Rachel Yang and Seif Chirchi; the modern room in a vintage building tends to be "crowded" and "a little too loud", but service is "pleasant" and fans agree it "can't be beat for the price."

Judy Fu's Snappy Dragon *Chinese* 20 | 10 | 17 | $22

Maple Leaf | 8917 Roosevelt Way NE (89th St.) | 206-528-5575 | www.snappydragon.com

When feeling the "need" for "top-notch" "homemade noodles and dumplings", surveyors head to this Maple Leaf Chinese serving affordable Mandarin and Sichuan dishes "you just can't find elsewhere"; service is "caring", and though the setting is simple, no one seems to care, but those who do can opt for takeout or delivery.

Julia's *American* 16 | 15 | 16 | $21

Capitol Hill | 300 Broadway E. (Thomas St.) | 206-860-1818
Wallingford | 4401 Wallingford Ave. N. (44th St.) | 206-633-1175
Issaquah | 375 Gilman Blvd. NW (7th Ave.) | 425-557-1919
www.juliasrestaurantseattle.com

For "breakfast like mom should have made", locals look to this affordable trio and its "wholesome", "innovative" American dishes that "fortify" patrons for the day; raters call the Wallingford branch "the best" of the bunch for dining, while Capitol Hill offers "drag shows" on the weekends (Issaquah serves only through lunch).

June *American* - | - | - | M

Madrona | 1423 34th Ave. (Union St.) | 206-323-4000 | www.juneseattle.com

Old-money types fill this "sophisticated" Madrona New American (sister to Queen Anne's Portage) for midpriced locavore fare that includes a "killer burger" on brioche and a signature "stuffed rabbit leg"; the "beautiful" room is decorated with vintage paintings.

Kabab House *Indian/Pakistani* ▽ 19 | 5 | 14 | $19

Greenwood | 8202 Greenwood Ave. N. (82nd St.) | 206-782-3611
Lynnwood | 1120 164th St. (bet. Meadow Rd. & 10th Ave.) | 425-745-2949
www.kababhouse.com

"Flavors pop" with "some of the best Indian-Pakistani food" going, "done well and inexpensively" by a "caring staff" at this Greenwood eatery; while some think an expanded menu might signal that the signature "kebabs are no longer the stars of the show", it's still "a stellar choice"; P.S. the newer Lynwood location is separately owned.

Kabul Afghan Cuisine *Afghan* 23 | 16 | 23 | $28

Wallingford | 2301 N. 45th St. (Corliss Ave.) | 206-545-9000 | www.kabulrestaurant.com

Since 1992, this Wallingford Afghan has been a "favorite" for its "amazing", "affordable" specialties including eggplant *borani* and lamb kebabs with a "delightful mélange of spices" in "every bite"; "white linen-topped tables" enhance the room decorated with maps and old photos, and the "friendly staff" is "helpful when ordering."

Kaname Izakaya 🅼 *Japanese* | - | - | - | I |

International District | 610 S. Jackson St. (6th Ave.) | 206-682-1828 | www.kaname-izakaya.com

"Authentic" Japanese pub grub is the draw at this family-run ID cafe offering "real-deal" ramen with homemade broth and a bar with shochu cocktails and sake; the dark-wood interior looks and feels like a Tokyo haunt complete with a TV playing Japanese DVDs - no surprise since the owner's previous career was making commercials in Japan.

Kaosamai *Thai* | - | - | - | I |

Fremont | 404 N. 36th St. (Phinney Ave.) | 206-925-9979
Location varies; see website | No phone
www.kaosamai.com

This brightly painted Fremont "favorite" for "delicious" budget-minded Thai favorites including curries has a friendly staff and has undergone an expansion adding more seats and an even bigger fair-weather deck; two food trucks also serve lunch weekdays around town.

Kasbah 🅼 *Moroccan* | - | - | - | M |

Ballard | 1471 NW 85th St. (Mary Ave.) | 206-788-0777 | www.kasbahmoroccanrestaurant.com

"Exotic", "delicious" fare at moderate prices is the draw at this Ballard Moroccan - especially the five-course $30 feast offering lots of options; belly dancing on weekends and "sumptuous" decor with arches, pillowed seating and swirling colors seem worlds away from the commercial-area location, and there's a bar menu too.

Kauai Family Restaurant 🅂🅼 *Hawaiian* ▽ | 23 | 13 | 17 | $17 |

Georgetown | 6324 Sixth Ave. S. (Michigan St.) | 206-762-3469 | www.kauaifamilyrestaurant.com

"Homesick" expats and locals "enjoy" the "aloha spirit" as much as the "real-deal" loco moco breakfasts, plate lunches and kalua pork at this Georgetown Hawaiian; the "hole-in-the-wall" setting filled with Hawaiiana memorabilia "really feels like" the islands, and they're open for dinner till 7:30 PM Thursdays and Fridays.

Kau Kau Barbeque Market *Chinese* | 24 | 4 | 11 | $16 |

International District | 656 S. King St. (Maynard Ave.) | 206-682-4006

Partisans praise "the best barbecue pork and duck" hanging in the window of this ID Chinese where "takeout" by the pound is a popular option given the no-frills setting and service; fare including "tasty" fried rice and egg foo yong comes in "big portions", and whether eaten in or out, the price is always right.

Kells Irish Restaurant & Pub *Irish* | 17 | 19 | 19 | $26 |

Pike Place Market | Pike Place Mkt. | 1916 Post Alley (bet. Stewart & Virginia Sts.) | 206-728-1916 | www.kellsirish.com

"It feels like" Dublin at this "crowded" Irish pub in the Pike Place Market where "soda bread and a Guinness" segue to shepherd's pie

FOOD | DECOR | SERVICE | COST

or Irish stew, all for a "wee price"; the "authentic", "dark" setting is a local favorite on St. Patrick's Day, and weekend nights it's the place to "party"; P.S. live music nightly.

Kidd Valley *Burgers* 18 | 10 | 16 | $11

Green Lake | 4910 Green Lake Way N. (Stone Way) | 206-547-0121
North Seattle | 14303 Aurora Ave. N. (143rd St.) | 206-364-8493
Queen Anne | 531 Queen Anne Ave. N. (Mercer St.) | 206-284-0184
Ravenna | 5502 25th Ave. NE (55th St.) | 206-522-0890
Bellevue | 15259 NE Bellevue-Redmond Rd. (152nd Ave.) | 425-643-4165
Kirkland | 5910 Lake Washington Blvd. NE (59th St.) | 425-827-5858
Kenmore | 6434 Bothell Way NE (65th Ave.) | 425-485-5514
Renton | 1201 Lake Washington Blvd. (Park Dr.) | 425-277-3324
www.kiddvalley.com

"Excellent" local burgers, "fresh fruit milkshakes" and "wow"-inducing fries and onion rings help to make this homegrown chain a local favorite; there's no decor to speak of and service is spotty, but since the grub's "cheap and consistent", no one's complaining.

Kikuya *Japanese* ▽ 19 | 16 | 17 | $24

Redmond | 8105 161st Ave. NE (bet. 83rd St. & Redmond Way) | 425-881-8771

"Be sure to order the appetizers of the day" at this Redmond Japanese offering up "reasonably priced" combo dinners and sushi; though it's in a strip mall, the vibe is contemporary with an Asian feel, and while some say it's "nothing outstanding", it's convenient for lunch.

Kimchi Bistro *Korean* ▽ 23 | 9 | 16 | $17

Capitol Hill | 219 Broadway E. (Alder St.) | 206-323-4472

The kimchi in the name says it all at this Capitol Hill Korean that dishes out "tasty" bibimbop and hot pots that "warm you from the inside out"; it might be a "hole-in-the-wall" in a Broadway mini-mall, but the staff is "nice."

Kingfish *Soul Food* 24 | 20 | 20 | $32

Capitol Hill | 602 19th Ave. E. (Mercer St.) | 206-320-8757 | www.thekingfishcafe.com

"Forget the diet" advise admirers of "soul food" at its "warmhearted best" including fried chicken and "famous" red-velvet cake at this midpriced Capitol Hill "temple of Southern cooking"; the "hospitable owners" and a setting featuring "nostalgic" family photographs "put everyone at ease", so it's "always ridiculously crowded" despite "no reservations" - and "rockin' cocktails" ease the wait.

Z Kisaku Sushi *Japanese* 27 | 20 | 23 | $37

Green Lake | 2101 N. 55th St. (Meridian Ave.) | 206-545-9050 | www.kisaku.com

At this "go-to" Japanese sushi spot in Green Lake, chef-owner Ryuichi Nakano transforms a "wide variety" of the "freshest seafood" into "classic and innovative" rolls and much-lauded omakase dinners; it's "always busy", so generally "attentive" service can get a bit "rushed", but prices are "reasonable" and it's "kid-friendly" - a welcome touch in this family-centric neighborhood; P.S. closed Tuesday.

	FOOD	DECOR	SERVICE	COST

Korean Tofu House *Korean* — - | - | - | I

University District | 4142 Brooklyn Ave. NE (NE 42nd St.) | 206-632-3119
U of W students and Korean expats count on the bibimbop, hearty soups and BBQ at this bargain-priced University District staple; the down-to-earth space gets cozy when crowded and the service is on the move-'em-in, move-'em-out side, but that's all part of its charm.

Krittika Noodles & Thai Cuisine *Noodle Shop/Thai* — - | - | - | I

Green Lake | 6411 Latona Ave. NE (bet. 64th & 65th Sts.) | 206-985-1182 | www.krittikas.com
"Locals" come for the "excellent pad Thai" and other noodle dishes among the Siamese fare offered at this Green Laker situated in an old mercantile building; the cozy dining room is a "go-to" for nine-to-fivers looking for a budget-friendly lunch or dinner without a "wait."

Kushibar ◐ *Japanese* — 20 | 19 | 22 | $29

Belltown | 2319 Second Ave. (bet. Battery & Bell Sts.) | 206-448-2488 | www.kushibar.com
Belltowners cheer the "huge selection" of grilled kushiyaki skewers and "inventive small bites" dished out at reasonable prices at this local Japanese; the rough wood, steel and cement interiors recall a "Tokyo izakaya", while specialty cocktails, shochu and sake keep things lively.

Kylie's Chicago Pizza *Pizza* — - | - | - | I

Fremont | 3601 Fremont Ave. N. (bet. N. 36th St. & 38th Sts.) | 206-632-2266 | www.kylieschicagopizza.com
Windy City transplants find deep-dish and regular pizzas with that unique Chicago crust and a truckload of toppings at this bargain-priced Fremont parlor; the space, entered via 36th Street, is simple and the staff buzzes around filling drinks while diners wait for the behemoth pies to emerge from the oven.

La Bête *Pacific NW* — - | - | - | M

Capitol Hill | 1802 Bellevue Ave. (Howell St.) | 206-329-4047 | www.labeteseattle.com
This cool Capitol Hill Pacific NWer is making waves with its owner-chefs (Ethan Stowell vets) and up-to-the-minute midpriced menu focused on local foods in snacks and medium-sized plates; the dark, vintage-style room features candlelight, found-object decorations and alt rock, drawing a hip, multigenerational crowd; P.S. on Monday nights it hosts a pop-up restaurant, Little Uncle, featuring 'roots Thai food' that's unlike any other available locally.

Z La Carta de Oaxaca ⊠ *Mexican* — 27 | 17 | 19 | $23

Ballard | 5431 Ballard Ave. NW (22nd Ave.) | 206-782-8722

Z NEW Mezcaleria Oaxaca ⊠ *Mexican*

Queen Anne | 2123 Queen Anne Ave. N. (bet. Boston & Crockett Sts.) | 206-216-4446
www.lacartadeoaxaca.com
"It tastes like Mexico" say fans of the "spectacular" "authentic Oaxacan cuisine" at this "buzzing" Ballard cantina (with a Queen

Anne offshoot that opened post-Survey) where the "affordable" "full-bodied" fare features "wow"-inducing mole and "even the salsa and chips are out of the ordinary"; though the "space can get a little cramped" with "long lines", a "friendly", "bustling staff" and margaritas that "hit the spot" ease "waits"; P.S. on Monday nights it hosts Shophouse, the Thai pop-up restaurant.

La Cocina del Puerco *Mexican* ▽ 17 | 12 | 14 | $12

Bellevue | 10246 Main St. (103rd Ave.) | 425-455-1151

At this Mexican mainstay in Bellevue's chic Old Main Street neighborhood, the "tasty" "homestyle" grub not only boasts a "minimum of cheese and fat", it's "cheap" too; the "rickety metal tables" and indoor-outdoor seating remind taco hounds of "Tijuana", and what's more, the "beer's cold" and the service generally "snappy."

La Côte Crêperie M *Dessert/French* ▽ 20 | 13 | 17 | $19

Madison Valley | 2811 E. Madison St. (29th Ave.) | 206-323-9800 | www.lacotecreperie.com

This "small" Madison Valley crêperie is "genuinely French", offering "delectable" buckwheat "savory" main course crêpes and sweet dessert versions that can be accompanied by wine or beer; the "welcoming" atmosphere includes a blue-and-white scheme that furthers the Gallic feel, and though prices are always gentle, the $18 dinner special (appetizer, crêpe and wine) is a real deal.

La Fontana Siciliana *Italian* 23 | 21 | 22 | $37

Belltown | 120 Blanchard St. (bet. 1st & 2nd Aves.) | 206-441-1045 | www.lafontanasiciliana.com

"Excellent" Sicilian dishes including pasta with sardines or anything topped with the "fantastic, fresh tomato sauce" keep this midpriced old-school Southern Italian on the Belltown "go-list"; tucked behind a "beautiful" gated brick courtyard complete with the titular fountain, the "warm" quarters with vintage library tables recall a "small" trattoria in Italy, and "friendly" service also helps make it a "lovely place for a date."

La Isla ◐ *Puerto Rican* 21 | 16 | 17 | $22

Ballard | 2320 NW Market St. (24th Ave.) | 206-789-0516 | www.laislaseattle.com

Located near the Ballard bar scene, this Puerto Rican spot with "garlicky", "rib-sticking" tropical fare backed by a "festive" vibe is especially "popular" on weekend nights; prices are reasonable and the "mojitos are strong", so it gets "crowded" from happy hour to 2 AM.

NEW **La Luna** *Mexican* - | - | - | M

Queen Anne | 2 Boston St. (Queen Anne Ave. N.) | 206-282-2511 | www.lalunaseattle.com

Anchoring a prime see-and-be-seen Queen Anne corner, this midpriced Nuevo Mexicano takes tasty liberties with south-of-the-border cuisine, luring passersby with its fresh enchiladas and tacos; it rocks at night, when the patio's tabletop fire pits allow you to toast your own s'mores, offered gratis.

	FOOD	DECOR	SERVICE	COST

Z La Medusa S M *Italian/Mediterranean* 27 | 18 | 23 | $36

Columbia City | 4857 Rainier Ave. S. (Edmunds St.) | 206-723-2192 | www.lamedusarestaurant.com

"A real find" for "satisfying" Sicilian cuisine, this Columbia City Italian-Med offers an "inventive" seasonal menu and is delivered with "outstanding service"; though "you may feel a little close to your neighbor" in the "cozy" space, that just "adds to the ambiance"; P.S. on Wednesdays May-October there's a $30 prix fix dinner built around goods from the farmer's market half a block away.

Laredos ◐ *Mexican/Tex-Mex* - | - | - | M

Queen Anne | 555 Aloha St. (Taylor Ave.) | 206-218-1040 | www.laredosgrill.com

Moderate prices and "awesome" regional Mexican and Tex-Mex cuisine converge at this "solid" Queen Anne cantina where specialties include "out-of-this-world" freshly made tortillas and "amazing" avocado margaritas; though service varies, the border cafe decor pleases partyers who revel in the late hours (till 1 AM weekends).

Z Lark M *American* 27 | 22 | 25 | $51

Capitol Hill | 926 12th Ave. (bet. Marion & Spring Sts.) | 206-323-5275 | www.larkseattle.com

The "exceptional" menu "takes small plates to a new level" with "local, seasonal ingredients" at John Sundstrom's "rustic" New American on Capitol Hill; the wood-beamed room is "tasteful" and "intimate", and though some say it seems "expensive" because "you can't help" over-ordering, it's agreed "every bite's a winner"; P.S. though primarily walk-in, it does accept same-day reservations.

La Rustica M *Italian* 24 | 19 | 20 | $36

West Seattle | 4100 Beach Dr. SW (Carroll St.) | 206-932-3020 | www.larusticarestaurant.com

From "perfect" pasta to "divine" braised lamb shank right through dolci, West Seattleites say "you can't go wrong" at this midpriced Italian across the street from the beach where the emphasis is on "quality ingredients"; service is decent, and while one surveyor's "cozy" quarters is another's "need to expand", fans agree "it isn't summer" until you've dined on the "romantic" "tiny patio."

La Vita É Bella *Italian* 22 | 19 | 22 | $34

Belltown | 2411 Second Ave. (bet. Battery & Wall Sts.) | 206-441-5322 | www.lavitaebella.us

"Top-notch" "homestyle" Italian fare has made a Belltown "favorite" of this midpriced ristorante where the "smell of garlic" and "wonderful pizza" draws you in; "friendly" staffers have you "feeling like one of the *familia*", while sunny weather brings people-watching on the patio.

Lecosho *American* - | - | - | M

Downtown | 89 University St. (bet. 1st & Western Aves.) | 206-623-2101 | www.lecosho.com

Matt Janke (ex Matt's in the Market) returns with this comfortable, eye-catching modern American in the middle of Downtown's

Harbor Steps hill climb; the midpriced menu reflects the food he craves, like espresso-rubbed short ribs and housemade sausage, backed up with cool cocktails and an easygoing atmosphere in a wood-filled setting.

Lee's Asian *Asian* 24 10 18 $19

West Seattle | 4510 California Ave. SW (Oregon St.) | 206-932-8209

Supporters are "never disappointed" in the "amazing" Pan-Asian dishes ("try the seven-flavor beef") at prices that are "so reasonable" at this West Seattle "gem"; though "decor is nonexistent", service is "efficient", and if you get "carryout you will be in heaven" at home.

Le Fournil French Bakery M *Bakery/French* 21 12 14 $14

Eastlake | 3230 Eastlake Ave. E. (bet. Fuhrman & Harvard Aves.) | 206-328-6523 | www.le-fournil.com

You have to look carefully to find this "authentic" French patisserie "hidden" in a commercial building near the University Bridge on busy Eastlake Avenue East, but the payoff's "beautiful pastries" and some of the "best croissants" around; the simple setting sports a Gallic theme with pictures of France, and there's also a real "lunch deal" with baguette sandwiches.

Le Gourmand S M *French* 26 22 25 $68

Ballard | 425 NW Market St. (6th Ave.) | 206-784-3463 | www.legourmandrestaurant.com

Chef Bruce Naftaly was a "locavore before it was trendy" remind regulars who call him a "master at blending" the "freshest" organic and sustainable ingredients (some from his own garden) into "superb" dinners at his and Sara Naftaly's "long-standing" French in Ballard; the "lovely" white modern dining room is "quiet" and service is "unobtrusive", all lending to its "romantic" appeal as an "expensive special-occasion" choice; P.S. open Wednesday-Saturday.

Lemongrass *Vietnamese* 21 16 16 $18

Capitol Hill | 514 12th Ave. (Jefferson St.) | 206-860-8164

International District | 1207 S. Jackson St. (12th Ave.) | 206-568-8788

Renton | Uwajimaya Plaza | 365 S. Grady Way (Shattuck Ave.) | 206-860-8164

www.originallemongrass.com

"Delightful" Vietnamese cuisine with its "classic, subtle interplay of flavors" distinguishes this trio of budget-friendly eateries whose menus span "classic" dishes to more unusual meals; "simple" modern spaces and "consistent" service make for a "pleasant" experience.

Le Panier *Bakery/French* 24 16 17 $12

Pike Place Market | 1902 Pike Pl. (Stewart St.) | 206-441-3669 | www.lepanier.com

The "smell of fresh-baked bread lures you in" at this Pike Place Market French bakery and cafe where raters revel in a "fabulous" croissant and coffee or a pâté sandwich for not much dough; the "line moves fast", and while some then grab a seat and "make up their market shopping list", others "sit at the window" reliving "memories of Paris."

	FOOD	DECOR	SERVICE	COST

Le Pichet ◐ *French* 25 | 21 | 21 | $32

Pike Place Market | 1933 First Ave. (Virginia St.) | 206-256-1499 | www.lepichetseattle.com

"Worth the trip" for "the roast chicken alone" (made to order for two), this Pike Place Market cafe (sibling of Café Presse) is loved for its "simple, straightforward" Gallic bistro fare at "reasonable prices"; the "aloof service" and decor with a zinc bar lend an air of "one of those old French movies" – especially if you order a *pichet* (pitcher) of wine.

NEW Lloyd Martin ⊠ *American* - | - | - | M

Queen Anne | 1525 Queen Anne Ave. N. (bet. Galer & Garfield Sts.) | 206-420-7602 | www.lloydmartinseattle.com

Lush takes on tried-and-true favorites, influenced by circa-1900 recipes, distinguish this midpriced Eclectic on Queen Anne, named for the two grandfathers of chef-owner Sam Cranell (ex Quinn's Pub); the handsome room with dark woods and soft lighting is comfortable for dropping by, though it's nice enough for date night too.

NEW Local 360 ◐ *American/Pacific NW* - | - | - | M

Belltown | 2234 First Ave. (Bell St.) | 206-441-9360 | www.local360.org

Ingredients and a beer-and-wine list sourced from within 360 miles of this hip Belltowner make for affordable, up-to-the-minute Pacific Northwest meals that lean toward groovy comfort food; formerly home to the modern-looking Flying Fish, the space has been redone in rustically woodsy style, seemingly a nod to the local farms that supply its kitchen, while the staff is well versed in the sustainable ethos that governs the place.

Local Vine *Eclectic* - | - | - | M

Capitol Hill | 1410 12th Ave. (at Madison & Union Sts.) | 206-257-5653 ◐

NEW University Village | 2620 NE University Village St. (25th Ave.) | 206-527-6222

www.thelocalvine.com

This urbane Capitol Hill wine bar pours some 80 wines by the glass, boasts a full bar and offers a midpriced menu of seasonally changing Eclectic small plates (think mac 'n' cheese with apple and shallot shoestrings); the ultramodern room has tables, but also low sofas and lots of pillows for a living-room feel; P.S. a University Village offshoot opened recently.

Lockspot Cafe *American/Seafood* 18 | 11 | 17 | $15

Ballard | 3005 NW 54th St. (32nd Ave.) | 206-789-4865

"Fish and beer" reel in Ballard locals and "visitors" for "old-fashioned" American seafood dishes in an old wood-tavern setting; be aware the place is "nothing special" though it's next to the Hiram M. Chittenden Locks so visitors can walk over and "watch the boats."

Z Lola ◐ *Greek* 25 | 22 | 23 | $39

Downtown | Hotel Andra | 2000B Fourth Ave. (Virginia St.) | 206-441-1430 | www.tomdouglas.com

Tom Douglas' take on modern Greek cooking has "nailed it" at this Downtowner next to the Hotel Andra, known for its "to-die-for" goat tagine and "unbelievable" breakfasts, all "reasonably priced" for the quality and quantity; service is "top-notch" and the cocoa-and-caramel decor is quite "snazzy", adding up to an experience that's "memorably good."

Long Provincial Vietnamese ◐ *Vietnamese* 21 | 19 | 19 | $27

Downtown | 1901 Second Ave. (Stewart St.) | 206-443-6266 | www.longprovincial.com

A sibling of the popular Tamarind Tree, this Downtowner offers a "huge" Vietnamese menu that includes "original and delightful" dishes not often tasted around town at prices that don't "break the piggy bank"; service is "usually attentive", and the "elegant" dining room has a striking jellyfish tank that leads the way to the Jelly Bar "scene."

Louie's Cuisine of China *Chinese* - | - | - | I

Ballard | 5100 15th Ave. NW (51st St.) | 206-782-8855 | www.louiescuisine.com

"Old-fashioned" Cantonese-Mandarin fare makes this Ballard stalwart a favorite with locals "craving" dim sum plates (no carts here) and "American-Chinese" classics like almond chicken (and General Tso's) at low prices; fans forgive the lackluster setting and service, and night owls note that it's open till midnight on Fridays and Saturdays.

Louisa's Café & Bakery *American* ▽ 16 | 12 | 15 | $22

Eastlake | 2379 Eastlake Ave. E. (Louisa St.) | 206-325-0081 | www.louisascafe.com

Just "blocks away" from the houseboats and residential areas of Eastlake, this "popular" American bakery and cafe is filled with neighbors seeking "affordable" breakfasts and "homemade" comfort food; the "casual" setting features artwork by locals, and if the service seems "pedestrian", that's only part of its hippie-ish charm; P.S. it now serves wine.

Lowell's *American* 20 | 15 | 16 | $25

Pike Place Market | 1519 Pike Pl. (bet. Pike & Pine Sts.) | 206-622-2036 | www.eatatlowells.com

This tri-level Pike Place Market "favorite" remains a "hangout" for its "unbeatable views" of Elliott Bay plus the "basic" American "classic diner" fare (think Seattle fish 'n' chips) that's "super-fresh, plentiful" and low-priced; granted it's "not big on decor" or service and some say a "tourist trap", but the "crowds" would indicate that most don't care.

Luc *American/French* 25 | 22 | 22 | $39

Madison Valley | 2800 E. Madison St. (28th Ave.) | 206-328-6645 | www.luc-seattle.com

"Talented" chef Thierry Rautureau "scores big" with his wildly anticipated casual French-American in tony Madison Valley, a "class act" offering "impeccably prepared bistro-style fare" delivered with "courteous service" at prices that are "more than reasonable"; the vintage-look setting with a zinc bar is just steps from "haute-cuisine" sibling Rover's and is "hopping" with the "din" of celebs and the near-famous.

	FOOD	DECOR	SERVICE	COST

Luigi's Pizza & Pasta 🄼 *Italian* — | - | - | - | I |

Magnolia | 3213 W. McGraw St. (32nd Ave.) | 206-286-9000

"Excellent thin-crust" pizza starts with homemade dough and sauce at this family-owned spot that's a standby for Magnolia residents for its pies, "decent" pastas and salads; the quarters are small and so are the prices, and it's also popular for "takeout."

Luisa's Mexican Grill *Mexican* — ▽ 23 | 18 | 22 | $20

Greenwood | 9776 Holman Rd. NW (6th Ave.) | 206-784-4132 | www.luisasmexicangrill.com

A Greenwood "favorite for years", this Mexican is loved for its "to-die-for" pork carnitas and its grilled corn tortillas "made in the *casita*" at the entrance and "served with butter"; the hacienda decor and "quick service" only make it better - especially for families with "kids."

Luna Park Cafe *American* — 18 | 19 | 16 | $18

West Seattle | 2918 SW Avalon Way (Manning St.) | 206-935-7250 | www.lunaparkcafe.com

Fans "love" the "quirky" "flair" of this low-budget American that pairs "West Seattle history" with "burgers and shakes" and they encourage newcomers to "try the breakfasts - any of them" offered all day; named for an old amusement park, the tavern setting is filled with local memorabilia and "reminiscent of the 1950s", while the service roller-coasters from surly to "sweet."

Lunchbox Laboratory *Burgers* — 24 | 10 | 14 | $17

South Lake Union | 1253 Thomas St. (Pontius Ave.) | 206-621-1090 | www.lunchboxlaboratory.com

With "a myriad of choices" from classic and "exotic" meats, cheeses, toppings and even salt, hamburger hounds can select each element at this South Lake Union American, resulting in "amazing" creations "huge" enough to "feed two adults" (and "worth the splurge").

Lynn's Bistro 🄼 *French* — 25 | 18 | 23 | $41

Kirkland | 214 Central Way (Main St.) | 425-889-2808 | www.lynnsbistro.com

Chef-owner Lynn Tran's "exquisite" French cuisine with Asian touches comes at "most reasonable prices" and with accommodating service, making her Kirkland kitchen a "favorite" of locals who dub it a "keeper" for a "romantic dinner" or a "business meeting"; with its setting of soft-green walls and flower-topped tablecloths, acolytes attest that as long as you don't expect a "trendy" evening, you'll be "well satisfied"; P.S. it now serves wine.

Machiavelli ⊠ *Italian* — 24 | 17 | 22 | $26

Capitol Hill | 1215 Pine St. (Melsose Ave.) | 206-621-7941 | www.machiavellis.com

"Delicious" Italian pastas that "won't break the bank" keep the crowds coming to this "down-to-earth" Capitol Hill trattoria that just simply "always works"; the "lively" setting is old-world "quaint" and service "friendly and efficient", but keep in mind that the "no-reservations policy" spells a "wait", unless you "arrive when it opens."

	FOOD	DECOR	SERVICE	COST

Macrina Bakery & Cafe *Bakery/Dessert* 25 | 17 | 19 | $15

Belltown | 2408 First Ave. (bet. Battery & Wall Sts.) | 206-448-4032
SODO | 1943 First Ave. S. (Holgate St.) | 206-623-0919
Queen Anne | 615 W. McGraw St. (bet. 6th & 7th Aves.) | 206-283-5900
www.macrinabakery.com

"Fantabulous" rustic sandwiches, soups and "addictive" baked goods warm up surveyors who praise these "gastronomic landmarks"; the "lofty" bakery/cafe settings make a "perfect lunch spot", but some caution "eat before you go" because you'll "wait a long time for a table."

NEW Madison Park Conservatory *American* - | - | - | E

Madison Park | 1927 43rd Ave. E. (bet. E. Madison & Newton Sts.) | 206-324-9701 | www.madisonparkconservatory.com

Cormac Mahoney presents ingenious takes on au courant New American dishes at this slightly spendy Madison Parker serving dinner and Saturday brunch; with tables and cabinets crafted out of old barge wood, the rustically antique rooms spread over two floors are spacious, a bit clubby and filled with A-listers every night; P.S. it hosts the pop-up Tako Truk on Sundays (4-8 PM).

Mae Phim Thai *Thai* 23 | 8 | 19 | $13

Downtown | 213 Pike St. (bet. 2nd & 3rd Aves.) | 206-623-7453 | www.maephimpike.com
Downtown | 94 Columbia St. (1st Ave.) | 206-624-2979 | www.maephim.com

Located Downtown, this "awesome" Thai doubleheader is Siamese cuisine "at its speedy best" - and "cheap" to boot; both locations are "jam-packed at lunch", and Pike Street is "an excellent choice" before "going to Beniroya Hall" for a concert.

Mae's Phinney Ridge Cafe *American* 15 | 13 | 15 | $16

Phinney Ridge | 6412 Phinney Ave. N. (65th St.) | 206-782-1222 | www.maescafe.com

Phinney Ridge's "cow-themed" American is where neighbors "stuff" themselves with "big heaping plates" of homemade cinnamon rolls, corned beef hash and other diner fare for not much moo-la; the staff is "friendly" and there's lots of bovine knick-knackery to check out, and since it's a "favorite" stop before a trip to the Woodland Park Zoo, it can be a "madhouse on the weekends"; P.S. not open for dinner.

Maggie Bluff's *Burgers* 19 | 19 | 20 | $21

Magnolia | Elliott Bay Marina | 2601 W. Marina Pl. (Magnolia Bridge) | 206-283-8322 | www.maggiebluffs.com

"Excellent" French-dip sandwiches, "one of the better burgers" around and a "terrific view" of the ocean from the patio keep boaters and the brunch-and-lunch bunch coming to this "reliable", affordable Magnolia eatery, part of the Restaurants Unlimited chain; the "nice staff" makes it an easy place to "kick back" - likewise the "nautical"-leaning decor that was recently spiffed up (post-Survey).

	FOOD	DECOR	SERVICE	COST

Malay Satay Hut *Malaysian* | 21 | 11 | 15 | $22 |

International District | Orient Plaza | 212 12th Ave. S. (Boren Ave. S.) | 206-324-4091
Redmond | 15230 NE 24th St. (152nd St.) | 425-564-0888
www.malaysatayhut.com
"Even the unadventurous" can find "mouthwatering" eats on the "extensive menus" at this "affordable" Malaysian duo where the no-frills rooms get "insanely jammed" at lunch (Redmond has "throngs of Microsofties swarming"); service is lackluster, and if some say it's "gone downhill", others still keep it on their "regular rotation."

Malena's Taco Shop ⊄ *Mexican* | 18 | 6 | 16 | $11 |

Ballard | 2010 NW 56th St. (bet. 20th & 22nd Aves.) | 206-789-8207
Queen Anne | 620 W. McGraw St. (bet. 6th & 7th Aves.) | 206-284-0304
At this south-of-the-border pair in Queen Anne and Ballard, the "namesake tacos are the thing to try" for their "flavorful Mexican goodness" and admirable "price-to-quality ratio"; decor and service are as "simple" as the grub, which fans find "pretty authentic."

Maltby Cafe *American* | 22 | 15 | 22 | $19 |

Maltby | 8809 Maltby Rd. (Broadway Ave.) | 425-483-3123 | www.maltbycafe.com
Visitors to Maltby's "nearby nurseries" and wineries stop in for "cinnamon rolls the size of hubcaps" and "mounds" of breakfast and lunch fare (no dinner) at this affordable "country-style" converted schoolhouse with helpful service; some sniff it's "nothing to write home about", but those waiting in "long lines" on weekends disagree.

Mama's Mexican Kitchen *Mexican* | 18 | 17 | 18 | $19 |

Belltown | 2234 Second Ave. (Bell St.) | 206-728-6262 | www.mamas.com
Before hitting a "show at The Crocodile", hearty eaters stop by this "divey" Belltown Mexican "landmark" for "ginormous burritos" and "gloppy, sloppy", "cheesy" grub washed down with "wicked" margaritas; while the place is festooned in "brilliantly beautiful kitsch" – including the Elvis Room – "to say service is sporadic is being generous."

Mamma Melina *Italian* | 23 | 19 | 22 | $32 |

University Village | 5101 25th Ave. NE (Blakeley St.) | 206-632-2271 | www.mammamelina.com
At this Varchetta family Italian, the move from a "rustic" University District storefront to "lovely" modern digs near University Village didn't deter the crowds from coming for the moderately priced "comfort" fare and "fresh-made" pastas and pizzas; though Mamma's retired, her sons (who also own Barolo) are in charge catering to everyone from those "bicycling on the Burke-Gilman Trail" to power-shoppers from the posh U-Village mall nearby.

Maneki Ⓜ *Japanese* | 25 | 15 | 20 | $29 |

International District | 304 Sixth Ave. S. (bet. Jackson & Main Sts.) | 206-622-2631 | www.manekirestaurant.com
The true "old standard" for "authentic, nontrendy" traditional Japanese cuisine in the ID comes via this "Seattle establishment"

(the original opened in 1904) offering "excellent sushi and home-style dishes" at a "superb value for the money"; service can be "slow" and it's always busy in the wait-list-only dining room, but those who reserve ahead can "enjoy dinner seated on the floor" in the "tatami rooms."

Maple Leaf Grill *Eclectic* ▽ 20 | 17 | 24 | $27

Maple Leaf | 8929 Roosevelt Way NE (90th St.) | 206-523-8449 | www.mapleleafgrill.com

"Unique, tasty" midpriced entrees and sandwiches provide comfort food for Maple Leaf denizens at this old house turned Eclectic eatery; "warm, friendly" service, craft beers and wine add to reasons "locals" have "mixed feelings" about "word getting out about the place", as some are tempted to "keep it all" to themselves.

NEW Marché *French* - | - | - | M

Pike Place Market | 86 Pine St. (bet. First Ave. & Pike Pl.) | 206-728-2800 | www.marcheseattle.com

Chef-owner Daisley Gordon revs up contemporary French bistro dishes in small and large plats, adds house charcuterie and 60 wines by the bottle, then keeps the bill midpriced at this new entry upstairs from sibling Cafe Campagne; the space is Parisian-modern in textured cement grays and red, with an old wooden wagon in the window and a view of market goings-on and Elliott Bay beyond.

Z NEW Marination Station *Hawaii/Korean* 27 | 11 | 20 | $11

Capitol Hill | 1412 Harvard Ave. (bet. Pike & Union Sts.) | No phone

Z Marination Mobile *Hawaii/Korean*

Location varies; see website | No phone
www.marinationmobile.com

A "taste explosion" of Korean-Hawaiian eats is "the bomb" at this blue food truck offering "cheap" options from "pork-centric" sliders and tacos to the "savory, spicy splendor" of "kimchi rice" and bulgogi and even "Spam musubi"; "be prepared to wait in line", but you can also expect "friendly" smiles from the servers; P.S. a brick-and-mortar Capitol Hill offshoot opened post-Survey.

Marjorie *Eclectic* 25 | 21 | 22 | $44

Capitol Hill | 1412 E. Union (14th St.) | 206-441-9842 | www.marjorierestaurant.com

"Happy" campers declare this former Belltowner is "better than ever" on Capitol Hill, where the "culinary magic" is "wrapped in warmth" and the Eclectic menu "takes chances, hitting more than it misses" with "masterful dishes" and "killer desserts"; what's more, the staff "makes you feel like family" in a recently (post-Survey) expanded setting that's industrial yet colorful and "cozy."

Marrakesh Moroccan *Moroccan* ▽ 21 | 22 | 19 | $33

Belltown | 2334 Second Ave. (bet. Bell & Wall Sts.) | 206-956-0500 | www.marrakeshseattle.com

With b'steeya "to die for" among the "delicious" Moroccan dishes on its midpriced menu, this Belltowner pleases with its unique dining "experience"; you sit at low tables while eating with "your bare hands" and getting "entertained by belly dancers", and the initiated ask "what's not to like?"

NEW Marrow American — - | - | - | M

Tacoma | 2717 Sixth Ave. (N. Anderson St.) | 253-267-5299 | www.marrowtacoma.com

Tacoma food lovers cheered when this inventive, reasonably priced New American eatery opened recently offering rich, up-to-the-minute cooking ordered from two distinctly named menus: the carnivorous Marrow and the vegetarian Arrow; the lively dining room is decked out in arty light-bulb chandeliers and Bulleit bourbon bottles, and reservations are a must.

Mashiko *Japanese* — 28 | 19 | 22 | $39

West Seattle | 4725 California Ave. SW (bet. Alaska & Edmunds Sts.) | 206-935-4339 | www.sushiwhore.com

An "amazing assortment" of sustainable seafood "not to be had elsewhere" plus moderate prices equal lines and "a decent wait" at this "edgy", "inventive" West Seattle Japanese "joint"; afishionados sit at the sushi bar and order chef-owner Hajime Sato's "omakase to die for", so never mind if the decor is a mite "dated."

Matt's Famous Chili Dogs *Hot Dogs* — 23 | 8 | 17 | $9

South Seattle | 6615 E. Marginal Way S. (4th Ave.) | 206-768-0418 | www.mattshotdogs.com

This South Seattle counter-service standout gets kudos for franks "anyway you want them" "piled high" with toppings, as in the "fabulous Chicago-style dogs"; its wide variety of wieners and sausages makes it a "hot-dog lover's dream", but there are also burgers and fries - and all of 'em take only the smallest of bite out of your wallet.

Matt's in the Market *Pacific NW/Seafood* — 25 | 21 | 23 | $42

Pike Place Market | 94 Pike St. (1st Ave.) | 206-467-7909 | www.mattsinthemarket.com

The "quintessential" low-key Pacific Northwest dining experience keeps fin-atics coming to this Pike Place Market "standby" where the "honkin' tuna or catfish top the list" of seafood "worth the price"; though Matt's gone (he opened Lecosho) you still "can't go wrong" here, as service is "terrific" and there's a "view over the market" through tall arched windows.

Matts' Rotisserie & Oyster Lounge *American* — 21 | 19 | 21 | $32

Redmond | Redmond Town Ctr. | 16551 NE 74th St. (bet. 164th & 166th Aves.) | 425-376-0909 | www.mattsrotisserie.com

Hailed as a "surprising find" in Redmond Town Center, this "excellent" American seafood/rotisserie offers the likes of "steak, chicken, fish, oysters and clams" at a "medium price" and "served fast"; it fills a variety of needs from "romantic" dinner to a "nice hangout" after a "show at the nearby theater", plus there's a "decent happy hour."

	FOOD	DECOR	SERVICE	COST

Maximilien *French* | 23 | 22 | 23 | $37 |

Pike Place Market | 81A Pike St. (1st Ave.) | 206-682-7270 | www.maximilienrestaurant.com

"You can't beat the view" of Elliott Bay from the upstairs dining room of this "unpretentious" Pike Place Market hideaway serving "traditional" midpriced French fare made with "delectable" "seasonal" local ingredients; service is "pleasant" in its "cozy" white-tablecloth setting filled with antique mirrors (plus outdoor seating), and best of all, an "indulgent" three-course Sunday Supper is $35.

Maxwell's Restaurant + Lounge ☒ *Pacific NW* | - | - | - | E |

Tacoma | Walker Bldg. | 454 St. Helens Ave. (6th Ave.) | 253-683-4115 | www.maxwells-tacoma.com

Situated in an "uncrowded" area of Downtown Tacoma in the historic 1927 Walker Building, this Pacific Northwester offers an "upscale" menu featuring "excellent" dishes including cioppino; with "classy" art deco decor and expensive prices to match, it's a noteworthy member of the city's growing restaurant scene; P.S. it features all-day happy hour on Mondays and Saturdays.

May ◐ *Thai* | ▽ 26 | 20 | 21 | $25 |

Wallingford | 1612 N. 45th St. (Woodlawn Ave.) | 206-675-0037 | www.maythaiseattle.com

"Luscious", "beautifully presented" Thai cuisine boasts a "complexity" of "unusual flavors" at this "upscale" Wallingford standout embellished with "intricate" decor including an upstairs dining room featuring hanging lamps and teak wood reclaimed from a house in Thailand; gentle prices are made even more palatable with two daily happy hours.

Mayuri *Indian* | 23 | 13 | 18 | $20 |

Bellevue | 15400 NE 20th St. (156th Ave.) | 425-641-4442
Bothell | 20611 Bothell-Everett Hwy. (Maltby Rd.) | 425-481-6900
www.mayuriseattle.com

This duo is a "hands-down" "favorite" for its "slightly unusual" pennywise Northern and Southern Indian fare that fans call "authentic" and full-flavored from freshly ground spices; decor is nothing special but the staff is "attentive", and while lunch is strictly "buffet", dinner brings a full menu that includes a multidish "Thali" at the Bellevue branch.

McCormick & Schmick's *Seafood* | 21 | 20 | 21 | $42 |

Downtown | 1103 First Ave. (Spring St.) | 206-623-5500
Bellevue | Lincoln Sq. | 700 Bellevue Way NE (8th St.) | 425-454-2606
www.mccormickandschmicks.com

Locals depend on these Downtown and Bellevue "bustling, noisy fish house" chain links in "tasteful" dark-wood settings for "always excellent" wild and farmed salmon, oysters and even fish 'n' chips; the menu with "lots of options" is suitable even for a "large group", and patrons profess that it's "worth the cost" for the quality - although the "happy-hour deals" lure in bargain-hunters.

	FOOD	DECOR	SERVICE	COST

McCormick's Fish House & Bar *Seafood* 23 | 21 | 23 | $36

Downtown | 722 Fourth Ave. (bet. Cherry & Columbia Sts.) | 206-682-3900 | www.mccormickandschmicks.com

Look to the "huge fresh fish and shellfish list" for the daily catch at this "outstanding" Downtown seafood "institution" offering "tasty" lunches and dinners at a "sensible price" and "friendly, efficient service" in a classic East Coast–style setting of dark wood and brass; the "bargain happy-hour food" is an office-drone favorite, and on game days there are specials tailored for sports fans.

Mediterranean Kitchen *Lebanese/Mediterranean* 26 | 14 | 22 | $25

Bellevue | 103 Bellevue Way NE (1st St.) | 425-462-9422
Kirkland | 11412 NE 124th St. (bet. 113th & 116th Aves.) | 425-823-8101
www.mediterraneankitchens.net

"It's hard to miss" the "giant portions" of "carefully spiced" Lebanese-Mediterranean couscous and "garlic"-infused dishes making their way through the dining room at this "excellent" Bellevue spot (with a Kirkland sibling); though the decor isn't much, prices are "reasonable" and the service adds to reasons fans "keep coming back.

Mee Sum Pastry *Chinese/Dessert* ∇ 24 | 8 | 16 | $10

Pike Place Market | 1526 Pike Pl. (bet. Pike & Pine Sts.) | 206-682-6780
University District | 4343 University Way NE (bet. 43rd & 45th Sts.) | 206-632-7298 ◐
www.meesum.com

Just a "stand across from" the main Pike Place Market, this Chinese is "loved" for its "must"-have barbecue pork hum bow, dumplings and pastries at a beyond-cheap price; for many locals it's a "regular stop on a market noshing tour"; P.S. the University District offshoot is sit-down.

Melrose Grill *Steak* ∇ 27 | 16 | 21 | $37

Renton | 819 Houser Way S. (bet. Wells Ave. & Williams St.) | 425-254-0759 | www.melrosegrill.com

"Excellent steaks" plus "local wines and beers" keep this Renton oldie where the "price is right" understandably "very busy on weekends"; set in a "historic building" that was a hotel and eatery in 1901, the mirrored back bar still remains; P.S. it takes only limited reservations (see website for specifics), so regulars advise to "go early to grab a table."

Melting Pot *Fondue* 19 | 18 | 19 | $44

Seattle Center | 14 Mercer St. (Queen Anne Ave.) | 206-378-1208
Bellevue | 302 108th Ave. NE (2nd Pl.) | 425-646-2744
Tacoma | 2121 Pacific Ave. (21st St.) | 253-535-3939
www.meltingpot.com

"It's all about sharing" and "cooking your own food" at this chain serving "every kind of fondue", including "delicious" chocolate pots; while it's a "romantic" "treat" for "younger couples" and "fun to do with a group", critics contend it's "overpriced" and "pretentious", and would prefer a "more casual" setup; P.S. go with a large party if you want "two burners."

Z Metropolitan Grill *Steak* 26 | 24 | 25 | $63

Downtown | 820 Second Ave. (Marion St.) | 206-624-3287 | www.themetropolitangrill.com

"Bring it on" cheer meat mavens at this Downtown "steakhouse par excellence" where beef rules but "anything on the menu is good" and comes in "huge portions"; the "friendly" staff makes everyone "feel comfortable" in the "old-style", "clubby" environs (now equipped with a new bar), leaving the big-spenders who dine here chuckling "healthy, shmealthy."

Mexico Cantina Y Cocina *Mexican* - | - | - | M

Downtown | Pacific Pl. | 600 Pine St. (6th Ave.) | 206-405-3400 | www.eatatmexico.com

"High-quality" Mexican cuisine with modern twists attracts Pacific Place visitors with "tastefully presented" seasonal dishes; the colorful spot is a respite for shoppers and a place to grab a bite before a movie just a few steps away, but is "worth a visit" even for non galleria-goers.

Meza *S American* - | - | - | I

Capitol Hill | 1515 14th Ave. (Pike St.) | 206-922-2399 | www.mezaseattle.com

"Extremely good", budget-friendly South American tapas and bocadilla sandwiches are on the bill of fare at this smallish Capitol Hill cafe, which also mixes "sangria by the pitcher" to "wet your whistle"; locals stop by for a quick bite, and it's gaining a "late-night scene" with its full bar and 3 AM weekend closing time.

Mike's Noodle House ⇏ *Noodle Shop* 23 | 8 | 12 | $12

International District | 418 Maynard Ave. S. (bet. Jackson & Kings Sts.) | 206-389-7099

Slurpers clamor for the "delicious" authentic soups, congee and *sui kau* dumplings at this "tasty" and "frugal"-minded noodle nook in the ID; filled with expats, it's "ultracramped", service is "nonexistent" and it's "cash-only", so come prepared.

NEW Milagro Cantina *Mexican* - | - | - | M

Kirkland | 148 Lake St. S. (bet. Kirkland & 2nd Aves.) | 425-952-6270 | www.milagrocantina.com

Kirklanders collect at this contemporary Mexican eatery for stylish takes on Latin favorites at prices that aren't over-the-top; the stunningly modern room is right on the Lake Street social drag, making it date-worthy, while the comely staff is welcoming and attentive.

Mioposto *Italian* ▽ 23 | 19 | 20 | $17

Mt. Baker | 3601 S. McClellan St. (Mt. Baker Blvd.) | 206-760-3400 | www.seattle-eats.com

Seattle Eats is behind this "nicely priced" Mt. Baker haunt serving "bacon-and-egg" breakfast pizzas, thin-crust regular pies and other dishes from the wood oven; the "pleasant" wood-and-brick setting across from the park is manned by a "friendly" staff, and you can also "call in your order" for pickup.

Mission ◐ *Pan-Latin* 20 | 19 | 17 | $21

West Seattle | 2325 California Ave. SW (bet. Admiral Way & College St.) | 206-937-8220 | www.missionbar.com

"Simple, delightful" made-from-scratch tacos, tamales and enchiladas are part of the "fresh" appeal at this Pan-Latin West Seattle canteen; the high-ceilinged space with a rock wall and candles sets a dramatic backdrop, and two "awesome" happy hours lubricate the scene.

Z Mistral Kitchen *American* 26 | 24 | 24 | $62

South Lake Union | 2020 Westlake Ave. (8th Ave.) | 206-623-1922 | www.mistral-kitchen.com

Chef-owner William Belickis walks a "no-net culinary tightrope" at his "stunning", "ambitious" South Lake Union New American proffering multiple "creative" menus and "dazzling cocktails" in a variety of settings; the modern dining room is casual and less costly than the "beautiful" Jewel Box room and "marvelous" chef's table where tasting menus are served, and there are lounge bites too; P.S. it goes Middle Eastern on Monday nights with Arabesque, a pop-up offering dishes from Egypt, Morocco, Israel and beyond.

Moghul Palace *Indian* - | - | - | M

Bellevue | 677 120th Ave. NE (8th St.) | 425-451-1909 | www.moghulpalace.net

A Bellevue "favorite", this moderately priced Indian Moghul dishes out chicken tikka masala, curries and tandoori dishes; though decor and service are nothing special, the long menu provides scads of choices and a lunch buffet gets you in and out for around $10.

Mojito *Pan-Latin* ▽ 25 | 16 | 25 | $22
(fka La Casa del Mojito)

Lake City | 7545 Lake City Way NE (11th Ave.) | 206-525-3162 | www.mojito1.com

"Delicious" fare leans to Cuba, Venezuela, Colombia and environs for regional specialties washed down with mojitos at this Lake City Pan-Latin; the bright-yellow building is filled with rustic furniture and "rhythmic energy" - and there's often live music on weekends too.

Molly Moon Truck ⊠ Ⓜ *American/Dessert* - | - | - | I

Location varies; see website | No phone | www.mollymoonicecream.com

Folks line up for the handmade ice cream dished out in crazy-good flavors (salted caramel, balsamic-strawberry) when this pretty blue truck rolls into the neighborhood; the mobile unit of a local ice cream maker, it's so popular that it still gets takers even in the chill of winter.

NEW Momiji *Japanese* - | - | - | M

Capitol Hill | 1522 12th Ave. (bet. E. Pike & Pine Sts.) | 206-457-4068 | www.momijiseattle.com

Already a hit, this Capitol Hill Japanese lures the young crowd with modern sushi rolls sporting monikers like Rockstar and Casanova, along with traditional kaiseki dinners and shochu cocktails; a sibling of Umi Sake House and Kushibar, it features minimalist rooms surrounding a tranquil courtyard, with immense woven light fixtures illuminating hand-carved tables and a sushi bar.

Mondello Ristorante *Italian* ▽ 25 | 21 | 25 | $38

Magnolia | 2435 33rd Ave. W. (McGraw St.) | 206-352-8700 | www.mondelloristorante.com

This "top-notch" "family-run" Magnolia Italian sibling of Queen Margherita Pizza turns out homemade pastas and sauces made with "fresh ingredients" from Mamma's recipes; the "not-too-fancy" sea-centric setting, moderate pricing and "friendly staff" make it "perfect for an intimate dinner" with friends or one's significant other; P.S. there's now outdoor seating.

Monkey Bridge *Vietnamese* 21 | 20 | 18 | $20

Ballard | 1723 NW Market St. (17th Ave.) | 206-297-6048 | www.themonkeybridge.com

Boosters of this Ballard Vietnamese say they "could eat here daily", given the "affordable", "delicious" pho soups, banh mi sandwiches and other specialties accented with "interesting spices" and dished out in "generous portions"; an "accommodating staff" and colorful "modern" setting also figure into a "deal" of a "comfortable" "authentic meal."

Monsoon *Vietnamese* 25 | 21 | 21 | $38

Capitol Hill | 615 19th Ave. E. (bet. Mercer & Roy Sts.) | 206-325-2111

Monsoon East *Vietnamese*

Bellevue | 10245 Main St. (bet. Bellevue Way & 102nd Ave.) | 425-635-1112

www.monsoonseattle.com

"Fabulous" Vietnamese dishes such as clay-pot catfish and crispy drunken chicken have made fans for this Capitol Hill-Bellevue twin-set that turns out "interesting" fare "presented with flair"; despite spotty service, there's a "soothing atmosphere" in the stylish settings for an overall "satisfying" evening that "warrants the tariff"; P.S. there's also Sunday brunch.

Morton's The Steakhouse *Steak* 25 | 23 | 25 | $69

Downtown | 1511 Sixth Ave. (bet. Pike & Pine Sts.) | 206-223-0550 | www.mortons.com

"They do it right every time" at this Downtown link in the Chicago-born chain of "old-school" steakhouses, where "outstanding" meat and famously "huge portions" make it the "king of the hill"; clubby decor with leather booths and "friendly", "attentive service" factor in for an all-around "excellent" experience - that's even better when on an "expense account."

Moshi Moshi *Japanese* 23 | 25 | 21 | $31

Ballard | 5324 Ballard Ave. NW (bet. 22nd Ave. & Vernon Pl.) | 206-971-7424 | www.moremoshi.com

Under a "beautiful" 22-ft.-tall "lighted" sakura cherry blossom tree, Ballard fin fanciers and clubbers chow down on "excellent" midpriced sushi and other Japanese fare at this "unpretentious" eatery; a "crazy-genius bartender" pours specialty cocktails, making the "energy" "perfect" for a "night out" or an "after-work respite."

Musashi's *Japanese* 23 10 18 $21

Wallingford | 1400 N. 45th St. (Interlake Ave.) | 206-633-0212

"With a line always running out the door", it's clear that locals and nearby U of W students approve of the "awesome, fresh" sushi at this "tiny" Wallingford Japanese with "friendly service"; it's a "cash-only" operation but tabs are small, so as long as "you don't need atmosphere", it's considered a "bang for your buck."

Muy Macho *Mexican* - - - I

South Park | 8515 14th Ave. S. (bet. Cloverdale & Sullivan Sts.) | 206-763-3484

Fans of Mexican fare don't let the temporary "loss of the South Park bridge" keep them away from what they call one of the "absolute best" taquerias around, known for its tacos al pastor (with marinated pork) and dishes including pozole; though the atmosphere is slight, tabs are too, making it attractive to expats and workers from nearby Boeing alike.

Z Nell's *American* 27 22 25 $48

Green Lake | 6804 E. Green Lake Way N. (1st Ave.) | 206-524-4044 | www.nellsrestaurant.com

From a "superb", "innovative" menu spotlighting "fresh" local meats, seafood and produce, chef-owner Philip Mihalski cooks up "consistently first-rate" fare at his "beautiful" and expensive Green Lake New American; the "quiet setting" is conducive to conversation (some say "boring") and service is "elegant", so acolytes attest it's an experience "you can count on" all-around.

Neville's at the British Pantry *British* - - - I

Redmond | 8125 161st Ave. NE (bet. 83rd St. & Redmond Way) | 425-883-7511 | www.thebritishpantryltd.com

"British favorites" like "authentic" sausage rolls and beef Wellington, plus homemade bread, pastries and desserts keep expats and others coming to this "cute" Redmond English "charmer"; sophisticates can get a traditional afternoon tea while the working class chows down on "bangers and mash", and it's all wallet-friendly.

New Orleans Creole *Cajun/Creole* ∇ 19 17 21 $23

Pioneer Square | 114 First Ave. S. (bet. Washington St. & Yesler Way) | 206-622-2563 | www.neworleanscreolerestaurant.com

Big Easy enthusiasts head to this "inexpensive" Pioneer Square Cajun-Creole for "authentic" étouffée that's "to die for" and "real Abita beer" downed to the beat of "live" jazz, zydeco and blues nightly; the dining room is dominated by the stage and old brick walls lined with black-and-white photos of musicians, and if hardliners say "you won't think you're in the French Quarter", Seahawks Sundays bring a pre-game New Orleans-style brunch.

FOOD | DECOR | SERVICE | COST

New Star *Chinese/Seafood* — - | - | - | I

International District | 516 S. Jackson St. (bet. 5th & 6th Aves.) | 206-622-8801 | www.newstarseafood.com

Local government workers and software cubicle jockeys call this spacious, modern IDer "one of the better Chinese" around for "solid" Cantonese and Hong Kong-style fare including "fresh seafood" from the live tanks and pan-fried noodles; expats have the advantage of being able to order from the specials written on the walls in *Hanzi*, but the cheap bills benefit all.

Nishino *Japanese* — 27 | 23 | 25 | $52

Madison Park | 3130 E. Madison St. (Lake Washington Blvd.) | 206-322-5800 | www.nishinorestaurant.com

"Supreme sushi" "sparkling with creativity" pleases the well-heeled patrons of this "mellow" Madison Park Japanese, where "beautiful" fish is fashioned into "traditional" and "contemporary" fare by Nobu-trained co-owner Tatsu Nishino; insiders "go omakase" and let the masters "do their work" in the "lovely", stylish room that's comfortable whether you're in "jeans or a suit", and don't mind a bill that's a "splurge."

Noah's Bagels *Bakery* — 17 | 10 | 14 | $10

Downtown | 600 Fourth Ave. (Cherry St.) | 206-264-4817
Queen Anne | 2133 Queen Anne Ave. N. (bet. Boston & Crockett Sts.) | 206-282-6744
University Village | 2746 NE 45th St. (25th Ave.) | 206-522-1998
Kirkland | Parkplace Ctr. | 320 Parkplace Ctr. (Central Way) | 425-827-7382
Mercer Island | 7808 SE 28th St. (78th St.) | 206-232-8539
www.noahs.com

Noshers say the bagels with a "schmear" or made into sandwiches "hit the spot" for a "quick breakfast or lunch" at these bakery chain links; they're "far from the authentic" New York model, but "loved" enough that the no-frills shops get "crowded" and even "sell out" regularly; that said, "servers don't waste much time and you get what you pay for."

Noble Court *Chinese* — 18 | 12 | 14 | $21

Bellevue | 1644 140th Ave. NE (Bellevue-Redmond Rd.) | 425-641-6011

The "food flows freely" during the dim sum service at this "dependable" and affordable Bellevue Chinese that "tends to be packed on weekends", in part because some regulars "go with a big party" to "try out as many different dishes as possible"; decor and service don't rate any raves (though it might help to "speak the language"), but it's all "well worth it."

Noodle Boat *Thai* — ▽ 26 | 21 | 25 | $19

Issaquah | 700 NW Gilman Blvd. (7th Ave.) | 425-391-8096 | www.noodleboat.com

Issaquah locals laud the "exceptional", "fresh" Thai curries, noodles and "amazing variety" of dishes with "exciting presentations" at this "family-owned", inexpensive "gem"; "service is polite and efficient", and the fare is MSG-free, but just know its strip-mall locale is a little "hard-to-find."

Northlake Tavern & Pizza House *Pizza* 22 | 10 | 16 | $20

University District | 660 Northlake Way NE (7th Ave.) | 206-633-5317 | www.northlaketavern.com

Since 1954, this "old favorite" near the U of W campus has fed students and locals alike with "killer" "gargantuan" pizzas built with "thick, chewy crusts" and a "ton of cheese and condiments"; patrons profess that you'll "waddle home" and warn that on Husky "game days", it's so "packed" you "may never see the inside."

O'Asian *Chinese* 20 | 21 | 20 | $27

Downtown | 800 Fifth Ave. (bet. Columbia & Marion Sts.) | 206-264-1789 | www.oasiankitchen.com

This "upper-class" Chinese in Downtown's Fifth Avenue Building gets kudos for "fabulous" dim sum made fresh daily in the kitchen; a "pleasant" staff and "handsome" contemporary decor make it an "elegant" "lunch option" for the "office crowd", even if it's "slightly higher priced" than humbler ID options.

Ocho ◐ *Spanish* 24 | 19 | 17 | $28

Ballard | 2325 NW Market St. (24th Ave.) | 206-784-0699 | www.ochoballard.com

Ballard's "hip" are on hand for the "terrific", "authentic" tapas at this "nook" of a Spaniard with coppery walls, outdoor seating and a "convivial" staff; "servings are tiny", but then you can "order and try a lot" - especially since it's "reasonably priced."

'Ohana ◐ *Hawaiian* 21 | 19 | 19 | $25

Belltown | 2207 First Ave. (Blanchard St.) | 206-956-9329 | www.ohanabelltown.com

The "quirky atmosphere" includes a thatched-roof tiki bar and bamboo booths at this affordable Belltown Hawaiian serving "creative" sushi and Island specialties including kalua pork and loco moco; happy hour means sake and pupus, and the bar scene heats up on weekends.

Z Olivar M *Spanish* 26 | 25 | 24 | $38

Capitol Hill | Loveless Bldg. | 806 E. Roy St. (Harvard Ave.) | 206-322-0409 | www.olivarrestaurant.com

"Unusual" tapas "set the scene for wonderful entrees" at chef-owner Philippe Thomelin's "welcoming" Capitol Hill Spaniard that "consistently excites" with seasonally changing "authentic" fare that's both "daring" and "delicious"; "gracious" service and "gorgeous" Russian murals make for a "charming" ambiance that's "perfect" for a "little dinner" paired with a movie at the Harvard Exit across the street.

Oliver's Twist *Pacific NW* 23 | 21 | 19 | $25

Phinney Ridge | 6822 Greenwood Ave. N. (70th St.) | 206-706-6673 | www.oliverstwistseattle.com

"Delectable small plates" are on the "short-and-sweet" menu of "shareable" meals at this affordable Phinney Ridge Pacific NWer that's really "more of a drinks with nibbles" spot where the "cocktails have kick"; though "it gets crowded so service can be slow", "comfy sofas" help make it a fine "hangout."

Olympia Pizza & Spaghetti House *Greek/Pizza* 19 | 12 | 19 | $17

Capitol Hill | 516 15th Ave. E. (bet. Mercer & Republican Sts.) | 206-329-4500 | www.olympiapizza3.com ◐
Wallingford | 4501 Interlake Ave. N. (45th St.) | 206-633-3655 | www.olypizza.net
Queen Anne | 1500 Queen Anne Ave. N. (Galer St.) | 206-285-5550 | www.olympiapizzaonqueenanne.com
West Seattle | 5605 Delridge Way SW (bet. Findlay & Juneau Sts.) | 206-933-7550 | www.olypizza.net

"Leave your pizza expectations at the door" of these Greek-style parlors and enjoy the "reasonably priced", "extra-cheesy" 'za with a world of toppings like Hawaiian or, fittingly, feta cheese; service is "friendly", and while Queen Anne, Wallingford and West Seattle are no-frills settings, Capitol Hill has a "beautiful bar."

Ooba's Mexican Grill *Mexican* 24 | 13 | 18 | $14

Bellevue | 555 108th Ave. NE (bet. 4th & 8th Sts.) | 425-646-4500 ⊠
Redmond | 15802 NE 83rd St. (158th Ave.) | 425-702-1694
Woodinville | 17302 140th Ave. NE (175th St.) | 425-481-5252 ⊠
www.oobatooba.com

"High-quality" yet "inexpensive" Mexican fare including "fish tacos", "portobello quesadillas" and "multiple salsas" are "*bueno*" thanks to a focus on "better ingredients" at this trio of "highly regarded" "solid performers"; the setting is "very casual", and though service is "fast", "lunch lines can spill outside."

Original Pancake House *American* 21 | 13 | 19 | $17

Ballard | 8037 15th Ave. NW (bet. 80th & 83rd Sts.) | 206-781-3344
Kirkland | Parkplace Ctr. | 130 Parkplace Ctr. (Central Way) | 425-827-7575
www.originalpancakehouse.com

Some of the "best pancakes on the planet" (including the "decadent" Dutch Baby) can be found at these Ballard and Kirkland outposts of the "popular", "competitively priced" chain that also pleases with "puffed-up" omelets and other "delicious" morning items; it's "a bit worn around the edges", but "inviting" and "quick" once you sit down - just "get there early on the weekends, or your breakfast will end up being lunch."

Osteria La Spiga *Italian* 23 | 23 | 21 | $43

Capitol Hill | 1429 12th Ave. (bet. Pike & Union Sts.) | 206-323-8881 | www.laspiga.com

"Artful, intriguing" homemade pastas and breads in the style of Emilia-Romagna induce "wows" from regulars of this chic Capitol Hill Italian; service is improving and "casual" yet "sophisticated" industrial decor (plus a large patio) adds to the dining "pleasure", all making it "so worth the money."

	FOOD	DECOR	SERVICE	COST

Other Coast Cafe *Sandwiches* ▽ 26 | 6 | 15 | $12

Ballard | 5315 Ballard Ave. NW (bet. 22nd Ave. & Vernon Pl.) | 206-789-0936
Capitol Hill | 721 E. Pike St. (Harvard Ave.) | 206-257-5927
www.othercoastcafe.com

"Unbelievable" sandwiches "the size of a spare tire" and full of thin-sliced meats drive this cheap "old-school" Ballard shrine to East Coast-inspired subs and sammies - but "fortunately you can order a half"; while the no-frills setting doesn't daunt devotees, they suggest "a few more" staffers and "another oven" might speed the process; P.S. the Capitol Hill branch opened post-Survey.

Ototo Sushi *Japanese* 19 | 15 | 19 | $31

Queen Anne | 7 Boston St. (Queen Anne Ave.) | 206-691-3838 | www.ototosushi.com

Regulars "sit at the sushi bar" with sake cocktails while "talking to the chefs" for something of "dinner and a show" at this neighborhood Japanese just off Queen Anne Avenue; the simple "Tokyo modern" room, moderate prices and "pleasant" staff all add up to an "enjoyable" visit.

Outback Steakhouse *Steak* 15 | 14 | 17 | $28

Bellevue | 15100 SE 38th St. (150th Ave.) | 425-746-4647
Kirkland | 12120 NE 85th St. (122nd Ave.) | 425-803-6880
Bothell | 22606 Bothell-Everett Hwy. (228th St.) | 425-486-7340
Everett | 10121 Evergreen Way (100th St.) | 425-513-2181
Federal Way | 2210 S. 320th St. (23rd Ave.) | 253-839-1340
Tacoma | 3111 S. 38th St. (Cedar St.) | 253-473-3669
Olympia | 2615 Capital Mall Dr. SW (bet. Black Lake Blvd. & Cooper Point Rd.) | 360-352-4692
Tukwila | 16510 Southcenter Pkwy. (Strander Blvd.) | 206-575-9705
www.outback.com

"Reliable" (if "not prime") seasoned steaks provide "real value for the dollar" at this "Aussie-themed" "middle-of-the-road" chain where folks love to "overindulge in the bloomin' onion"; it's too "kitschy" and "packaged" for pickier patrons and the "cute" service is "hit-or-miss", but "you can take all of your kids and your neighbors too" since you'll blend right into the "noisy" surroundings; P.S. the North Seattle and South Lake Union locations have closed.

Oyster Bar on Chuckanut Drive *Seafood* 25 | 24 | 24 | $44

Bow | 2578 Chuckanut Dr. (Oyster Creek Ln.) | 360-766-6185 | www.theoysterbaronchuckanutdrive.com

A "must day-trip from Seattle", it's "well worth" the scenic drive up to the small town of Bow for "stellar" seafood coupled with a "spectacular" panoramic view of Samish Bay and the San Juan Islands at this "pricey" lodgelike landmark; you can "see where your oysters were plucked down below", and service is "perfection with a capital 'P.'"

Pabla Indian Cuisine *Indian* 22 | 13 | 19 | $21

Downtown | 1516 Second Ave. (bet. Pike & Pine Sts.) | 206-623-2868

Pabla Punjabi Cuisine *Indian*

Downtown | 999 Third Ave. (Madison St.) | 206-623-5587

(continued)

Pabla Punjabi Palace ☒ *Indian*

SeaTac | 15245 International Blvd. (Military Rd.) | 206-623-0580
www.pablaindiancuisine.com

"Convenient" for Downtown office workers and SeaTac folks, these Punjabi cafes are sought out for their "delicious" "great selection" of Indian dishes, with simple decor and cordial service completing the picture; the newer Third Avenue spot is open for lunch only.

Pacific Café Hong Kong Kitchen Ⓜ *Chinese* | - | - | - | I |

International District | 416 Fifth Ave. S. (Jackson St.) | 206-682-0908 | www.pacifichkcafe.com

Cha chaan teng (Hong Kong-Cantonese-Western fusion cuisine) draws surveyors to this IDer where "to-die-for" chicken wings and "tasty" soft-shell crabs are washed down with "fresh" fruit or red bean shakes; the simple room's 30 seats fill up fast with expats and office drones, since it's also a "good value."

Pacific Grill ☒ *Seafood/Steak* | 26 | 23 | 23 | $43 |

Tacoma | Waddell Bldg. | 1502 Pacific Ave. (15th St.) | 253-627-3535 | www.pacificgrilltacoma.com

Chef-owner Gordon Naccarato "pours his heart and soul" into this "amazing" Tacoma "find" serving "quality steaks and fish" with an emphasis on seasonal ingredients that "shine"; service is "pleasing", as is the stylish brick-walled room in the historic Waddell Building, and while tabs can be "a bit high", a noodle bar pops up in the lounge Monday-Saturday and "happy-hour deals" are "awesome."

Paddy Coynes Irish Pub ◐ *Pub Food* | 16 | 18 | 18 | $23 |

South Lake Union | 1190 Thomas St. (bet. Fairview & Minor Aves.) | 206-405-1548

Bellevue | Lincoln Sq. | 700 Bellevue Way NE (8th St.) | 425-453-8080

Tacoma | Hotel Olympus | 815 Pacific Ave. (bet. 8th & 9th Sts.) | 253-272-6963

www.paddycoynes.net

"Satisfying", "decently priced" Irish pub grub includes Gaelic classics such as shepherd's pie and soda bread at this trio where locals give "two thumbs-up" to "a wee bit of Ireland"; woody decor and amiable service make it a "comfortable" spot for "dinner or a Guinness."

Pagliacci Pizza *Pizza* | 23 | 12 | 19 | $17 |

Capitol Hill | 2400 10th Ave. E. (Miller St.) | 206-726-1717

Capitol Hill | 426 Broadway E. (Harrison St.) | 206-726-1717

Greenwood | 851 NW 85th St. (Dibble Ave. NW) | 206-726-1717

Interbay | 1614 W. Dravus St. (bet. 16th & 17th Aves.) | 206-726-1717

North Seattle | 315 N. 145th St. (bet. Greenwood & Phinney Aves.) | 206-726-1717

Sand Point | 6244 Sand Point Way NE (bet. 62nd & 63rd Sts.) | 206-726-1717

Queen Anne | 550 Queen Anne Ave. N. (Mercer St.) | 206-726-1717

(continued)

(continued)

Pagliacci Pizza

University District | 4529 University Way NE (bet. 45th & 47th Sts.) | 206-726-1717
Bellevue | Bellevue Sq. | 563 Bellevue Sq. (bet. Bellevue Way & 8th St.) | 425-453-1717
NEW Bellevue | 8 100th Ave. NE (Main St.) | 206-726-1717
www.pagliacci.com
Additional locations throughout the Seattle area

"High-end", thin-crust pizzas made with "fresh" artisan ingredients like local meats from Salumi and "wow"-inducing seasonal toppings (pear and Gorgonzola, anyone?) give this chainlet's 'za its added "value"; sure, it's "not New York" pie, but fans say it's "Seattle's standard" and give kudos for quick delivery and a "nice" staff - and some locations even have a small dining area.

Pair S M *American/Mediterranean* 26 | 21 | 22 | $36

Ravenna | 5501 30th Ave. NE (55th St.) | 206-526-7655 | www.pairseattle.com

Ravenna locals call this midpriced New American-Med in a French farmhouse setting such a "find" that "excellent does not do it justice"; the "tasty" small plates are paired - hence the name - with wine, and though "they don't take reservations" except for large groups, those willing to wait concede it's "worth the minor frustration."

Palace Kitchen ◐ *American* 25 | 21 | 23 | $39

Downtown | 2030 Fifth Ave. (Lenora St.) | 206-448-2001 | www.tomdouglas.com

Possibly "the best chicken you will ever have" and an "amazing burger" are among the "excellent", "not-too-spendy" fare featuring seasonal "local ingredients" at this Tom Douglas New American Downtowner; decorated in a "funky" yet "chic" palace theme and manned by a "friendly, attentive staff", it's open until 1 AM - with a late-night breakfast that begins at 10 PM.

Z Palisade *Seafood* 24 | 27 | 25 | $49

Magnolia | Elliott Bay Marina | 2601 W. Marina Pl. (Garfield St.) | 206-285-1000 | www.palisaderestaurant.com

Regulars "go at sunset" for the "superb views" of Elliott Bay and the marina at this "pricey-but-worth-it" Pacific Northwest seafooder in Magnolia, where the "fresh" shore fare is "amazing" and the staff "rolls out the red carpet for each guest"; though the supper-club decor seems a little "dated, it still works", especially for "special occasions."

Palomino *Italian* 20 | 20 | 20 | $35

Downtown | City Centre Bldg. | 1420 Fifth Ave. (bet. Pike & Union Sts.) | 206-623-1300
Bellevue | 610 Bellevue Way NE (6th St.) | 425-455-7600
www.palomino.com

An "institution" for the "posh" business crowd, shoppers and theatergoers, these "see-and-be-seen" scenes offer "modern" Italiana made with "quality" ingredients including particularly "fantastic pizza" at moderate prices; the "ultraslick Italian-chic" decor (it's part of the Restaurants Unlimited chain) and "friendly staff" guarantee it's "always crowded", especially during the "fabulous" happy hour.

Pan Africa Market ☒ *African* - - - I

Pike Place Market | 1521 First Ave. (bet. Pike & Pine Sts.) | 206-652-2461 | www.panafricamarket.com

With its "delicious", "affordable" African meaty stews and vegetable dishes, this Pike Place Market cafe leans to Ethiopian offerings and is a "nice change of pace" from the "fish and more fish" menus typical in this seafood-heavy part of town; "don't be put off by the bare-bones decor" - it's a relaxing refuge from the market's bustle.

Panos Kleftiko ☒ *Greek* 22 15 20 $30

Queen Anne | 815 Fifth Ave. N. (bet. Aloha & Valley Sts.) | 206-301-0393 | www.panoskleftiko.com

"If you like garlic" you'll be "in heaven" at this "down-home" Queen Anne Greek with "authenticity to spare" in addition to "fresh" flavors and reasonable prices; located close to the Seattle Center, the "typical taverna atmosphere" is a draw "before the opera" or a play, since "it's only a couple of blocks' walk."

Paragon Restaurant & Bar *American* ∇ 19 17 17 $30

Queen Anne | 2125 Queen Anne Ave. N. (bet. Boston & Crockett Sts.) | 206-283-4548 | www.paragonseattle.com

It may be "quiet and sedate" at the booths in back where a mid-priced American menu with a Southern twist is served, but there's a "rocking-with-the-band" feel at the 30-ft. front bar where there's live music most nights at this "popular" Queen Anne fixture; weekend brunch adds to the options.

☒ Paseo ☒☒☒ *Cuban* 28 9 16 $13

Shilshole | 6226 Seaview Ave. NW (62nd St.) | 206-789-3100
Fremont | 4225 Fremont Ave. N. (bet. 42nd & 43rd Sts.) | 206-545-7440
www.paseoseattle.com

"Magnificent" and "messy" Cuban sandwiches stuffed with "pork that melts in your mouth" practically "inspire poetry" at this "busy", wallet-friendly duo; it may "run out of bread" and is "cash-only", but that doesn't stop fans from forming "lines out the door", especially at the "wee" Fremont original, though the newer Shilshole branch has "shorter" waits.

Pasta & Co. *Italian* 22 15 17 $19

University District | University Vill. | 4622 26th Ave. NE (Blakeley St.) | 206-523-8594
Bellevue | 10218 NE Eighth St. (bet. Bellevue Way & 102nd Ave.) | 425-453-8760
www.pastaco.com

These "dependable" Italian "delis" are a "no-brainer" for busy days or when "entertaining guests" with their "top-of-the-line" take-out options for "easy" meals that taste "homemade"; though some find the fare a little "overpriced", there are a few seats at each location for those who can't wait till they get home to dig in.

	FOOD	DECOR	SERVICE	COST

Pasta Bella *Italian* ▽ 21 | 23 | 21 | $27

Ballard | 5913 15th Ave. NW (bet. 59th & 60th Sts.) | 206-789-4933 | www.pastabellaseattle.com

This "dependable" Ballard pasta place is an everyday "favorite" for "consistent" midpriced Italian classics delivered by a "friendly" crew; "quaint" rustic decor makes it a natural for a low-key date.

Pearl *Pacific NW* 22 | 22 | 22 | $43

Bellevue | Lincoln Sq. | 700 Bellevue Way NE (8th St.) | 425-455-0181 | www.pearlbellevue.com

It "feels like a little slice of LA" at this "beautiful find" in Bellevue, where the "creative" Pacific NW menu has an "excellent presentation" and is served by a "trendy", "well-trained staff"; the "cool", dark decor is "definitely a step up" for the neighborhood options, and "complimentary valet service" is an additional plus; P.S. there's a hopping bar scene, and happy hour is "always packed."

Pecos Pit BBQ ☒ *BBQ* 26 | 9 | 21 | $11

SODO | 2260 First Ave. S. (bet. Holgate & Lander Sts.) | 206-623-0629

The "killer" BBQ is "juicy, flavorful" and "messy" at this SODO "shack" that's a "best bet" say fans who "drive miles to oink it up" with "spicy pulled-pork sandwiches" and other cheap 'cue at outdoor picnic tables; it's open weekdays only from 11 AM–4 PM, and cognoscenti warn "beware the spicy hot sauce."

Pegasus Pizza *Pizza* 21 | 11 | 16 | $19

West Seattle | 2770 Alki Ave. SW (bet. 61st & 62nd Aves.) | 206-932-4849 | www.pegasuspizza.com

"Hefty pizzas" draw pie partisans to this parlor that's "practically on the beach" in West Seattle, where the "value-sized" Greek-influenced creations have names like the Hercules; "kids love it" and in turn it's "warm and welcoming to families."

Perché No Pasta & Vino Ⓜ *Italian* 24 | 20 | 24 | $28

Green Lake | 1319 N. 49th St. (Green Lake Way) | 206-547-0222 | www.perchenopastaandvino.com

"Delicious" Italian "classics" with a "twist" draw locals to this Green Lake trattoria owned and run by the Kong family who "always make you feel welcome" and "aim to please" with an "extensive" menu of "freshly made" dishes at "good value"; the "lively" setting includes a "second-floor balcony" with "an entertaining view" of the dining and bar areas below.

Peso's Kitchen & Lounge ◐ *Mexican* 22 | 18 | 16 | $23

Queen Anne | 605 Queen Anne Ave. N. (bet. Mercer & Roy Sts.) | 206-283-9353 | www.pesoskitchen.com

Breakfasts are a "haven from the morning bustle" at this affordable Queen Anne cantina that dishes out "solid" "gourmet" Mexican eats morning through night; the decor is haute hacienda but "service is not its strong suit", and those looking for a quieter meal should arrive "early" since it turns into a "lively night club" and "singles" scene as the evening progresses.

	FOOD	DECOR	SERVICE	COST

P.F. Chang's China Bistro *Chinese*

18	19	18	$30

Downtown | Westlake Ctr. | 400 Pine St. (4th Ave.) | 206-393-0070
Bellevue | Bellevue Sq. | 525 Bellevue Sq. (8th St.) | 425-637-3582
Lynnwood | Alderwood Mall | 3000 184th St. SW (Alderwood Mall Pkwy.) | 425-921-2100
www.pfchangs.com

"Light, delicious", "Americanized" Chinese food keeps fans "coming back" - especially for the "standout" lettuce wraps - at these "trendy", "stylish" chain links; though not everyone is convinced ("overpriced", "ordinary", "loud"), the "consistent" service is a plus, as is the "smart" menu "catering to people with allergies" and other needs.

Philadelphia Fevre *Deli*

-	-	-	I

Madison Valley | 2332 E. Madison St. (John St.) | 206-323-1000 | www.phillysteakshop.com

Philly cheesesteaks provide a taste of the City of Brotherly Love at this Madison Valley storefront with a menu of regional favorites that also includes hoagies, scrapple and Tastykake; the setting is no-frills, and the bill rings up budget-friendly.

Phnom Penh *Cambodian*

-	-	-	I

International District | 660 S. King St. (bet. Maynard & 7th Aves.) | 206-748-9825 | www.phnompenhnoodles.com

"Awesome", inexpensive rice noodle dishes draw slurpers to this Cambodian eatery in the ID where the bamboo decor suggests a rural Southeast Asian grass hut; fans say it's a "great place to finish off a tour" of Chinatown; P.S. closed Wednesdays.

Pho Bac *Vietnamese*

▽ 24	7	14	$12

International District | 1314 S. Jackson St. (bet. Ranier & 12th Aves.) | 206-323-4387

One of the first and "arguably the best" pho shop in Seattle, this IDer ladles out a "rich broth" packed with noodles, "quality meats" and more for little money; the no-frills setting is in a "funky location" and service "needs improvement", but "don't let that stop you."

Pho Cyclo Café *Vietnamese*

22	16	15	$14

Capitol Hill | 406 Broadway E. (Harrison St.) | 206-329-9256
NEW **Downtown** | Wells Fargo Ctr. | 999 Third Ave., Plaza One (Marion St.) | 206-623-3958 ☒
SODO | 2414 First Ave. S. (bet. Lander & Stacy Sts.) | 206-382-9256 ☒
www.phocyclocafe.com

"Popular" for its "authentic" and "quick" pho soups and banh mi sandwiches, this trio also offers budgetwise entrees for more options than at most Saigon noodle shops; service varies, but the interiors complete with cyclo bicycle carts recall a "Vietnamese street eatery" and fans favor them as a "fast-food alternative."

Phoenecia *Eclectic*

▽ 27	21	25	$33

West Seattle | 2716 Alki Ave. SW (bet. 60th & 61st Aves.) | 206-935-6550 | www.phoeneciawestseattle.com

This reinvented longtime West Seattle spot is "better than ever" offering a "hip" take on artisan pizza plus reasonably priced Eclectic small plates made with local, sustainable ingredients; it's already a neighborhood "favorite" where patrons "are treated like old friends" in a stylishly "cool" room that looks out on Alki Beach.

Pho Thân Brothers *Vietnamese* 22 | 8 | 15 | $10

Ballard | 2021 NW Market St. (20th Ave.) | 206-782-5715
Capitol Hill | 516 Broadway E. (Republican St.) | 206-568-7218
Green Lake | 7714 Aurora Ave. N. (77th St.) | 206-527-5973
University District | 4207 University Way NE (bet. 42nd & 43rd Sts.) | 206-632-7272
West Seattle | 4822 California Ave. SW (Edmunds St.) | 206-937-6264
Bellevue | 1299 156th Ave. NE (13th St.) | 425-818-4905
Redmond | 7844 Leary Way NE (Cleveland St.) | 425-881-3299
Edmonds | 22618 Hwy. 99 (76th Ave.) | 425-744-0212 ⊄
Everett | 500 SE Everett Mall Way (bet. 3rd & 7th Aves.) | 425-353-8906 ⊄
Tacoma | 10435 Pacific Ave. S. (bet. 104th & 106th Sts.) | 253-548-8886
www.thanbrothers.com
Additional locations throughout the Seattle area

"You can't go wrong" with 17 kinds of "delicious" steaming pho soup plus a free cream puff that make up the "cheap", "quintessential comfort meals" at this local Vietnamese chain; the "spartan environment" and "minimal service" don't deter those looking for a quick lunch or who don't care to "cook at home."

Piecora's NY Pizza *Pizza* 21 | 11 | 15 | $17

Capitol Hill | 1401 E. Madison St. (14th Ave.) | 206-322-9411 | www.piecoras.com

"All the right smells" greet patrons at this "old-fashioned" Capitol Hill "pizza joint" owned by New York expats, where a "brusque-but-polite" staff dishes out affordable "classic cheese" 'za in "by-the-slice" or pie-sized options; while the setting's "nothing special", there's a "strong microbrew selection" and pro sports to watch on the big TV, so "who cares?"

Pig Iron Bar-B-Q Ⓢ Ⓜ *BBQ* 24 | 17 | 19 | $25

South Seattle | 5602 First Ave. S. (Findlay St.) | 206-768-1009 | www.pigironbbq.net

"Finger-licking good" slow-smoked BBQ draws followers to this affordable South Seattle joint (a sibling of Slim's Last Chance Chili Shack next door) for "succulent ribs" and such plus homemade sweet tea and margaritas; "tattooed servers" fit in with a clientele that includes Harley enthusiasts; just forget about getting dinner since they close at 4 PM.

Pike Pub & Brewery *Pub Food* 17 | 17 | 17 | $22
(aka Pike Brewing Co.)

Pike Place Market | 1415 First Ave. (Union St.) | 206-622-6044 | www.pikebrewing.com

It's not just the "amazing beer museum" and on-site brewery that make this "hip" Pike Place Market pub a "favorite" – the affordable grub is made with "local ingredients", all the better to match with "heavenly seasonal ales (if you're lucky)"; service is "solid", and it's one of the few local options to "go with the kids" and still get an "adult" meal.

Pike Street Fish Fry ◐ *American/Seafood* 22 | 11 | 17 | $18

Capitol Hill | 925 E. Pike St. (10th Ave.) | 206-329-7453 | www.pikestreetfishfry.net

"Fish 'n' chips the way they were meant to be" reel in throngs to this small American next to Nuemo's on Capitol Hill, where "delicious" "cheap eats" are often made with unusual sustainable seafood and frites come with lots of sauces; though it "takes a while" to get served, the "cool" atmosphere adds to its "late-night" draw.

Pink Door ◐ *Italian* 22 | 22 | 21 | $37

Pike Place Market | 1919 Post Alley (bet. Stewart & Virginia Sts.) | 206-443-3241 | www.thepinkdoor.net

"Well-done" midpriced Italian fare is only part of the picture at this "unique" Pike Place Market perennial offering "delightful lunches" "outside on the deck" and classy "outré" cabaret acts during the "dinner show"; service is "friendly" amid "whimsical" decor in a downstairs setting that's pure "baroque basement", and half the "quirky fun" is finding the "speakeasy" pink door on Post Alley.

Piroshky Piroshky *Russian* 24 | 10 | 17 | $10

Pike Place Market | 1908 Pike Pl. (bet. Stewart & Virginia Sts.) | 206-441-6068 | www.piroshkybakery.com

"Wonderful smells" beckon boosters of "handmade" pastry to this Russian bakery in the Pike Place Market, where the inexpensive "warm" and "hearty" stuffed *piroshky* come in over 20 "sweet and savory" flavors; what's more, as customers stand in the "fast"-moving line, they can watch the "little pockets of heaven" being made.

Pizzeria Pulcinella *Pizza* - | - | - | I

South Seattle | 10003 Rainier Ave. S. (68th Ave.) | 206-772-6861 | www.pulcinellapizza.com

With some of the "best Neapolitan pizza" around, this Napoli-certified pizzeria on the old Lake Washington driving route in South Seattle offers wallet-pleasing classic pies baked in an imported Valoriani "wood-burning oven" plus beer "straight from Italy"; located in a vintage building, the room is decked out with mahogany woodwork and marble tables.

Place Pigalle Restaurant & Bar *Pacific NW* 25 | 25 | 24 | $46

Pike Place Market | 81 Pike St. (Pike Pl.) | 206-624-1756 | www.placepigalle-seattle.com

Francophiles find "one of Seattle's best dining experiences" at this "sweet little" pricey Pacific Northwest bistro in the Pike Place Market where "inventive" and "beautiful" cuisine is made with "local and seasonal" ingredients; "hidden" in the market labyrinth, the "romantic" dining room gets extra appeal from its Elliott Bay view with a "100-mile perspective."

	FOOD	DECOR	SERVICE	COST

Plaka Estiatorio Ⓜ *Greek* — ▽ 27 | 22 | 22 | $27

Ballard | 5407 20th Ave. NW (Russell Ave.) | 206-829-8934 | www.plakaballard.com

"Some of the tastiest Greek dishes in the city" come from the kitchen of this Ballard "family-run" taverna turning out "amazing", "authentic" specialties from the owner's native Athens; the "rustic" setting is filled with vintage "family pictures" and since there are also "great prices", surveyors ask "what more could you want?"

Plum Vegan Bistro *Vegan/Vegetarian* — 25 | 21 | 22 | $23

Capitol Hill | 1429 12th Ave. E. (bet. Pike & Union Sts.) | 206-838-5333 | www.plumbistro.com

This stylish, airy Capitol Hill cafe on trendy 12th Avenue East is "proof" positive that vegan vittles can be made "as greasy and tasty" as "anything else" that's "damn good"; devotees bring their "carnivore friends" for the signature "mac 'n' yease" and happy hour, and the "special deals" make herbivores "love the experience" even more.

Poco Wine Room ◐ *Mediterranean/Pacific NW* — ▽ 19 | 20 | 21 | $34

Capitol Hill | 1408 E. Pine St. (14th Ave.) | 206-322-9463 | www.pocowineroom.com

An "absolute gem" for its "well-prepared" bites, "varied, creative wine selection" and cocktails, this Capitol Hill Med-Pacific NWer appeals to locals with small and shareable plates and entrees; the "well-designed" bi-level space is "lively" some nights and "peaceful" on others, and the upstairs is "especially great for get-togethers."

Pogacha *Croatian/Pacific NW* — 17 | 14 | 18 | $24

Bellevue | Bellevue Plaza | 119 106th Ave. NE (Main St.) | 425-455-5670

Issaquah | 120 NW Gilman Blvd. (Front St.) | 425-392-5550

www.pogacha.com

Café Pogacha Ⓢ *Croatian/Pacific NW*

Bellevue | 10885 NE 4th St. (108th Ave.) | 425-450-0333

The "memorable" Croatian pogacha flatbread baked at these eateries sets the stage for "delightful", "properly priced" Pacific Northwest fare delivered with pleasant service; Issaquah is a "low-key" spot with occasional "live music in the bar", the Bellevue strip-maller is cheery and casual, and the nearby Café offers breakfast, lunch and coffee.

Pomegranate Bistro *American* — 25 | 18 | 20 | $26

Redmond | 18005 NE 68th St. (180th Ave.) | 425-556-5972 | www.pomegranitebistro.com

"Fabulous", "creative" American fare comes courtesy of chef-owner-caterer Lisa Dupar at this Redmond bistro where the aptly named (pizzalike) firebread arrives right out of the oven and everything is "seasonal" and "reasonably priced"; the staff is "accommodating", and diners can sit and watch the kitchen action through a large "viewing window", plus it's "kid-friendly."

	FOOD	DECOR	SERVICE	COST

Ponti Seafood Grill *Seafood* | 24 | 23 | 22 | $46 |

Queen Anne | 3014 Third Ave. N. (Nickerson St.) | 206-284-3000 | www.pontiseafoodgrill.com

The "sublime" view of the Lake Washington Ship Canal adds to the "ambiance" at this Queen Anne "favorite" where the return of original chef Alvin Binuya brings "fresh", "fabulous" Pacific NW seafood that's "not to be missed"; it's "expensive but worth it", with a "convivial" staff and a "romantic" room with a Tuscan feel; P.S. the adjacent Café Ponti offers small plates plus a two-course $20 deal.

Poppy *American* | 25 | 20 | 23 | $45 |

Capitol Hill | 622 Broadway E. (Roy St.) | 206-324-1108 | www.poppyseattle.com

Chef-owner Jerry Traunfeld creates a "sense of adventure" at his Capitol Hill New American offering "terrific", "innovative" Thali-based locavore dinners with a "panoply" of small plates served all at once; "charming service" and "stunning" Scandinavian-inspired decor add to an "experience" that acolytes consider "quite reasonably priced."

NEW **Poquitos** ◐ *Mexican* | - | - | - | M |

Capitol Hill | 1000 E. Pike St. (10th Ave.) | 206-453-4216 | www.vivapoquitos.com

Tacos, burritos and goat *birria* (stew) are made with quality local meats at Capitol Hill's fun, midpriced Mexican cantina, a Bastille sib; its big digs wow with bright tiles and swooping ironwork, and you can watch the tortillas and guacamole being made by hand in kitchen niches; P.S. it offers two happy hours daily as well as weekend brunch.

Portage *French/Pacific NW* | 25 | 21 | 23 | $44 |

Queen Anne | 2209 Queen Anne Ave. N. (Boston St.) | 206-352-6213 | www.portagerestaurant.com

"Stunningly delicious" dinners with "fresh-from-the-market" flavors and "nuanced sauces" draw surveyors to this pricey Queen Anne French-Pacific NWer that's a sibling of June; the staff "radiates charm" in a "romantic" room that's "tiny" but "comfortable."

Portalis Wine Bar M *American/European* | - | - | - | M |

Ballard | 5205 Ballard Ave. NW (20th Ave.) | 206-783-2007 | www.portaliswines.com

This Ballard wine shop/bar turns out "well-prepared" bites including cheese and charcuterie plates plus other "reasonably priced" vino-friendly fare; the store dominates the "lovely" brick-walled room where the bar lures shoppers for a leisurely break.

Primo Grill *Mediterranean* | - | - | - | M |

Tacoma | 601 S. Pine St. (6th Ave.) | 253-383-7000 | www.primogrilltacoma.com

"Fantastic" Mediterranean cuisine plus steaks and pizzas are on the menu at Charlie McManus' midpriced Tacoma grill, which also offers a "well-chosen wine list"; the "classy casual" space has a "welcoming" feel, and locals like to "grab a stool in front of the bar" and watch the action in the open kitchen.

	FOOD	DECOR	SERVICE	COST

Proletariat Pizza *Pizza* — - | - | - | I

White Center | 9622 16th Ave. S. (bet. 98th & Roxbury Sts.) | 206-432-9765 | www.proletariatpizza.com

"Who knew White Center was a pizza mecca?" muse admirers citing "some of the best" handmade pies around with "delish" toppings turned out at this affordable eatery; though it's a bit "ambiance"-challenged, "all's forgiven" once the goods arrive.

Purple Café & Wine Bar *Pacific NW* — 20 | 21 | 20 | $36

Downtown | 1225 Fourth Ave. (University St.) | 206-829-2280
Bellevue | 430 106th Ave. NE (4th St.) | 425-502-6292
Kirkland | Parkplace Ctr. | 323 Parkplace Ctr. (Central Way) | 425-828-3772
Woodinville | 14459 Woodinville-Redmond Rd. NE (145th St.) | 425-483-7129
www.thepurplecafe.com

"Interesting" wines by the glass, flight or bottle pair up with "tasty" midpriced Pacific NW small plates at this grape-centric local mini-chain; decor ranges from "cool" to "upscale" (there's an "awesome wine tower" at the Downtown branch), service is generally "knowledgeable" and all locations are undeniably "popular."

Purple Dot Cafe ◐ *Chinese* — ∇ 17 | 11 | 14 | $19

International District | 515 Maynard Ave. S. (King St.) | 206-622-0288

Thrifty types chow down at this International District Chinese specializing in Hong Kong-style fare and "better-than-average dim sum"; the discolike purple-and-chrome room sees a lot of "big groups" and late-night action from nightcrawlers looking to sober up (it's open until 3:30 AM on the weekend).

Pyramid Alehouse *Pub Food* — 16 | 15 | 17 | $23

SODO | 1201 First Ave. S. (bet. Atlantic St. & Royal Brougham Way) | 206-682-3377 | www.pyramidbrew.com

Located across from the stadiums where the Mariners, Sounders and Seahawks play, this microbrewery fills with fans looking for "excellent" "housemade" tap beer and reasonably priced "pub grub to soak it all up"; it's "loud and crowded" and on game days the service can get a bit "slow", but the "staff will make you merry."

Queen City Grill *American* — 21 | 21 | 23 | $43

Belltown | 2201 First Ave. (Blanchard St.) | 206-443-0975 | www.queencitygrill.com

This "bustling", "reliable" Belltown American "classic" delivers its pricey seafood and other dishes with a "warm Northwest vibe" and a "friendly, professional staff"; the "clubby" interior is all dark wood and vintage booths, and the "comfy surroundings" make for great "people-watching" of "old-time Seattlelites."

Queen Margherita Pizza *Pizza* — - | - | - | M

Magnolia | 3111 W. McGraw St. (bet. Condon Way & 32nd Ave.) | 206-548-4908 | www.queenmargheritaseattle.com

Well-heeled Magnolia locals now have this midpriced pizza royal in their midst serving Neapolitan-style pies hot and blistered from the wood-fired imported oven; a sibling of the popular Mondello down the street, it offers Italian-focused wines to boot and serves it all in a '20s-style setting that incorporates industrial touches.

Queen Mary Tea Room 🅼 *Tearoom* 21 | 21 | 19 | $25

Ravenna | 2912 NE 55th St. (bet. 29th & 30th Aves.) | 206-527-2770 | www.queenmarytea.com

A "happy place" for a British breakfast or to spend the afternoon "with the girls", this Ravenna classic is known for its traditional tea service complete with "tasty" sandwiches, house-baked pastries and over 60 kinds of brews; "friendly, knowledgeable service and a gently priced bill all figure into the "delightful experience."

Quinn's Pub ◐ *American* 24 | 20 | 21 | $32

Capitol Hill | 1001 E. Pike St. (bet. 10th & 11th Aves.) | 206-325-7711 | www.quinnspubseattle.com

With its "unique slant" on artisanal gastropub grub, this midpriced Capitol Hill American gets kudos from fans for its "deliciously rich" fare including "fantastic" marrow bones and wild boar sloppy joes, bucked up by an "awesome" beer and booze list; situated in a "masterfully remodeled" old space on "happening" East Pike Street, it gets "noisy" and busy, but though it's "hip", it's "not limited to hipsters."

Racha *Thai* 20 | 19 | 19 | $23

Seattle Center | 23 Mercer St. (1st Ave.) | 206-281-8883 | www.rachathai.com

Tukwila | Westfield Southcenter | 1150 Southcenter Mall (bet. Andover Park & Southcenter Pkwy.) | 206-768-8883 | www.rachathai.com

Woodinville | 13317 NE 175th St. (bet. 133rd & 135th Aves.) | 425-481-8833 | www.rachawoodinville.com

Spicy chicken wings "like the devil's candy" are among the "taste treats" served in "generous" portions at this "upscale" Thai mini-chain; it's a "solid" choice for lunch, family dinners or "pre-function" meals and drinks for ACT theatergoers, with "friendly" staffers adding to the appeal.

Rancho Bravo *Mexican* 24 | 3 | 13 | $8

Capitol Hill | 1001 E. Pine St. (bet. 10th & 11th Aves.) | 206-322-9399

"Serious taco-truck food" that's "authentic", "cheap" and "amazingly delicious" gets a permanent home by way of the Rancho Bravo folks behind this Capitol Hill brick-and-mortar shop; it's a "far superior late-night option" to the usual burgers or dogs, "just keep your expectations low for atmosphere and service and all will be fine."

R&L Home of Good Bar-B-Que 🅂 🅼 ⊄ *BBQ* - | - | - | I

Capitol Hill | 1816 E. Yesler Way (bet. 18th & 19th Aves.) | 206-322-0271

"Absolutely fabulous" BBQ earns applause at this Capitol Hill institution where homestyle house-smoked pork ribs, brisket and pulled pork are served with a slice of bread; followers say it's "some of the best" in town and the staff's the "nicest" , though there's little decor; just be sure to bring cash (you won't need much).

	FOOD	DECOR	SERVICE	COST

☒ Ray's Boathouse *Pacific NW/Seafood* — 24 | 24 | 23 | $45

Shilshole | 6049 Seaview Ave. NW (60th St.) | 206-789-3770 | www.rays.com

A "splendid menu" of "melt-in-your-mouth" Pacific NW wild seafood coupled with "stunning views" across Shilshole Bay and service that's "all you can ask for" make this spendy "Seattle tradition" a "must" for impressing "out-of-town" visitors - especially during the Copper River salmon run; P.S. it changed chefs post-Survey.

Ray's Cafe *Pacific NW/Seafood* — 22 | 22 | 22 | $31

Shilshole | 6049 Seaview Ave. NW (60th St.) | 206-782-0094 | www.rays.com

It's pure "ecstasy" to "sit out on the deck" and watch the "bald eagles" above or "the salmon jump below" while noshing on "fine" seafood including crab cakes or sake kasu black cod at this Shilshole Pacific NWer; the "less-expensive cousin of Ray's Boathouse downstairs", it gets "a tad crowded", but nonetheless the "happy hour can't be beat" and the "friendly staff is exceptionally attentive."

Red Door ◐ *Pub Food* — ▽ 16 | 19 | 17 | $26

Fremont | 3401 Evanston Ave. N. (34th St.) | 206-547-7521 | www.reddoorseattle.com

Look for the red door to find this Fremont old faithful that's still a popular weekday "lunch spot" and "ale-and-nibbles" destination on the weekends; it "makes you feel like you're back in college" (but without the midterms) with gentle prices to match.

Red Fin ◐ *Japanese* — 21 | 21 | 19 | $35

Downtown | Hotel Max | 612 Stewart St. (7th Ave.) | 206-441-4340 | www.redfinsushi.com

A "pleasant surprise" in Downtown's Hotel Max, this Japanese has "something for everyone" in its "mix of sushi" and hot dishes, some with a modern twist - and in the morning, there's American breakfast; the "unrushed" tempo is "perfect" at the "end of a long day."

Red Lantern ☒ *Asian* — - | - | - | M

International District | 520 S. Jackson St. (bet. 5th & 6th Aves.) | 206-682-7211 | www.redlanternseattle.com

Modern Asian flavors hit the spot at this affordable ID cafe run by the Li family, which specializes in deeply flavored Northern Chinese and Korean dishes along the lines of beef lettuce wraps or Sichuan peppercorn shrimp; the contemporary dining room is comfortable and bright, and manned by an efficient staff that seems happy you're there.

Red Mill Burgers Ⓜ ⊄ *Burgers* — 24 | 11 | 15 | $12

Phinney Ridge | 312 N. 67th St. (Phinney Ave.) | 206-783-6362

Interbay | 1613 W. Dravus St. (15th Ave.) | 206-284-6363

NEW Red Mill Totem House ☒ Ⓜ *Burgers*

Ballard | 3058 NW 54th St. (32nd St.) | 206-784-1400

www.redmillburgers.com

Offering some of the most "amazing" burgers in town "greasy hands down", fans say this "old-fashioned" duo in Phinney Ridge and

Interbay completes the "perfect meal" with "onion rings that taste like onions" plus "must" milkshakes; it's definitely "worth the three days it shaves off your life", healthwise, and for lining up for "half your lunchtime", given the "bang for the buck"; P.S. the Ballard location, which adds fish 'n' chips to the formula, opened post-Survey.

Red Robin *Burgers* 16 | 15 | 17 | $19

Seattle Waterfront | Pier 55 | 1101 Alaskan Way (Spring St.) | 206-623-1942
Bellevue | Factoria Mall | 3909 Factoria Blvd. SE (40th Ct.) | 425-641-3989
Bellevue | 408 Bellevue Sq. (4th St.) | 425-453-9522
Issaquah | 1085 Lake Dr. (11th Ave.) | 425-313-0950
Redmond | 2390 148th Ave. NE (bet. 22nd & 24th Sts.) | 425-641-3810
Redmond | Redmond Town Ctr. | 7597 170th Ave. NE (76th St.) | 425-895-1870
Des Moines | 22705 Marine View Dr. S. (Kent Des Moines Rd.) | 206-824-2214
Everett | 1305 SE Everett Mall Way (Mall Dr.) | 425-355-7330
Lynnwood | 18410 33rd Ave. W. (184th St.) | 425-771-6492
Woodinville | 18029 Garden Way NE (140th Ave.) | 425-488-6300
www.redrobin.com
Additional locations throughout the Seattle area

"Deservedly popular", this chain attracts crowds with its 29 kinds of "delicious" burgers "done any way you like" and gets "woo-hoo's" for the "bottomless fries"; "kids love" birthdays here, and adults like the "fast service", "casual" setting and inexpensive tabs, plus you "know what to expect"; P.S. most locations offer gluten-free options.

Re:Public *Pacific NW* - | - | - | M

South Lake Union | 429 Westlake Ave. N. (bet. Harrison & Republican Sts.) | 206-467-5300 | www.republicseattle.com

In the heart of happening South Lake Union, this Pacific NWer in a vintage building is both approachable and au courant, dishing out moderately priced farm-to-table fare in a setting of old bricks and wood beams with modern straight-edged design and sexy, dark colors; elevated booths line a wall across from the bar so diners can survey the young, smart crowd.

NEW **Revel** *American/Korean* - | - | - | M

Fremont | 403 N. 36th St. (Phinney Ave. N.) | 206-547-2040 | www.revelseattle.com

Gussied-up, moderately priced Korean comfort food shines in the hands of Seif Chirchi and Rachel Yang (Joule) at this urbane Fremonter where everything's handmade and the flavors are strong and sophisticated; housed in an old building, its modern-industrial interior bustles with a younger crowd, while next door its 21-and-over lounge adjunct, Quoin, rocks the neighborhood at night.

Rikki Rikki *Japanese* 18 | 16 | 16 | $29

Kirkland | Parkplace Ctr. | 442 Parkplace Ctr. (Central Way) | 425-828-0707 | www.rikkirikki.com

Whether Kirklanders are shopping Parkplace Center or catching "dinner and a movie" at the nearby cinema, this "busy" Japanese haunt lures them in with sushi, noodles and tempura, all at midlevel prices; though service is a mixed bag, the orders "come out quickly" and the Asian comics on the walls and the tatami room only make it better.

Ristorante Italianissimo *Italian* ▽ 26 | 22 | 26 | $36

Woodinville | 15608 NE Woodinville-Duvall Pl. (156th Ave.) | 425-485-6888 | www.italianissimoristorante.com

Woodinville Wine Country habitués rely on this Northern Italian for "superb" fare such as "wafer-thin layers" of the "best lasagna in town" served in an "intimate" white-tablecloth room; the "friendly" staff gets a nod, as does the wine list featuring distinguished local labels, and it all makes a "relaxed" ending to a day of touring.

Ristorante Paradiso *Italian* 20 | 17 | 20 | $31

Kirkland | 120A Park Ln. (Lake Washington Blvd.) | 425-889-8601 | www.ristoranteparadiso.com

In the "heart of the Kirkland arts scene", this "quaint", midpriced Italian has "dependable" pastas and entrees including spinach, mozzarella and prosciutto-stuffed chicken in Marsala sauce; the "intimate" room and "great service" make it feel like "that little" cafe in Italy.

NEW RN74 *French* - | - | - | E

Downtown | Joshua Green Building | 1433 Fourth Ave. (Pike St.) | 206-456-7474 | www.michaelmina.net

A fave with flush Downtowners, Michael Mina's spendy, *vin*-centric eatery pleases with a French regional menu designed to go with the bottles on offer; its snazzy room - a spiffed-up former Rite-Aid pharmacy - buzzes with lively chatter while a French train board lists wine specials and apprises patrons of the last bottle served, minute by minute.

Romio's Pizza & Pasta *Pizza* 19 | 12 | 15 | $18

Downtown | 917 Howell St. (9th Ave.) | 206-622-6878 | www.downtownromios.com
Eastlake | 3242 Eastlake Ave. E. (bet. Fuhrman & Harvard Aves.) | 206-322-4453 | www.eastlakeromios.com
Magnolia | 2001 W. Dravus St. (20th Ave.) | 206-284-5420 | www.romiosmagnolia.com
Lake City | 12534 Lake City Way NE (125th St.) | 206-362-8080 | www.romioslakecity.com
Redmond | 16801 Redmond Way (Avondale Way) | 425-702-2466 | www.romiosredmond.com
Everett | 11223 19th Ave. SE (Silver Lake Rd.) | 425-316-0305 | www.silverlakeromios.com
Everett | 2803 Colby Ave. (California St.) | 425-252-0800 | www.romioseverett.com
Mountlake Terrace | 24225 56th Ave. W. (bet. 242nd & 244th Sts.) | 425-673-2187 | www.e-romios.com

The links in this Greek pizza chain dish out "substantial", "delicious" pies with "fresh toppings" plus pastas and "amazing salads", and some locations even have gluten-free items (a "rarity" in these parts); they aren't much to look at or for service, though, so many just do "takeout."

	FOOD	DECOR	SERVICE	COST

Rose's Bakery Cafe ⊠ *Pacific NW* | - | - | - | I |

Eastsound | 382 Prune Alley (Rose St.) | 360-376-4292
"Imaginative" soups, sandwiches and thin-crust pizzas can be found on Orcas Island at this affordable, family-friendly Eastsound Pacific NWer where everything is "made from scratch" and desserts are "not to be missed"; neighbors drop by and visitors "are made to feel at home" with hospitality that sweetens a "dose" of espresso.

Rosita's Mexican Grill *Mexican* ∇ 17 | 15 | 15 | $19

Green Lake | 7210 Woodlawn Ave. NE (bet. 71st & 72nd Sts.) | 206-523-3031 | www.rositasrestaurant.com
Locals feel the "love" for this Green Lake Mexican where the salsa verde is so tasty fans could "bathe" in it but instead pair it with "warm tortillas" "fresh off the grill"; the cantina setting is welcoming, the bill is reasonable and it's also family-friendly.

Roti Cuisine of India *Indian* ∇ 21 | 18 | 18 | $23

Queen Anne | 530 Queen Anne Ave. N. (Mercer St.) | 206-216-7684 | www.rotirestaurantseattle.com
"Bring lots of people" and "order everything" instruct enthusiasts of this affordable Queen Anne Northern Indian where "tasty" from-scratch naan, mango chicken and other dishes get a boost from fresh-ground spices; traditional paintings decorate the room, service is "friendly" and there's a weekday lunch buffet too.

Z Rover's Ⓜ *French* 28 | 25 | 27 | $94

Madison Valley | 2808 E. Madison St. (28th Ave.) | 206-325-7442 | www.thechefinthehat.com
"Charming", "talented chef-owner" Thierry Rautureau "reinterprets" French cuisine in "gorgeous", "imaginative" dishes fashioned from the "finest Pacific Northwest ingredients" at his genteel Madison Valley house enhanced by "flowers, linens" and a "phenomenal staff" that exhibits the "right combination of proper and friendly"; while it's not cheap, tasting menus start at $59 and Friday lunches are a local favorite.

NEW Rub With Love Shack *American* - | - | - | I

Pike Place Market | 2010 Western Ave. (bet. Lenora & Virginia Sts.) | 206-436-0390 | www.tomdouglas.com
Wedged like a tomato slice between Etta's and Seatown Seabar, this inexpensive Tom Douglas deli draws the happy hordes visiting Pike Place Market for plump sandwiches and rotisserie meats (it also vends the chef's famed spice rubs and sauces); the tiny space has counter seating plus some tables outside, and once a month a pop-up restaurant appears for a single night, with a theme like Tokyo or South Africa.

Russell's *American* ∇ 20 | 15 | 18 | $33

Bothell | 3305 Monte Villa Pkwy. (35th Ave.) | 425-486-4072 | www.russelllowell.com
In a repurposed white barn in Bothell, celebrity caterer Russell Lowell turns out "fantastic" midpriced American classics all day to

devotees who declare he "never disappoints" with "rich and savory" dishes "worth the drive all the way from Seattle"; the client list reads like a worldly "who's who", and it's convenient to Woodinville Wine Country, with breakfast and lunch more low-key affairs.

Ruth's Chris Steak House *Steak* | 24 | 21 | 23 | $63

Downtown | Grand Hyatt Hotel | 727 Pine St. (bet. 7th & 8th Aves.) | 206-624-8524
Bellevue | 565 Bellevue Sq. (8th St.) | 425-451-1550
www.ruthschris.com

Loyalists "love the sizzling platters" of "oh-so-good buttery steaks" at these "top-quality" Downtown and Bellevue links in a chophouse chain that come through with "winning" sides too; delivering "old-style service" in a "traditional" setting, it's "expensive" (and "not for the dieter"), but "utterly reliable", especially when you're "entertaining friends and clients."

Saint, The *Mexican* | - | - | - | M

Capitol Hill | 1416 E. Olive Way (Olive Pl.) | 206-323-9922 | www.thesaintsocialclub.com

"You can't go wrong" assert surveyors taken with the "real-deal" made-from-scratch Mexican dishes and "superb" margaritas at this midpriced Capitol Hill cantina with 80 tequilas on hand; "service is like a homecoming" in a "lovely" "two-tiered" space decorated with vintage black-and-white matador portraits.

Saley Crêpes Ⓜ *French* | - | - | - | I

Capitol Hill | 1361 E. Olive Way (Bellevue Ave.) | 206-405-3444

The inexpensive savory and sweet crêpes at this Capitol Hill cafe cause a "Pavlovian reaction" in fans who come to "savor every bite" of the cooked-to-order specialty; it's set in a "small" storefront tucked into an old building with the cheery flowers painted on the front window making it easier to find.

Ⓩ Salish Lodge Dining Room *Pacific NW* | 23 | 27 | 23 | $56

Snoqualmie | Salish Lodge & Spa | 6501 Railroad Ave. SE (Hwy. 202) | 425-888-2556 | www.salishlodge.com

"Romantically breathtaking" views from the top of Snoqualmie Falls are a "magnificent" backdrop for "elegant" Pacific NW cuisine made with "fresh" local ingredients and served by a "warm, hospitable" staff at this "serene" destination for "special occasions" and "getaways"; dinner tabs are expensive, but breakfast and lunch are also offered.

Saltoro *American* | 20 | 17 | 20 | $34

North Seattle | 14051 Greenwood Ave. N. (143rd St.) | 206-365-6025

Something of a neighborhood secret, this North Seattle "hangout" just outside the Highlands gated community turns out "solid" New American fare such as steak and truffle-frites at moderate prices; the sister restaurant of nearby Bick's, it features casual-clubby decor with artisan glass fixtures and a fireplace.

FOOD	DECOR	SERVICE	COST

Salty's *Seafood*

20 | 22 | 21 | $43

West Seattle | 1936 Harbor Ave. SW (Fairmont Ave.) | 206-937-1600
Redondo | 28201 Redondo Beach Dr. S. (282nd St.) | 253-946-0636
www.saltys.com

"Breathtaking" views right "on the water" enhance this duo known for its "well-prepared, fresh" seafood and "unbeatable" Sunday brunch buffets (Saturday too at Alki Beach) where the bar/cafe features a build-your-own Bloody Mary option; service is "helpful", and if tabs run "a pretty penny", it's all "worth it."

Z Salumi S M *Italian/Sandwiches*

27 | 11 | 18 | $16

Pioneer Square | 309 Third Ave. S. (bet. Jackson & Main Sts.) | 206-621-8772 | www.salumicuredmeats.com

Hot sopressata sandwiches and salami from Gina Batali (Mario's sister) induce "OMGs" from surveyors who bow to this affordable Pioneer Square Italian "cured piggy product" shrine started by papa Armandino; though lines aren't quite as long as they once were at Seattle's "worst-kept secret", there's still a "wait" - but plan ahead and you can book a lunch party in the private back room; P.S. closes at 4 PM.

Salvatore Ristorante M *Italian*

∇ 24 | 19 | 22 | $35

Ravenna | 6100 Roosevelt Way NE (61st St.) | 206-527-9301 | www.salvatoreristoranteitaliano.com

For more than 20 years, chef-owner Salvatore Anania has presided over his midpriced Ravenna Italian where there is "no pretense" but there are "superb" dishes including "specials so marvelous the menu is superfluous"; the murals of Portofino further transport patrons who find it one of the "closest experiences" to Italy without "actually traveling."

Sam's Sushi *Japanese*

∇ 22 | 13 | 19 | $24

Ballard | 5506 22nd Ave. NW (bet. 56th & Market Sts.) | 206-783-2262 | www.sams-sushi.co.nr
Seattle Center | 521 Queen Anne Ave. N. (bet. Mercer & Republican Sts.) | 206-282-4612

Some of the "freshest" sushi in Seattle is cut at these unassuming, "no-nonsense" Japanese twins in Ballard and Seattle Center that also dish out affordable udon and yakisoba; there's not much atmosphere, but service is "friendly" and "you can be in and out in 45 minutes and be totally happy."

Sand Point Grill *Eclectic*

19 | 19 | 22 | $35

Sand Point | Sand Point Vill. | 5412 Sand Point Way NE (55th St.) | 206-729-1303 | www.sandpointgrillseattle.com

A "neighborhood hangout" with "something for everyone", this midpriced Sand Point Eclectic gets "creative" with "seasonal ingredients" and popular "daily additions" while also serving "fabulous" hamburgers and made-from-"scratch" desserts; the casual setting and "flexible service" are a good fit "for families", though it's equally "pleasant" to just "sit at the bar and enjoy the vibe."

	FOOD	DECOR	SERVICE	COST

Santa Fe Cafe *New Mexican* ▽ 20 | 18 | 18 | $25

Phinney Ridge | 5910 Phinney Ave. N. (bet. 59th & 60th Sts.) | 206-783-9755 | www.santafecafeseattle.com

The "place to go" on Phinney Ridge for a taste of Sante Fe, this midpriced New Mexican "doesn't skimp on quality" or "heat" say chile-head fans of its "awesome" cooking; "comfy" digs with a Southwest feel are a respite "on a cold Seattle night."

Santorini Greek Grill *Greek* ▽ 29 | 14 | 24 | $19

Kirkland | 106 Central Way (1st St.) | 425-822-0555

Everybody is treated "like family" at this inexpensive Kirklander where the "yum-m-my", "garlicky" gyros, souvlaki and the like are what fans call some of the "best" Greek eats around; the "really small place" on busy Central Way gets a steady stream of customers, and the owner "serves a side of hospitality with every order."

Sazerac *Pacific NW/Southern* 20 | 21 | 21 | $36

Downtown | Hotel Monaco | 1101 Fourth Ave. (Spring St.) | 206-624-7755 | www.sazeracrestaurant.com

"Dressed-up comfort food" comes with Pacific NW flavors and some Southern twists at this midpriced Downtowner in the Hotel Monaco known for "fabulous" breakfasts, business meals and an extended "happy-hour deal"; service can be "slow", but then the bright and brick-walled setting is a good "place to people-watch."

Scandinavian Cafe *Scandinavian* - | - | - | I

Ballard | Scandinavian Specialties | 6719 15th Ave. NW (bet. 67th & 70th Sts.) | 206-784-7020 | www.scanspecialties.com

This "last vestige" of "old" Scandinavian Ballard spotlights all things Norwegian, Swedish and thereabouts with lunch specialties including old-fashioned, "tasty open-faced sandwiches with shrimp or salmon" and "yellow-pea soup"; during the holidays the 14-seat cafe, which is located within the import shop, is packed with locals seeking "lutefisk, lingonberry jam and rommegrot."

Sea Garden ◐ *Chinese/Seafood* 20 | 10 | 14 | $26

International District | 509 Seventh Ave. S. (King St.) | 206-623-2100

"Go early, go late, just go" urge afishionados of this "high-quality", low-budget Chinese seafood "institution" in the ID dishing out the likes of salt-and-pepper squid and crab in black bean sauce; the "no-nonsense" setting features live tanks for the fin fare, and on weekends it's a "hot spot" that stays open until 3 AM.

Seastar Restaurant & Raw Bar *Seafood* 25 | 23 | 24 | $47

South Lake Union | 2200 | 2121 Terry Ave. (bet. Denny Way & Lenora St.) | 206-462-4364

Bellevue | Civica Office Commons | 205 108th Ave. NE (2nd St.) | 425-456-0010

www.seastarrestaurant.com

Some of "the best seafood" around is dished up at this "power" duo offering "superb" fish and shellfish and a raw bar open all day for oysters, sushi and ceviche; Bellevue is "where to be seen with the beautiful people", South Lake Union is a hot area, and if tabs are "a bit pricey", there's "lovely" decor and "classy service" to compensate.

Seatown Seabar & Rotisserie *Seafood* - | - | - | M

Pike Place Market | 2010 Western Ave. (bet. Lenora & Virginia Sts.) | 206-436-0390 | www.tomdouglas.com

Next to his Etta's Seafood in the Pike Place Market, Tom Douglas' contemporary deli-seafooder dishes out midpriced housemade local eats (some gleaned from the family farm) that are baked, roasted, rotisseried, smoked, pickled or preserved; the space is divided into two areas: the stylish cafe serves breakfast, lunch or dinner with seating at a cool counter or at comfortable tables, while the Rub With Love Shack to-go annex is next door.

Señor Moose Café *Mexican* 26 | 13 | 21 | $24

Ballard | 5242 Leary Ave. NW (bet. Ione Pl. & 20th Ave.) | 206-784-5568 | www.senormoose.com

Comida tipica from Mexico's Central Plateau is "fresh" and "consistent" at this "down-home", "real-deal" Ballard joint where the "phenomenal" affordable fare features lots of moles and tacos; it "won't win any prizes for decor", but the "spicy breakfasts" have a devoted following among those who "cram in" - and now there's a full bar too.

Serafina ◐ *Italian* 25 | 23 | 23 | $42

Eastlake | 2043 Eastlake Ave. E. (Boston St.) | 206-323-0807 | www.serafinaseattle.com

"Spectacular" Italian cuisine "delights" at this spendy Eastlake "favorite" where housemade pasta meets "creative specials" and "marvelous service"; the "hip", "rustic" room with ochre walls looks "romantic" but can get "boisterous", as it's open until midnight for late bites or after-theater dining; P.S. Cicchetti, its more casual sibling, is next door, and at lunch there's now a panini window.

NEW Serious Biscuit *Southern* - | - | - | I

South Lake Union | 401 Westlake Ave. N. (Harrison St.) | 206-436-0050 | www.dahliaworkshop.com

Fluffy biscuits and fixin's draw the South Lake Union office crowd to this hopping, inexpensive Southern cafe downstairs from Serious Pie, which stuffs hot buttered biscuits with everything from slow-braised meats and housemade cheeses to peanut butter and jam made with fruit from Tom Douglas' own Prosser farm; the digs are artisan-cool and the vibe friendly - a good thing, since sometimes there's a wait while the goods puff up in the oven behind the counter; P.S. weekday happy hour is from 2-6 PM.

Z Serious Pie *Pizza* 26 | 18 | 21 | $26

Downtown | 316 Virginia St. (bet. 3rd & 4th Aves.) | 206-838-7388

NEW South Lake Union | 401 Westlake Ave. N. (Harrison St.) | 206-436-0050

www.tomdouglas.com

"Seriously good pizza" for "not-too-serious people" makes this relatively "spendy" Downtowner "not your typical" pie joint, turning out "addictive", "thin wood-fired crusts" with "sophisticated toppings" like "truffled cheese and chanterelles"; true, "you're crammed in like anchovies", but the "communal tables spark conversation" and the "staff is courteous" - all in all, "deservedly a crowd-pleaser"; P.S. the South Lake Union branch opened post-Survey.

74th Street Ale House *Pub Food* 21 | 17 | 19 | $20

Phinney Ridge | 7401 Greenwood Ave. N. (74th St.) | 206-784-2955 | www.seattlealehouses.com

This Phinney Ridge "joint is jumping" with patrons who pop in for the "imaginative" British pub fare, "local microbrews" and cask beer at wallet-friendly prices; the English-style "trendy tavern" feel and "friendly service" also make it a place to "hunker down" in the afternoon before the evening quaffers arrive; P.S. it's a sibling of the Columbia City and Hilltop Ale Houses.

Shamiana *Indian/Pakistani* ▽ 21 | 18 | 16 | $39

Kirkland | Houghton Vill. | 10724 NE 68th St. (108th Ave.) | 425-827-4902 | www.shamianarestaurant.com

An Indian-Pakistani longtimer in Kirkland's Houghton Village mall, this "favorite" has a "lighter" touch with midpriced classics including the signature Major Grey's chicken curry; the stylish room is "not too casual or too fancy" for a "sit-down" lunch ($9.95 buffet) or dinner.

Shanghai Garden *Chinese* 24 | 12 | 19 | $24

International District | 524 Sixth Ave. S. (Weller St.) | 206-625-1689

Issaquah | 80 Front St. N. (Sunset Way) | 425-313-3188 M

"Fantastic" dumplings and hand-shaved noodles are a "guilty pleasure" at this ID-Issaquah Chinese duo serving "fresh", "impressive" spicy dishes that are budget-friendly; "you don't go for the decor", but the "efficient" staff brings meals "out of the kitchen lightning-fast."

Sharp's Roasthouse ◐ *American* - | - | - | M

SeaTac | 18427 International Blvd. (188th St.) | 206-241-5744 | www.sharpsroasthouse.com

"One of the better places" near Sea-Tac airport, this American offers a menu of roasted beef, poultry and pork plus BBQ that's a "bargain for the quality"; the bar has over 400 spirits and 26 draft beers plus a wagering wheel to determine prices, and those who look up find a ceiling filled with bent airplane propellers.

Shiki Japanese M *Japanese* ▽ 25 | 13 | 21 | $34

Queen Anne | 4 W. Roy St. (Queen Anne Ave.) | 206-281-1352

Acolytes attest some of "the best sushi in Seattle" is found at this moderately priced Queen Anne "mom-and-pop" Japanese that's not for the "squeamish" since the house specialty is the deadly (if improperly handled) blowfish, offered in season; but "friendly" owner Ken Yamamoto is a "consummate sushi chef", so regulars advise "sit at the bar" and "put yourself in his hands" and "you won't regret it."

	FOOD	DECOR	SERVICE	COST

Shiku Sushi *Japanese* ▽ 23 | 18 | 22 | $41

Ballard | 5310 Ballard Ave. NW (Vernon Pl.) | 206-588-2151 | www.shikusushi.com

Both "traditional and nouveau" sushi and izakaya dishes are "excellent" choices at this slightly spendy contemporary Japanese; situated on busy Ballard Avenue, it's fine for an "after-dinner stroll", and it's also open for lunch on weekends.

Z Shiro's Sushi *Japanese* 27 | 15 | 23 | $48

Belltown | 2401 Second Ave. (Battery St.) | 206-443-9844 | www.shiros.com

"Master" Shiro Kashiba's Pacific NW-inspired Japanese is "pitch-perfect" and poised to "expand your sushi comfort-zone" say Belltowners who call the omakase at the sushi bar a "life-altering experience"; a "knowledgeable staff" helps explain "traditional delicacies", and though it's "pricey", there's "no attempt whatsoever to be cool or trendy" - plus "if you're lucky", you'll spot a celebrity.

Shuckers *Seafood* 23 | 22 | 23 | $47

Downtown | Fairmont Olympic Hotel | 411 University St., downstairs (enter at 4th Ave. & Seneca St.) | 206-621-1984 | www.fairmont.com

"Fabulous" seafood takes fin fans "to heaven" at this "busy" oyster bar in Downtown's "upper-crust" Fairmont Olympic Hotel; attracting a "business" and "theater crowd", the "clublike" oak-paneled room is "sophisticated" and the service "spot-on" for a "high-end" experience that's "old-school in the best sense."

Shultzy's ◐ *Sandwiches* 18 | 12 | 12 | $18

University District | 4114 University Way NE (bet. 41st & 42nd Sts.) | 206-548-9461 | www.shultzys.com

"Sausage, fries, beer - that's all that matters" for devotees of the cheap housemade wursts and cheesesteaks on the "extensive" menu of this "cute" UDer; with nine tap beers that rotate daily, it's a "great place to hang out" especially after a U of W Husky game.

Silence-Heart-Nest *Vegan/Vegetarian* ▽ 18 | 17 | 21 | $16

Fremont | 3508 Fremont Pl. N (35th St.) | 206-633-5169 | www.silenceheartnest.com

A haven in Fremont for vegans and vegetarians, this "cute" cafe offers "tasty", affordably priced 'neat loaf', egg scrambles, salads and such; the simple dining room reflects the Eastern spiritual thought of those operating it; P.S. there is no dinner.

Sip at the Wine Bar *American* 19 | 23 | 20 | $42

Downtown | 909 Fifth Ave. (Madison St.) | 206-682-2779 M

Issaquah | 1084 NE Park Dr. (bet. 10th Ave. & 11th Ln.) | 425-369-1181

www.siprestaurant.com

"Innovative", "tasty" New American dishes and wines from around the world make these "eclectic" twins the place to "try something" "adventurous"; even if "service is uneven" and the bill is a little "pricey", the "relaxing" upscale modern decor including outdoor seating adds to the "happy surprise."

	FOOD	DECOR	SERVICE	COST

Sitka & Spruce *Eclectic* 26 | 19 | 22 | $46

Capitol Hill | 1531 Melrose Ave. E. (bet. Pike & Pine Sts.) | 206-324-0662 | www.sitkaandspruce.com

Set in Capitol Hill's Melrose Building, this locally focused Eclectic from chef-owner Matthew Dillon (the Corson Building) turns out a "thoughtful", seasonal menu that's "creative without being strange" and "reasonably priced for the quality"; service is "efficient" in "relaxed" quarters filled with warehouselike "character", and Bar Ferd'nand is right next door; P.S. there's also weekday lunch and weekend brunch, plus on Monday nights it offers 'Malafacha-style' Mexican food.

611 Supreme *French* 21 | 19 | 19 | $20

Capitol Hill | 611 E. Pine St. (bet. Belmont & Boylston Aves.) | 206-328-0292 | www.611supreme.com

"Excellent" Breton buckwheat crêpes are made with "inventive" combinations of ingredients at this "cozy" Capitol Hill French situated in a brick-walled nook that feels like "a little bit of Paris"; "warm" servers, "fair prices" and a nighttime lounge add to the appeal.

Z Six Seven *Pacific NW* 23 | 26 | 22 | $47

Seattle Waterfront | Edgewater Hotel | 2411 Alaskan Way, Pier 67 (bet. Vine & Wall Sts.) | 206-269-4575 | www.edgewaterhotel.com

"Sublime" views and high-end Pacific NW "food that matches" might just "blow your socks off" suggest fans of this Seattle Waterfront eatery in the Edgewater Hotel; floor-to-ceiling windows secure its "elegant" contemporary appeal as a place to "chill out" and watch the boats on Elliott Bay.

NEW Skillet Diner ◐ *American* 23 | 9 | 15 | $14

Capitol Hill | 1400 E. Union St. (14th Ave.) | 206-420-7297

Skillet ◐ *American*

Location varies; see website | No phone
www.skilletstreetfood.com

It's easy to spot the Airstream trailer "from another era" that was transformed into a "sensational" "mobile vendor" dishing out "awesome" American "cheap" eats (think grass-fed beef burger with arugula and bacon jam); check the website for the day's location, and be prepared for service that "varies" and at least a short line; P.S. the Capitol Hill brick-and-mortar offshoot opened post-Survey and boasts a bar and more extensive menu than the truck.

Z SkyCity *Pacific NW* 22 | 27 | 23 | $62

Seattle Center | Space Needle | 400 Broad St. (4th Ave.) | 206-905-2111 | www.spaceneedle.com

"Sitting on top of the world", diners take in "360-degree views of Seattle" at this slowly revolving restaurant at the Space Needle, where the "delicious", "fresh" Pacific NW fare often made with local ingredients and delivered by a "savvy staff" is a "pleasant surprise"; the bill's equally "stratospheric", but then it includes the tariff for the ride up ($18), and brunches and lunches are less expensive while offering the same "awesome" perch.

	FOOD	DECOR	SERVICE	COST

Slim's Last Chance ◐ ☒ *Southern* | ▽ 26 | 15 | 17 | $19

Georgetown | 5606 First Ave. S. (Lucile St.) | 206-762-7900 | www.slimslastchance.com

"Simmering hot chili" with "that special tang" comes in "four styles" and is ladled over mac 'n' cheese or grits at this budget-friendly Georgetown Southern roadhouse; it's "friendly" in a "gruff" sort of way, with a clientele ranging from bikers to low-key business types, and though adjacent sibling Pig Iron Bar-B-Q closes after lunch, enthusiasts can get grub here till midnight with live bands on weekends; P.S. there's free pool on Mondays.

Smarty Pants ◐ *Sandwiches* | 23 | 16 | 17 | $15

Georgetown | 6017 Airport Way S. (Vale St.) | 206-762-4777 | www.smartypantsseattle.com

"Divine sandwiches" and weekend brunch are "creative", "inexpensive" and delivered with "quick" service at this "funky" Georgetown "establishment"; the decor is "all about the motorcycle", and the "nice outdoor patio" is enclosed so it's rainproof year-round.

Spazzo *Italian* | 16 | 18 | 19 | $30

Redmond | Redmond Town Ctr. | 16499 NE 74th St. (bet. 164th & 166th Aves.) | 425-881-4400 | www.schwartzbros.com

"Cheery" and "colorful", this Redmond sibling of Daniel's Broiler dishes out "dependable" pizza, pasta and other Italian fare for "reasonable" tabs; some lament it's "not as good as it used to be", yet it still gets lively and "noisy" in the bar - and there's a "quieter" area in the back for those who want to "talk."

Spencer's For Steaks & Chops ◐ *Steak* | - | - | - | E

SeaTac | Hilton Americas | 17620 Pacific Hwy. S. (176th St.) | 206-248-7153 | www.spencersforsteaksandchops.com

"First-rate", prime, hand-cut and aged Chicago steaks make carnivores' "mouths water" at this beef-eater's spot in the SeaTac Hilton that's "great for a hotel restaurant"; the wine list tops 250 labels, but unless you're on a corporate card it's all "very pricey."

Spiced *Chinese* | ▽ 22 | 8 | 11 | $17

Bellevue | 1299 156th Ave. NE (13th Pl.) | 425-644-8888 | www.spicedonline.com

This simple Bellevue Chinese buzzes with expats ordering "cold bar dishes" (pig's ears, tongues and the like) from the case in front or cooked specialties such as Chongqing spicy chicken or hot pots; though there isn't much decor or service, the menu is big and marked for degrees of spiciness, indicating the generous use of Sichuan peppercorns and fresh hot chile peppers.

Spicy Talk Bistro *Chinese* | - | - | - | I

Redmond | 16650 Redmond Way (bet. 166th & 168th Aves. NE) | 425-558-7858 | www.spicytalkbistro.com

Supple hand-shaved noodles and tasty hot pots are the draw at this Redmond Chinese where locals and techies come for peppery Sichuan cooking, swiftly served; a whiteboard listing specials and dark walls splashed with comic-y orange footprints add to the friendly, energetic mood.

Z Spinasse *Italian* 28 | 22 | 23 | $48

Capitol Hill | 1531 14th Ave. (bet. Pike & Pine Sts.) | 206-251-7673 | www.spinasse.com

"Fabulous" Piedmont cuisine and "light-as-a-feather" handmade pasta are the "real deal", channeling "little joints in Italy" for patrons of this Capitol Hill "gem" offering à la carte and family-style-tasting menus deemed "well worth the cost"; toque Jason Stratton keeps the recently expanded (post-Survey) quarters "buzzing with energy", and now, for a quick bite, there's Artusi, the new aperitivo bar next door.

Sport *Eclectic* ∇ 16 | 16 | 18 | $25

Seattle Center | Fisher Plaza | 140 Fourth Ave. N. (Broad St.) | 206-404-7767 | www.sportrestaurant.com

There's unique "memorabilia all over the place" at this "slick" sports bar (a sibling of Seastar and John Howie Steak) in the ABC/KOMO-TV building across from the Seattle Center, where fans are "pleasantly surprised" by affordable Eclectic fare including an American Kobe beef burger; service is "adequate", but equally important is the draw of dozens of flat-screen TVs - including personal screens in the booths - tuned to sports nonstop.

Spring Hill *Pacific NW* 25 | 20 | 22 | $49

West Seattle | 4437 California Ave. SW (Genessee St.) | 206-935-1075 | www.springhillnorthwest.com

Surveyors "expect good things" from Mark Fuller's "clever menu" featuring "fabulous" seasonal food and the "holy grail of hamburgers" at this "high-style" West Seattle Pacific Northwester; the "pro" staff is "friendly", and though tabs might be "a bit expensive", the "cool" industrial-chic room is "always crowded."

Spur Gastropub *American* 24 | 20 | 21 | $41

Belltown | 113 Blanchard St. (1st Ave.) | 206-728-6706 | www.spurseattle.com

"Complex yet vibrant" gastropub small plates with twinges of "molecular gastronomy" "amaze" diners at this Belltown New American that "showcases vegetables in the most exquisite manner" while turning out the likes of "sumptuous" pork-belly sliders and crudos; the stylish "nuevo spaghetti-Western-inspired decor" has a running photo show of iconic Americana, and no one much cares about the tab.

Stan's Bar-B-Q *BBQ* - | - | - | I

Issaquah | 58 Front St. N. (bet. NW Alder Pl. & W. Sunset Way) | 425-392-4551 | www.stansbarbq.com

Issaquah locals whoop it up at this affordable BBQ place, digging into juicy Kansas City smoked meats from owner/pit master Stan Phillips, who learned the craft in Missouri at his daddy's knee; the frontier-feeling room leans to KC football memorabilia, though it's a Seahawks spot too, and transcends the usual sports bar dishabille with prompt, cheerful service.

	FOOD	DECOR	SERVICE	COST

Staple & Fancy Mercantile *Italian* | - | - | - | M |

Ballard | Kolstrand Bldg. | 4739 Ballard Ave. NW (bet. Ballard Way & Dock Pl.) | 206-789-1200 | www.ethanstowellrestaurants.com

Busy chef Ethan Stowell's latest is this Ballard Italian offering mid-priced à la carte dishes or an adventurous $45 four-course menu; the brick space in the historic Kolstrand Building was once a grocery store (hence the name), and some of the original wood and metal has been recycled into the decor of the room.

St. Clouds *Pacific NW* | 23 | 19 | 24 | $31 |

Madrona | 1131 34th Ave. (Union St.) | 206-726-1522 | www.stclouds.com

It's "like going on vacation" for enthusiasts of this Madrona stalwart that gets a chorus of "yums" for "fresh" Pacific NW cuisine at "reasonable prices"; the "quaint", "comfortable" setting and "friendly, accommodating staff" are more reasons why it's a "favorite" for "dinner on Friday night after a long week" or for weekend brunch.

Z **Steelhead Diner** *Pacific NW* | 24 | 21 | 22 | $36 |

Pike Place Market | 95 Pine St. (1st Ave.) | 206-625-0129 | www.steelheaddiner.com

Regulars attest that chef-owner Kevin Davis' Pacific Northwester in Pike Place Market "keeps us coming back" for "reasonably priced" "comfort food at its finest" including jumbo crab cakes, caviar pie and "spiced-just-right" gumbo; the staff exudes "good energy", and the decor lends a "cool vibe" with fishing murals and fly boxes; there's also a kitchen bar where you can "watch the action" and "chat with the chefs", plus ample comfy booth and table seating.

Stellar Pizza, Ale & Cocktails M *Pizza* | 22 | 17 | 16 | $19 |

Georgetown | 5513 Airport Way S. (Lucile St.) | 206-763-1660 | www.stellarpizza.com

"Exuberant" combinations of toppings crown the "belly-busting" pizzas made with housemade dough and sauces at this Georgetown "hipster" hangout that also offers a "terrific assortment of beers"; the dark, "cavernous" digs and service flame the "funky" vibe, and it all comes at "awesome value."

NEW **Stopsky's Deli** *Deli/Jewish* | - | - | - | I |

Mercer Island | 3016 78th Ave. SE (bet. SE 30th & 32nd Sts.) | 206-236-4564 | www.stopskysdelicatessen.com

After a bumpy start, this Mercer Island deli has found its pace with homemade charcuterie, bagels and Jewish noshes that are notably non-kosher, but all about being healthy; it recently added entrees to the lunch menu and started serving dinner too, in a light-filled space with lots of pale wood and vintage black-and-white photographs.

Streamliner Diner *Diner/Italian* | 19 | 11 | 18 | $25 |

Bainbridge Island | 397 Winslow Way E. (Ericksen Ave.) | 206-842-8595 | www.streamlinerdiner.com

This "longtime" Bainbridge Island "favorite" for affordable "hearty breakfasts" is a mainstay that's "hard to beat" and definitely "worth a ferry trip" from Seattle; "during the day it's a diner" and at night it turns into a "surprisingly good bistro" with an Italian menu.

Stumbling Goat Bistro M *Pacific NW* 23 | 19 | 23 | $41

Greenwood | 6722 Greenwood Ave. N. (67th St.) | 206-784-3535 | www.stumblinggoatbistro.com

A "neighborhood place with Downtown quality", this Greenwood stalwart has "found its footing" with an "excellent" updated menu of Pacific NW organic-focused seasonal fare; the staff "never rushes you but is always on hand" in the "dimly lit" brick-walled setting, so even if prices are a tad high, it's still an "excellent job all around."

Sunfish M ≠ *Seafood* ∇ 21 | 11 | 12 | $15

West Seattle | 2800 Alki Ave. SW (62nd Ave.) | 206-938-4112

Located right on Alki Beach, this West Seattle fish 'n' chipper serves its "fresh", budget-friendly specialty with "perfect" tartar sauce and a house garlic-vinegar; the place is "not much for ambiance", but the view of the beach is "the best" and the service is "fast", so some confess "I eat there so often I should have a dorsal fin."

Sunlight Cafe *Eclectic/Vegetarian* - | - | - | I

Roosevelt | 6403 Roosevelt Way NE (bet. 64th & 65th Sts.) | 206-522-9060 | www.sunlightcafevegetarian.com

A vegetarian-vegan institution born in the '70s, this Roosevelt cafe dishes out cheap Eclectic "hippie food in a hippie atmosphere" for an experience that's a throwback "in the best possible way"; patrons promise the nut burgers et al. will "make you feel healthier", and you may just be inspired to "dread your hair."

Sushi Kappo Tamura *Japanese* - | - | - | M

Eastlake | 2968 Eastlake Ave. E. (Allison St.) | 206-547-0937 | www.sushikappotamura.com

Chef-owner Taichi Kitamura's latest is this midpriced kappo (counter) Japanese in Eastlake that replaces his spendy Chiso Kappo and showcases his sushi and sashimi skills along with unique locavore takes on *ippin* small plates and tasting menu options starting at $50; the dressy, modern room overlooks the gleaming kitchen with chefs at work, and the staff eagerly talks about the dishes served, omakase or not.

Sushiman M *Japanese* - | - | - | M

Issaquah | 670 NW Gilman Blvd. (7th Ave.) | 425-391-4295

Issaquah afishionados look to this Japanese eatery where the sushi is joined by *chankonabe* (a hearty stew known as a sumo-wrestler staple), grilled meats, teriyaki and 25 different sakes - a nod to the izakaya trend; chef-owner Bobbi Suetsugu is a retired sumo wrestler, and his contemporary cafe is family-friendly.

Sutra M *Eclectic/Vegetarian* ∇ 24 | 19 | 22 | $46

Wallingford | 1605 N. 45th St. (Woodlawn Ave.) | 206-547-1348 | www.sutraseattle.com

Appreciated as an "experience for your taste buds and senses", this "amazing" eco-conscious Wallingford Eclectic-vegetarian turns out elaborate prix fixe dinners so "inventive" that "omnivorous locavores" find it "hard to believe" there's "no meat in the meal"; incorporating "foraged greens" and produce grown in the back garden, the meals (served Wednesday-Saturday) start with the bang of a "big gong" made from a recycled scuba tank; the chef-owners also run the yoga school next door.

Sweet Iron Waffles *Belgian* — | — | — | I

Downtown | 1200 Third Ave. (University St.) | 206-682-3336
NEW **University District** | 4518 University Ave. NE (bet. 45th & 47th Sts.) | 206-545-4865
www.sweetironwaffles.com

Liège-style waffles made from local, natural ingredients and cooked on Belgian cast-iron presses are "heaven" for fans of this inexpensive Downtown nook and its new University District sibling; the goods recall treats found on the "streets of Europe" and come in both sweet and savory versions.

Szechuan Chef *Chinese* 23 | 10 | 18 | $19

Bellevue | Kelsey Creek Ctr. | 15015 Main St. (148th Ave.) | 425-746-9008 | www.szechuanchefbellevue.com

"Spicy food fiends" find "satisfaction" in this Bellevue Sichuan's "cheap", "fresh-out" dan dan noodles, wontons and "nuclear furnace" of a hot pot; the "unpretentious" strip-maller is hard to find but "worth the hunt", and service is "fast and polite."

Szmania's *Steakhouse* 25 | 21 | 21 | $38

Magnolia | 3321 W. McGraw St. (34th Ave.) | 206-284-7305 | www.szmanias.com

Steaks sizzle at the center of the new (post-Survey) menu at Austrian-born chef-owner Ludger Szmania's "longtime favorite" Magnolia clubhouse, though he's kept a few of the old Bavarian and American favorites for good measure; the dining room is newly freshened too, giving the neighborhood gentry a pleasing place for schmoozing, never mind if the bill can get a bit high.

Tai Tung *Chinese* ▽ 23 | 11 | 22 | $18

International District | 655 S. King St. (Maynard Ave.) | 206-622-7372

The "reliability" factor draws a devoted following to this 75-plus-year-old ID Chinese offering a "fresh, fast and good" taste of old Chinatown; those in the know "sit at the counter and eat like a regular", ordering off "the notes on the entry mirror" as the "patient" waiters answer questions about the fare.

Taki's Mad Greek ⊠ *Greek*

Ballard | 8539 15th Ave. NW (bet. 85th & 87th Sts.) | 206-297-9200 | www.takismadgreek.com

This Ballard family-owned Greek serves "generous" portions of from-scratch souvlaki, moussaka and such that are "clearly made with love" and are inexpensive too; "dad's at the stove" while mom "makes you feel at home", and on Saturday nights chef-owner Taki Dotis grabs his bouzouki and the music and dancing starts, so "plan to be plucked from your table to join in."

FOOD | DECOR | SERVICE | COST

Tamarind Tree *Vietnamese* 25 | 20 | 19 | $27

International District | 1036 S. Jackson St. (12th Ave.) | 206-860-1404 | www.tamarindtreerestaurant.com

The "exotic" upscale Vietnamese cuisine at this International District hideaway is an "all-star hit parade" of "delicious" dishes from "start to finish"; the "attention to detail" in the decor and service is "evident", and it's "reasonably priced" given the "experience."

Tango *Spanish* 20 | 19 | 19 | $36

Capitol Hill | 1100 Pike St. (Boren Ave.) | 206-583-0382 | www.tangorestaurant.com

"Innovative", "high-quality" tapas and other "delicious" Spanish fare draws fans to this moderately priced Capitol Hiller that's "famous" for its "sinful" chocolate-cayenne-tequila El Diablo dessert; though service is "spotty", the vibe in the rustic-chic room is "friendly and hip."

Tap House Grill *Eclectic* 17 | 16 | 18 | $26

Downtown | 1506 Sixth Ave. (bet. Pike & Pine Sts.) | 206-816-3314

Bellevue | 550 106th Ave. NE (4th St.) | 425-467-1730

www.taphousegrill.com

There are a whopping 160 beers on tap, but there's also a "varied" selection of midpriced grub like jambalaya, steak and sushi at these Downtown and Bellevue Eclectics; "friendly" service and modern digs add to reasons they're "popular" and sometimes "noisy" - especially during the "huge" happy hours (twice a day during the week and once on weekends).

Taqueria La Venadita *Mexican* - | - | - | I

Issaquah | 730 NW Gilman Blvd. (7th Ave.) | 425-391-6480

Authentic Mexican *comidas* for minimal pesos draw Issaquah locals to this small cafe with a big reputation for "fresh" and "tasty" tacos, tortas and menudo; the meat options include cabeza (beef cheeks) and lengua (tongue), and it's all dished out with "friendly service."

Taste *Pacific NW* 22 | 22 | 21 | $31

Downtown | Seattle Art Museum | 1300 First Ave. (bet. Union & University Sts.) | 206-903-5291 | www.tastesam.com

"Plates that could stand in for works of art" are "inventive and delicious" at this Pacific NW Downtowner in the Seattle Art Museum, where the ingredients are seasonal and sustainable and the drinks menu is "patterned after the theme of the exhibit"; the only quibble is that "portions are, indeed, just a taste" but they're delivered with "attentive service" in a room featuring rotating exhibits.

Taste of India *Indian* 22 | 14 | 21 | $21

University District | 5517 Roosevelt Way NE (56th St.) | 206-528-1575 | www.tasteofindiaseattle.com

A perennial "favorite" in the University District, this wallet-friendly Indian "never disappoints" with its "fantastic" curries and other "absolutely delicious" classics such as tikka masala washed down by "bottomless chai" refills; service is "fast" in the simple white rooms decorated with fabrics and artifacts.

FOOD DECOR SERVICE COST

Tat's Deli ⊠ *American* — | - | - | - | I |

Pioneer Square | 159 Yesler Way (2nd Ave.) | 206-264-8287 | www.tatsdeli.com

At this Pioneer Square lunch shack, East Coast-inspired pastrami sandwiches and hoagies loom large; its brick-walled digs are posted with ordering instructions, which you'd best follow or head to the back of the line - which goes out the door, though a live cam on its website can help you strategize.

Tavolàta *Italian* — | 25 | 22 | 22 | $40 |

Belltown | 2323 Second Ave. (bet. Battery & Bell Sts.) | 206-838-8008 | www.tavolata.com

"Fabulous" modern Italian cuisine with "excellent" housemade pastas from a "small and well-chosen menu" highlight Ethan Stowell's midpriced "winner" in trendy Belltown; its hip industrial space is popular with "the 20-30 group" who either love or hate the "long communal table" depending on if they're game to "meet new friends" (there are private tables if not), and who kick up a "noisy" scene at prime times; P.S. the kitchen's open till midnight on weekends.

Taxi Dogs *Hot Dogs*

| - | - | - | I |

Pike Place Market | 1928 Pike Pl. (bet. Stewart & Virginia Sts.) | 206-443-1919

For a regular hot dog or a more "German, Polish or British" pup, hit this storefront in the Pike Place Market that grills them and tucks them into a "soft bun"; there's no seating, but patrons are welcome to sit at the deli next door owned by the same family; P.S. closes at 4 PM.

Tempero do Brasil M *Brazilian* — | - | - | - | M |

University District | 5628 University Way NE (bet. 56th St. & Ravenna Blvd.) | 206-523-6229 | www.temperodobrasil.net

Locals, "homesick South Americans" and "struggling grad students" come for the "silky" Bahian fish stew of halibut in "coconut milk laced with lime" plus "fabulous" cachaça rum drinks at this "homestyle" midpriced Brazilian in the University District; situated in a "small" house at the end of The Ave, the "warm" brightly painted environs "erupt" with live music on Saturday nights.

Ten Mercer ◐ *American* — | 22 | 20 | 24 | $41 |

Queen Anne | 10 Mercer St. (bet. 1st & Queen Anne Aves.) | 206-691-3723 | www.tenmercer.com

This Queen Anne New American near the Seattle Opera and Seattle Repertory Company is a pre- and post-"theater favorite" for its "consistent" "comfort food" (including gluten-free dishes) accompanied by "efficient service"; the bi-level room has a cool "loft space", and floor-to-ceiling windows view the city streets and passersby.

NEW Terra Plata ⊠ M *American* — | - | - | - | M |

Capitol Hill | Melrose Mkt. | 1501 Melrose Ave. (Minor Ave.) | 206-325-1501 | www.terraplata.com

The latest from Tamara Murphy (Elliott Bay Café) is a stylish arrival in Capitol Hill's Melrose Market, presenting reasonably priced New

American fare that puts the spotlight on impeccable local ingredients; full of windows and light, its rustically modern dining room and bar boasts rough wood, steel and cement elements, plus there's a rooftop patio perfect for watching neighborhood goings on.

Thai Curry Simple *Thai* | - | - | - | I |

NEW **Capitol Hill** | 1122 E. Madison St. (bet. 11th & 12th Aves.) | 206-325-1494
International District | 406 Fifth Ave. S. (Jackson St. S.) | 206-327-4838
www.thaicurrysimple.com
Bangkok street food is the specialty of this cheap-eats duo slinging one-dish feasts for a five spot, chosen from a menu on the wall listing curries, panangs and rotis, spiked to suit with chili sauces; the ID location's no-frills digs suit its techie, neo-hippie clientele fine, as does the no-nonsense staff that keeps the line moving quickly, while the Capitol Hill location is strictly takeout.

Thai Ginger *Thai* | 22 | 18 | 19 | $28 |

Downtown | Pacific Pl. | 600 Pine St. (6th Ave.) | 206-749-9100
Madison Park | 1841 42nd Ave. E. (Madison St.) | 206-324-6467
Bellevue | 3717 Factoria Blvd. SE (bet. I-90 & 38th St.) | 425-641-4008
Issaquah | 4512 Klahanie Dr. SW (Issaquah Fall City Rd.) | 425-369-8233
Redmond | Redmond Town Ctr. | 16480 NE 74th St. (bet. 164th & 166th Aves.) | 425-558-4044
www.thaiginger.com
"Too good to pass over", this "reliable" Thai chain comes through with "aromatic and hearty curries", "addictive" crab fried rice, noodles and soups; the service varies by location but the prices are always moderate, just call before you go since some locations are always "busy-busy."

Thaiku *Thai* | 22 | 24 | 18 | $23 |

Ballard | 5410 Ballard Ave. NW (22nd Ave.) | 206-706-7807 | www.thaiku.com
This low-priced Ballard Thai offers "tasty" noodles and rice plus some dishes not usually seen "outside of Thailand"; while "service can be inattentive", the decor is attention-grabbing with a "rickshaw suspended from the ceiling", and the infamous back bar that "looks like old Shanghai" is also an herbal apothecary with drinks to match.

Thai Siam *Thai*

Ballard | 8305 15th Ave. NW (83rd St.) | 206-784-5465 | www.thaisiamrestaurant.com
The "Heavenly Chicken is heavenly" and the "black sticky rice is fabulous" at this inexpensive Ballard Thai that's "one of the best" and "most authentic" around; the smallish setting is decorated with Siamese statues, and it's still filled with locals after some 20 years.

Thai Tom *Thai* | 25 | 9 | 13 | $14 |

University District | 4543 University Way NE (bet. 45th & 47th Sts.) | 206-548-9548
"Day or night" it's "tightly packed" with Thai fanatics and U of W students at this low-budget University District fixture where the

"well-seasoned woks" are "fired in rapid succession" and the flavors change slightly since the chefs cook "from feel"; service can be "slightly surly", and the timid should know that the heat level "starts at very spicy"; P.S. it's cash-only and there's no alcohol.

Thanh Vi *Vietnamese* ∇ 19 | 10 | 18 | $11

University District | 4226 University Way NE (bet. 42nd & 43rd Sts.) | 206-633-7867 | www.thanhvi.net

"Bold, bountiful" Vietnamese dishes that taste like they're from "mom's kitchen" are the draw at this University Districter where University of Washington students and profs can be found downing "amazing" banh mi sandwiches and pho soups; the setting is simple and it's run by "the nicest people", but best of all, it's "cheap."

That's Amore *Italian* ∇ 24 | 18 | 21 | $31

Mt. Baker | 1425 31st Ave. S. (Atlantic St.) | 206-322-3677 | www.thatsamoreseattle.com

You wouldn't know it from the street, but this "sweet" Mt. Baker trattoria boasts "spectacular views of the Seattle skyline" from its window tables in addition to an "abundance" of Italian dishes (including "fantastic pizzas"); the atmosphere is "romantic" yet "informal" enough to be comfortable, with "attentive service", and on Sunday there's brunch.

Thin Pan *Thai* - | - | - | I

Kirkland | 170 Lake St. S. (2nd Ave.) | 425-827-4000

The "Thai green beans are worth a special trip" to this affordble Kirkland "neighborhood place" where locals head when they "have that craving"; the modern spot opens onto the sidewalk in warm weather and is decorated with Asian accents and art from local artists.

13 Coins ◐ *Italian* 19 | 17 | 21 | $32

South Lake Union | 125 Boren Ave. N. (Denny Way) | 206-682-2513

SeaTac | 18000 International Blvd. (opp. Sea-Tac Airport) | 206-243-9500

www.13coins.com

"Get your throwback on" at these "rich man's 24-hour" SeaTac-South Lake Union twins offering "tasty" Italian dishes, breakfast and lunch items from a "vast" menu delivered with "prompt service"; they're "da bomb" for "late-night eats", especially at the "high-back, swivel counter seats" where regulars soak in the "Rat Pack" vibe and "watch the flames" as the chefs cook.

35th Street Bistro Ⓜ *European* 22 | 20 | 21 | $37

Fremont | 709 N. 35th St. (Fremont Ave.) | 206-547-9850 | www.35bistro.com

It's "like France except it's Fremont" at this "charming" bistro dishing out "consistently fine" European fare at moderate prices; "friendly, informal service" in a "chic", high-ceilinged room hung with wine maps and vintage mirrors befits "an impromptu date", and there's an "interesting crowd" for people-watching, as long as you don't mind when it gets a little "noisy."

	FOOD	DECOR	SERVICE	COST

Three Girls Bakery *Bakery* | 24 | 10 | 20 | $11

Ballard | 6209 15th Ave. NW (bet. 62nd & 63rd Aves.) | 206-420-7613 ☒

Pike Place Market | 1514 Pike Pl. (Pike St.) | 206-622-1045

Operating in the Pike Place Market since 1912, this bakery is still a "must-stop" for "munching on" "terrific bread" (some 50 kinds) and "big, honest, gloppy" sandwiches while sitting at the "counter"; a "funky", "unpretentious" setting and "helpful" staff make it even more "enjoyable"; P.S. the Ballard branch is takeout only.

3 Pigs Bar-B-Que ☒ *BBQ* | 21 | 12 | 16 | $15

Bellevue | 1048 116th Ave. NE (bet. 10th & 12th Sts.) | 425-453-0888 | www.3pigsbarbq.com

The Harrell brothers hail from Atlanta, but draw "crowds" to Bellevue for "delicious" pulled pork, ribs and such considered some of the "best" around; prices are "reasonable", service "quick" and the "archetypal strip-mall" space across from Overlake Hospital features sports memorabilia and TV for those who like to linger.

Tilikum Place Café *European* | 25 | 19 | 23 | $36

Belltown | 407 Cedar St. (bet. Denny Way & 5th Ave.) | 206-282-4830 | www.tilikumplacecafe.com

Belltowners wanting a "real treat" find it at this European-style cafe located near the Chief Seattle statue and offering "amazing" home-baked goodies and other "innovative" fare; the "unassuming" room is "pretty" with wood beams and tin lamps, and "excellent" service helps make it a "nice respite from the city" bustle.

Z Tilth *American* | 28 | 21 | 25 | $53

Wallingford | 1411 N. 45th St. (International Ave.) | 206-633-0801 | www.tilthrestaurant.com

Eco-savvy chef Maria Hines dishes out "wonderful, inventive" locavore fare in "surprising preparations" tailored to both "vegans and carnivores" at her organic-certified Wallingford New American; a "welcoming", "knowledgeable" staff and a "cheerfully informal" Craftsman bungalow setting are more reasons fans "would eat here every day if [they] could afford it", plus weekend brunch is a "delight."

NEW Ting Momo ☒ *Tibetan* | - | - | - | I

South Lake Union | 310 Terry Ave. N. (bet. Harrison & Thomas Sts.) | 206-971-0720 | www.tingmomo.com

Though it had a bumpy start, this affordable, weekday-lunch-only South Lake Union cafe from Tom Douglas has stepped up its game with daily yak dumpling plates and hand-pulled noodle soups full of uncommon Tibetan tastes and textures; the cool Asian digs feature a counter by the door and a collection of tables for downing a quick bite.

Tin Room Bar *American* | - | - | - | M

Burien | 923 SW 152nd St. (bet. 9th & 10th Aves.) | 206-242-8040 | www.tinroombar.com

Locals like to "get there early" to get a place at the bar at this Burien "neighborhood pub" offering the likes of reasonably priced hamburgers; some remember when the place was a tin shop, and the old tin roller still hangs in a place of honor, while tables are made from the old workbenches - the other half of the building is the vintage movie house the Tin Theater.

Tin Table ◐ *Pacific NW* 20 | 22 | 19 | $31

Capitol Hill | 915 E. Pine St. (10th Ave.) | 206-320-8458 | www.thetintable.com

Patrons feel like "part of the 'in' crowd" at this Capitol Hill Pacific Northwester where they "rub elbows with dancers and hipsters" from the Century Ballroom next door while dining; part of the Oddfellows Hall revamp, the room sports a 12-seat tin table that was repurposed from old metal fire doors found in the walls during the restoration.

Top Gun Seafood ◐ *Chinese/Seafood* 22 | 12 | 14 | $24

Bellevue | 12450 SE 38th St. (124th Ave.) | 425-641-3386 | www.topgunrestaurants.com

With dim sum some deem "the best" around, this modern, authentic Chinese seafooder in Bellevue has "a long line waiting" for "a crack at the carts" that glide through the dining room doling out "delicious morsels"; there's also a Cantonese menu and it's all "a great value", even though it's "crowded" weekends and parking "is very limited."

Tosoni's Ⓢ Ⓜ *Continental* 26 | 18 | 24 | $55

Bellevue | 14320 NE 20th St. (bet. 140th & 148th Aves.) | 425-644-1668

Bellevue's "best-kept secret" "never disappoints" with its "fantastic", pricey Continental cuisine and "excellent wine list" served in an "intimate" setting that's surprisingly "hidden in a strip mall"; chef Walter Walcher "wears a tall toque" and when not preparing the likes of veal tenderloin with chanterelle sauce "will usually come out to greet you", enhancing "special nights out and celebrations."

Toulouse Petit ◐ *Cajun/Creole* 23 | 23 | 20 | $30

Queen Anne | 601 Queen Anne Ave. N. (Mercer St.) | 206-432-9069 | www.toulousepetit.com

An "outstanding" New Orleans-inspired menu makes surveyors "happily cry 'I surrender'" to the "divine" dishes at this midpriced Queen Anne hangout close to the Key Arena and the theater; the "vibrant" decor includes "shuttered windows 20 ft. high" and hundreds of candles that make it "full of energy", and happy-hour devotees "love it" for a whopping 50 dishes priced under $5.

Toyoda Sushi Ⓜ *Japanese* 26 | 18 | 23 | $30

Lake City | 12543 Lake City Way NE (bet. 125th & 127th Sts.) | 206-367-7972

Perennially popular, this Japanese in Lake City draws raw-fish fans with "the sushi trifecta: friendly, fresh and not froufrou"; "scrumptious" bites include both traditional rolls and some with "interesting twists", and even though it "gets too crowded", it's "worth the drive" for one of the "best values you can find."

	FOOD	DECOR	SERVICE	COST

Trellis *American* 22 19 20 $41

Kirkland | Heathman Hotel | 220 Kirkland Ave. (State St.) | 425-284-5900 | www.heathmankirkland.com

At the forefront of the farming chef trend, Brian Scheehser sustainably grows 10 acres of fruit, vegetables and herbs, which he "masterfully" tranforms into "terrific", "remarkably varied" dishes at this "upscale" Kirkland New American in the Heathman Hotel; though service is "hit-or-miss", foraged foods added in-season and housemade charcuterie and pasta plus a large patio add to reasons it's so "busy."

Tropea *Italian* 26 18 25 $27

Redmond | 8042 161st Ave. NE (Redmond Way) | 425-867-1082 | www.ristorantetropea.com

A "little Redmond treasure" in "a sea of subpar chains", this trattoria makes you "forget you're in a suburb" with its "to-die-for" veal chops, lasagna and classic pastas delivered with "friendly" service; the rustic, "intimate" setting is "a little slice of Italy" and "worth seeking out" even if you "aren't from the neighborhood."

Tsukushinbo ⌧ *Japanese* - - - I

International District | 515 S. Main St. (5th Ave.) | 206-467-4004

Reasonably priced and "friendly", this "mom-and-pop" Japanese in the International District pleases patrons with "authentic", "home-cooked" meals, "famous ramen" and "tasty" sushi; it's a lunchtime secret for the hip denizens of Japantown and local cubicleers, but with only a handful of seats, it gets "lines galore."

Tulio Ristorante *Italian* 25 23 24 $43

Downtown | Hotel Vintage Park | 1100 Fifth Ave. (Spring St.) | 206-624-5500 | www.tulio.com

Chef Walter Pisano turns out "meltingly delicious" Italian dishes including smoked salmon raviolis at this Downtown ristorante in the Hotel Vintage Park; "crisp, professional service" helps assure it's a staple for business lunches and "pre-theater" dining in a setting that's "old-style classy" with lots of dark woodwork; the crowd is "eclectic", and the smart money "reserves well in advance" because this "reasonably priced" spot is "always busy."

Turkish Delight ⌿ *Turkish* - - - I

Pike Place Market | 1930 Pike Pl. (bet. Stewart & Virginia Sts.) | 206-443-1387

This "delightful" family-run Turkish spot in the Pike Place Market is perfect for "a quick lunch" of inexpensive "boreks, stews and kebabs" topped off with "fabulous baklava"; the space is bright and modern with windows that open out to the market - perfect for watching the passing parade of characters.

Tutta Bella Neapolitan Pizzeria *Pizza* 22 17 20 $22

Columbia City | 4918 Rainier Ave. S. (Hudson St.) | 206-721-3501

Wallingford | 4411 Stone Way N. (44th St.) | 206-633-3800

(continued)

Tutta Bella Neapolitan Pizzeria

South Lake Union | 2200 Westlake Ave. (Denny Way) | 206-624-4422
Issaquah | 715 NW Gilman Blvd. (Front St.) | 425-391-6838
www.tuttabella.com

"Some of the best pizzas in town" are the "authentic" certified Napoli pies with a "wood-fired" "thin crust" at this local chain of artisan pizzerias where ingredients are from Italy and the gelato's from Bottega Italiana; the "friendly" staff makes it work as well for "a casual first date" as for a low-cost "family dinner."

Two Bells Bar & Grill *Pub Food* 22 | 9 | 16 | $17

Belltown | 2313 Fourth Ave. (bet. Battery & Bell Sts.) | 206-441-3050 | www.thetwobells.com

A "timeless" Belltown "institution" with "some of the greatest" sandwiches and "hand-formed" burgers "around", this "cozy" tavern and grill is a dandy "cheap dinner" choice before a movie at the Cinerama; though nitpickers note it could use some "freshening up", the room is home to rotating art shows and "music sometimes."

Typhoon! *Thai* 22 | 19 | 18 | $29

Redmond | Bella Bottega | 8936 161st Ave. NE (90th St.) | 425-558-7666 | www.typhoonrestaurants.com

Not just a Redmond "go-to" for classic noodles and soup, this mid-priced Thai with a "big menu" also serves "deliciously unique" specials in its bamboo-decorated quarters; whether for a "reliable lunch" or a "pleasant dinner" before a movie, fans consider it a "super value."

Umi Sake House ◐ *Japanese* 25 | 23 | 20 | $34

Belltown | 2230 First Ave. (Bell St.) | 206-374-8717 | www.umisakehouse.com

With its "mind-boggling list" of "innovative", "not-so-spendy" sushi and izakaya dishes, surveyors say this "hip" Belltown Japanese can "put a little spice" in your life; more than 60 hot and cold sakes keep the "cool" clientele lubricated in a room designed like a classic Nipponese country house, and if service varies, it's still "quite a scene" including two "happening" happy hours Sunday–Thursday.

NEW Uneeda Burger *Burgers* - | - | - | I

Fremont | 4302 Fremont Ave. N. (43rd St.) | 206-547-2600 | www.uneedaburger.com

The lil' bro of Quinn's Pub, this hip Fremonter delivers on its better-burger pledge with pedigreed patties paired with decadent milkshakes at affordable prices, while riding the trendy-joint-in-an-old-auto-repair-shop craze (complete with framed mechanics' name patches); its quality goods and fun feel attract foodies of all ages, especially when the garage door rolls up to reveal a big front deck.

Uptown China *Chinese* 22 | 16 | 21 | $22

Queen Anne | 200 Queen Anne Ave. N. (John St.) | 206-285-7710 | www.uptown-china.com

This "friendly" Queen Anne Chinese gets "love" for its "from-scratch" Hunan, Cantonese, Sichuan and Shanghainese dishes and for its proximity to Seattle Center events; the bill is modest, and for exhausted office types and hungry homebodies, there's "very fast" delivery.

Uptown Espresso *Coffeehouse* 19 | 15 | 19 | $8

Belltown | 2504 Fourth Ave. (Wall St.) | 206-441-1084
Downtown | 1933 Seventh Ave. (bet. Stewart & Virginia Sts.) | 206-728-8842
NEW Wallingford | 2300 N. 45th St. (Corliss Ave.) | 206-812-0404
NEW Magnolia | 3223 W. McGraw St. (33rd Ave.) | No phone
Queen Anne | 525 Queen Anne Ave. N. (bet. Mercer & Republican Sts.) | 206-285-3757
Seattle Waterfront | Pier 70 | 2801 Alaskan Way (Broad St.) | 206-770-7777
South Lake Union | 500 Westlake Ave. N. (Republican St.) | 206-621-2045
West Seattle | 3845 Delridge Way SW (Andover St.) | 206-933-9497
West Seattle | 4301 SW Edmunds St. (California Ave.) | 206-935-3753
www.velvetfoam.com

"Perfect foam" on "exceptional" lattes has caffeine cravers dubbing this local bean chain "the bomb" in a "coffee-saturated town"; even though the service runs hot and cold, the decor "feels like home", and thanks to free WiFi, locals wander in to work, tweet and Facebook at all hours.

Veraci Pizza *Pizza* 25 | 12 | 18 | $19

Ballard | 500 NW Market St. (bet. 5th & 6th Aves.) | 206-525-1813 | www.veracipizza.com

With its "crisp, thin crust" and "fresh", "delicious toppings", the wood-fired pizza at this affordable Ballardeer is a "hands-down favorite" of devotees who follow their pie with some homemade gelato; the decor is simple and contemporary, service is "friendly" and there's "usually a wait" for a table at lunch and dinner.

Via Tribunali *Pizza* 23 | 20 | 18 | $26

Capitol Hill | 913 E. Pike St. (bet. Broadway & 10th Ave.) | 206-322-9234 ◐
Fremont | 4303 Fremont Ave. N. (43rd St.) | 206-547-2144
Georgetown | 6009 12th Ave. S. (Vale St.) | 206-464-2880 ⊠
Queen Anne | 317 W. Galer St. (3rd Ave.) | 206-264-7768
www.viatribunali.com

For "cutting-edge" pizza with an "extra-thin crust" and "fresh ingredients", pie lovers line up at this Napoli-approved, midpriced local chain; service can be "leisurely", and the slightly "Gothic" settings can be so "dark", some joke "if seeing your slice is important, find another place."

Vios Cafe *Greek* 22 | 18 | 19 | $27

Capitol Hill | 903 19th Ave. E. (Aloha St.) | 206-329-3236 ⊠ M
Ravenna | Third Place Books | 6504 20th Ave. NE (65th St.) | 206-525-5701
www.vioscafe.com

This midpriced Greek twinset offers "platters" of "rich, delicious" fare including souvlaki and moussaka served with "care and love" in charming "family-style" settings; the original Capitol Hill location has become a "neighborhood" staple, while Ravenna in the Third Place Books bookstore is open for breakfast too; both spots have a children's menu and a play area to keep little ones occupied.

Voilà! Bistrot *French* 21 | 20 | 21 | $35

Madison Valley | 2805 E. Madison St. (28th Ave.) | 206-322-5460 | www.voilabistrot.com

"Get your cassoulet fix" at this "romantic" midpriced Madison Park bistro "favorite" where "it's hard to decide" between the French "comfort food" and the specials of Paris-born chef-owner Laurent Gabrel (Chloe); the "quaint" old-world decor and "really nice" staff add to the "charm and personality."

Volterra *Italian* 25 | 22 | 22 | $42

Ballard | 5411 Ballard Ave. NW (22nd Ave.) | 206-789-5100 | www.volterrarestaurant.com

This Ballard Italian "continues to roll along" thanks to chef-owner Don Curtiss' "superb" and "unique" offerings that are "very reasonably priced for the quality"; the "low-key" dining room is rustic yet "elegant" and the staff is "savvy and helpful", so fans insist "if you can get in, you must go."

Volunteer Park Cafe & Marketplace Ⓜ *American* 25 | 19 | 20 | $23

Capitol Hill | 1501 17th Ave. E. (Galer St.) | 206-328-3155 | www.alwaysfreshgoodness.com

"Hidden away" on a "sleepy" Capitol Hill residential street, this "darling" "little nook" in an old storefront "hits the spot" with its "homey" American comfort food dished out in a "pleasant", "casual" atmosphere; service is "friendly", and the affordable menu has "amazing" baked goods, lunches and dinners and a wine selection that's "fantastic"; P.S. it's home to a monthly pop-up called Savage Street Cuisine, focusing on a different world region at each dinner.

Walrus & the Carpenter ☒ *American/Seafood* - | - | - | M

Ballard | Kolstrand Bldg. | 4743 Ballard Ave. NW (bet. 17th Ave. & Shilshole Ave.) | 206-395-9227 | www.thewalrusbar.com

Don't let the oyster bar designation fool you - while this Ballard seafood sibling of the Boat Street Cafe is luring seafood lovers with its freshly shucked bivalves, it's also dishing out midpriced New American dinners and desserts, craft cocktails, wine and microbrews; the hip digs pack in all ages at the zinc bar and simple tables that ring the walls, and the smart money shows up early to snag a seat.

Wann Japanese Izakaya ◐ *Japanese* 20 | 20 | 19 | $31

Belltown | 2020 Second Ave. (bet. Lenora & Virginia Sts.) | 206-441-5637 | www.wann-izakaya.com

An "authentic izakaya" that's a Belltown branch of a Japanese chain has lots of sake and shochu to wash down "inventive bar food" including midpriced robata grill dishes, noodles and "fresh sushi"; it further "appeals to the cool" crowd with "clean, crisp decor" and a "Zen atmosphere", plus "great-value" happy hours.

	FOOD	DECOR	SERVICE	COST

Wasabi Bistro ◐ *Japanese* — 22 | 18 | 18 | $32

Belltown | 2311 Second Ave. (bet. Battery & Bell Sts.) | 206-441-6044 | www.wasabibistro.biz

After being closed for more than a year, this Belltowner is once again packing 'em in with its affordable takes on modern Japanese (including "creative sushi"); the room is more modern than ever, making it date-worthy for young hipsters with good jobs, or partyers getting the evening started at happy hour; P.S. book at least two days ahead for the five-course kaiseki ($105), a study in flavors and textures.

NEW Wheeler Street Kitchen ☒ Ⓜ *American/Pacific NW* — - | - | - | I

Magnolia | 3216 W. Wheeler St. (bet. 32nd & 33rd Aves.) | 206-257-0213 | www.wheelerstreetkitchen.com

Soups and burgers are the A-listers at Magnolia's wallet-friendly American hangout in the heart of the village; its teensy space, a former glass-art studio, has been snazzed up for the well-heeled ladies who meet here to lunch and catch up on the local goings on.

Where Ya At Matt ☒ *Creole/Soul Food* — - | - | - | I

Location varies (see website) | No phone | www.whereyaatmatt.com

Creole soul food from N'Awlins expat chef Matthew Lewis draws office workers and others to this big red truck dishing out gumbo, po' boys, big puffy beignets and other hot, moderately spicy grub for a wallet-friendly lunch to eat back at your desk; check its website for daily locations.

Wilde Rover *Pub Food* — ▽ 16 | 19 | 15 | $24

Kirkland | 111 Central Way (bet. 1st & Lake Sts.) | 425-822-8940 | www.wilderover.com

"Drinks, music and games" make this Kirklander the "perfect Irish pub" for locals who rove beyond the "bar food with inspiration from Ireland" to its real attractions; while the decor is "dark and rather inviting", "bartenders who know how to pour" a Guinness, live bands and trivia night are what really "pack the place."

Z Wild Ginger *Pacific Rim* — 25 | 23 | 22 | $42

Downtown | Mann Bldg. | 1401 Third Ave. (Union St.) | 206-623-4450
Bellevue | The Bravern | 11020 NE Sixth St. (110th Ave.) | 425-495-8889
www.wildginger.net

Once again Seattle's Most Popular, this "classy" Downtown and Bellevue duo proffers "pricey" "one-of-a-kind" Pacific Rim fare including "imaginative" dishes with housemade sauces and a specialty of "fragrant duck on cloudlike buns"; Bellevue's weekend dim sum brunches add to the appeal, and though the bustling, "sleek" dining rooms hold hundreds of diners, "reservations are a must."

Willows Inn Ⓜ *Pacific NW* — - | - | - | E

Lummi Island | 2579 West Shore Dr. (Melcher Ave.) | 360-758-2620 | www.willows-inn.com

Savvy eaters take the ferry to this rustic 1910 inn on Lummi Island to feast hyper-locally on finessed Pacific Northwest five-course prix fixe dinners from chef Blaine Wetzel (ex Copenhagen's Noma), who sources ingredients from the inn's Nettles Farm and local waters; its comely dining room is unpretentious, with pale tablecloths and unfettered views of trees and the sea; P.S. no children; diners can overnight at the inn.

Yanni's M *Greek* ▽ 26 | 16 | 17 | $26

Phinney Ridge | 7419 Greenwood Ave. N. (75th St.) | 206-783-6945 | www.yannisgreekrestaurant.com

Locals "love" this "amazing" family-run Phinney Ridge Greek for its "homemade", midpriced fare served in "large portions" by a "warm, friendly" staff; the owner's garden provides some of the fresh ingredients, and there's occasional belly dancing and live music, plus the happy hour is a "well-kept secret."

Yea's Wok M *Chinese*

Newcastle | Coal Creek Village Shopping Ctr. | 6969 Coal Creek Pkwy. SE (Newcastle Way) | 425-644-5546 | www.yeaswok.com

Eastsiders, Boeing employees and others collect at this budget-friendly stalwart in a Newcastle strip mall for Chinese dishes with crisp vegetables and zinging sauces that draw lines at dinner; the sparkling space features Boeing-oriented decor, including model planes atop the aquarium and a huge vintage photo of the aircraft giant's first engineer, Chinese-born and M.I.T.-trained Wong Tsoo.

Zaina *Mediterranean* ▽ 22 | 10 | 13 | $13

Downtown | 109 Pine St. (bet. 1st Ave. & News Ln.) | 206-623-1730
Pioneer Square | 108 Cherry St. (1st Ave.) | 206-624-5687

This Pioneer Square cafe's falafel and other Med street food comes at "reasonable prices" and with a side of atmospheric music; other than the Egyptian rugs, decor is basic, leading some to prefer takeout, and it's also "ideal" when you "need to feed vegan" family or friends; P.S. the Downtown branch opened post-Survey.

Zeeks Pizza *Pizza* 19 | 14 | 17 | $18

Belltown | 419 Denny Way (5th Ave.) | 206-285-8646
Green Lake | 7900 E. Green Lake Dr. N. (79th St.) | 206-285-8646
Phinney Ridge | 6000 Phinney Ave. N. (60th St.) | 206-285-8646
Queen Anne | 41 Dravus St. (Nickerson St.) | 206-285-8646
Ravenna | 2108 NE 65th St. (bet. Ravenna & 20th Aves.) | 206-285-8646
West Seattle | 6459 California Ave. SW (Fauntleroy Way) | 206-285-8646
Bellevue | 10201 NE 10th St. (102nd Ave.) | 425-893-8646
Issaquah | 2525 NE Park Dr. (25th Ave.) | 206-285-8646
Kirkland | 124 Park Ln. (Lake St.) | 206-285-8646
NEW Redmond | 16015 Cleveland St. (Redmond Way) | 425-893-8646
www.zeekspizza.com
Additional locations throughout the Seattle area

Known for "amusing" variations like the Thai One On chicken pie, this pizza chain also offers "unique" versions like the Tree Hugger (it's "all veggie") in its 'za lineup; the affordable "hangouts" have become "Seattle favorites" that fill the bill for hungry "soccer teams" and kids' "birthday parties."

	FOOD	DECOR	SERVICE	COST

Zippy's Giant Burgers *Burgers* | 23 | - | 15 | $10 |

White Center | 9614 14th Ave. SW (Roxbury St.) | 206-763-1347 | www.zippysgiantburgers.com

Die-hard fans say they'd "crawl on their hands and knees in the snow" to get to this White Center burger joint where 100% chuck is ground on-site each day for "simple", "thick" hamburgers "done up right"; it moved to new, roomier nearby digs post-Survey, and now serves beer.

Z'Tejas *Southwestern* | 18 | 17 | 19 | $26 |

Bellevue | Bellevue Sq. | 535 Bellevue Sq. (8th St.) | 425-467-5911 | www.ztejas.com

"Surprisingly good" for a "place in the mall", this Southwestern grill in Bellevue Square dishes out "reliable" enchiladas and "cornbread at its finest"; the "noisy, dark" spot with tile and wrought-iron decor attracts daytime shoppers, and later the "bar overflows" with tequila-drinking "young professionals" and "dates."

INDEXES

Cuisines

Includes names, locations and Food ratings.

AFGHAN

Kabul Afghan | **Wallingford** 23

AFRICAN

(See also Eritrean, Ethiopian, Moroccan)

Pan Africa Mkt. | **Pike Place** -

AMERICAN

Alki Bakery | **multi.** 21
Allium | **Eastsound** -
Americana | **Cap Hill** 20
Athenian | **Pike Place** 19
Barking Dog | **Ballard** 20
Beecher's Cheese | **Pike Place** 25
Bennett's | **Mercer Is** 18
Betty | **Queen Anne** 23
Bick's Broadview | **Greenwood** 21
Bing's Bar & Grill | **Madison Pk** 16
Bin on Lake | **Kirkland** 20
Bis on Main | **Bellevue** 24
Bleu Bistro | **Cap Hill** 21
Blue Star | **Wallingford** 18
BluWater | **multi.** 16
Book Bindery | **Queen Anne** -
NEW Brave Horse | **S Lake Union** -
Brix 25° | **Gig Harbor** -
Buckley's | **multi.** 17
Buns | **Location Varies** -
Cafe Nola | **Bainbridge Is** 21
Z Calcutta Grill | **Newcastle** 21
Cheesecake | **multi.** 17
Coastal Kitchen | **Cap Hill** 20
Columbia Ale | **Columbia City** 19
Costa's | **Univ Dist** 18
NEW Coterie Room | **Belltown** -
Crow | **Queen Anne** 25
Z Crush | **Madison Vly** 25
DeLuxe B&G | **Cap Hill** 17
Dish | **Fremont** 25
Earth & Ocean | **Dwtn** 22
Eats Mkt. Café | **W Seattle** 20
Elliott Bay | **multi.** 22
Elliott Bay Café | **multi.** 18
Emmer/Rye | **Queen Anne** 22
Endolyne Joe's | **W Seattle** 18
Eva | **Green Lk** 26
Ezell's | **multi.** 23
5 Point Café | **Belltown** 18
5 Spot | **Queen Anne** 21
14 Carrot Cafe | **Eastlake** 20
Frank's Oyster | **Ravenna** 20
Gallery Café/Frye | **Cap Hill** -
Geraldine's | **Columbia City** 24
Glo's | **Cap Hill** 25
Greenlake B&G | **Green Lk** 17
Grill on Broadway | **Cap Hill** 15
Hattie's Hat | **Ballard** 17
Hi-Life | **Ballard** 21
Hi Spot Cafe | **Madrona** 23
Honey Bear | **Lake Forest Pk** 19
Hudson | **Georgetown** 19
Icon Grill | **Dwtn** 20
Inn at Ship Bay | **Eastsound** -
Julia's | **multi.** 16
June | **Madrona** -
Kidd Valley | **multi.** 18
Z Lark | **Cap Hill** 27
Lecosho | **Dwtn** -
NEW Lloyd Martin | **Queen Anne** -
Lockspot Cafe | **Ballard** 18
Louisa's Café | **Eastlake** 16
Lowell's | **Pike Place** 20
Luc | **Madison Vly** 25

Luna Park Cafe | **W Seattle** 18
Lunchbox Lab | **S Lake Union** 24
NEW Madison Park Conserv. | **Madison Pk** –
Mae's | **Phinney R** 15
Maggie Bluff's | **Magnolia** 19
Maltby Cafe | **Maltby** 22
NEW Marrow | **Tacoma** –
Matts' Rotisserie | **Redmond** 21
Z Mistral | **S Lake Union** 26
Z Nell's | **Green Lk** 27
Original Pancake | **multi.** 21
Pacific Grill | **Tacoma** 26
Pair | **Ravenna** 26
Palace Kitchen | **Dwtn** 25
Pike Pub | **Pike Place** 17
Pike St. Fish | **Cap Hill** 22
Pomegranate Bistro | **Redmond** 25
Poppy | **Cap Hill** 25
Portalis Wine Bar | **Ballard** –
Pyramid Ale | **SODO** 16
Queen City Grill | **Belltown** 21
Quinn's Pub | **Cap Hill** 24
Red Door | **Fremont** 16
Red Robin | **multi.** 16
NEW Revel | **Fremont** –
NEW Rub With Love | **Pike Place** –
Russell's | **Bothell** 20
Saltoro | **N Seattle** 20
Sharp's Roasthse. | **SeaTac** –
Sip/Wine Bar | **multi.** 19
Skillet | **multi.** 23
Spur Gastropub | **Belltown** 24
Tat's Deli | **Pioneer Sq** –
Ten Mercer | **Queen Anne** 22
NEW Terra Plata | **Cap Hill** –
Z Tilth | **Wallingford** 28
Tin Room Bar | **Burien** –
Trellis | **Kirkland** 22
Volunteer Pk. Cafe | **Cap Hill** 25
Walrus/Carpenter | **Ballard** –
NEW Wheeler St. Kitchen | **Magnolia** –

ARGENTINEAN

Asado | **Tacoma** –
Buenos Aires Grill | **Dwtn** 21

ASIAN

Chinoise | **Queen Anne** 20
Dragonfish | **Dwtn** 19
Indochine | **Tacoma** 25
Lee's Asian | **W Seattle** 24

BAKERIES

Alki Bakery | **multi.** 21
Z Bakery Nouveau | **W Seattle** 29
Belle Epicurean | **multi.** 23
Belle Pastry | **multi.** 24
Z Cafe Besalu | **Ballard** 29
Crumpet Shop | **Pike Place** 24
Essential Baking Co. | **multi.** 22
Honey Bear | **Lake Forest Pk** 19
Il Fornaio | **Dwtn** 20
Le Fournil French Bakery | **Eastlake** 21
Le Panier | **Pike Place** 24
Louisa's Café | **Eastlake** 16
Macrina | **multi.** 25
Noah's Bagels | **multi.** 17
Piroshky Piroshky | **Pike Place** 24
Rose's Bakery | **Eastsound** –
3 Girls Bakery | **multi.** 24

BARBECUE

Bainbridge BBQ | **Bainbridge Is** 17
Carolina Smoke | **Bothell** –
Chuck's Hole In the Wall | **Pioneer Sq** –
Dixie's BBQ | **Bellevue** 21
Frontier Room | **Belltown** 22
Jones BBQ | **multi.** 21

CUISINES

Pecos Pit BBQ | **SODO** 26
Pig Iron BBQ | **S Seattle** 24
R&L BBQ | **Cap Hill** -
Stan's Bar-B-Q | **Issaquah** -
3 Pigs BBQ | **Bellevue** 21

BELGIAN

Brouwer's | **Fremont** 22
Sweet Iron | **multi.** -

BRAZILIAN

Tempero/Brasil | **Univ Dist** -

BRITISH

Neville's at the British Pantry | **Redmond** -
Queen Mary Tea | **Ravenna** 21
74th St. Ale | **Phinney R** 21

BURGERS

NEW Brave Horse | **S Lake Union** -
Buns | **Location Varies** -
Counter | **Ballard** 21
DeLuxe B&G | **Cap Hill** 17
Dick's Drive-In | **multi.** 19
Elliott Bay | **multi.** 22
Endolyne Joe's | **W Seattle** 18
Kidd Valley | **multi.** 18
Luna Park Cafe | **W Seattle** 18
Lunchbox Lab | **S Lake Union** 24
Maggie Bluff's | **Magnolia** 19
Red Mill | **multi.** 24
Red Robin | **multi.** 16
Two Bells B&G | **Belltown** 22
NEW Uneeda Burger | **Fremont** -
NEW Wheeler St. Kitchen | **Magnolia** -
Zippy's | **White Ctr** 23

CAJUN/CREOLE

Bayou on 1st | **Pike Place** -
New Orleans | **Pioneer Sq** 19

Toulouse | **Queen Anne** 23
Where Ya At Matt | **Location Varies** -

CAMBODIAN

Phnom Penh | **Intl Dist** -

CARIBBEAN

(See also Cuban)

Island Soul Caribbean | **Columbia City** -

CHEESE SPECIALISTS

Beecher's Cheese | **Pike Place** 25
Bennett's | **Mercer Is** 18

CHEESESTEAKS

Phila. Fevre | **Madison Vly** -

CHINESE

(* dim sum specialist)

Bamboo Garden Szechuan | **Bellevue** 25
Bamboo Garden Vegetarian | **Queen Anne** 20
Black Pearl | **multi.** 17
Café Ori | **Bellevue** 18
Chiang's Gourmet* | **multi.** 23
NEW Din Tai Fung | **Bellevue** -
Fu Man Dumpling | **Greenwood** 24
Harbor City BBQ* | **Intl Dist** -
Henry's Taiwan | **multi.** -
Ho Ho Seafood | **Intl Dist** 20
Honey Court* | **Intl Dist** 19
Hue Ky Mi Gia | **multi.** -
Jade Garden* | **Intl Dist** 22
Judy Fu's | **Maple Leaf** 20
Kau Kau BBQ | **Intl Dist** 24
Louie's* | **Ballard** -
Mee Sum | **multi.** 24
New Star | **Intl Dist** -
Noble Court* | **Bellevue** 18
O'Asian* | **Dwtn** 20

Pacific Café | **Intl Dist** —

P.F. Chang's | **multi.** 18

Purple Dot* | **Intl Dist** 17

Red Lantern | **Intl Dist** —

Sea Garden | **Intl Dist** 20

Shanghai Gdn. | **multi.** 24

Spiced | **Bellevue** 22

Spicy Talk Bistro | **Redmond** —

Szechuan Chef | **Bellevue** 23

Tai Tung | **Intl Dist** 23

Top Gun* | **Bellevue** 22

Uptown China | **Queen Anne** 22

Yea's Wok | **Newcastle** —

COFFEEHOUSES

B&O Espresso | **Cap Hill** 20

Z Cafe Besalu | **Ballard** 29

Fonte | **Dwtn** 20

Uptown Espresso | **multi.** 19

COFFEE SHOPS/ DINERS

Bayou on 1st | **Pike Place** —

CJ's Eatery | **Belltown** 18

5 Point Café | **Belltown** 18

Geraldine's | **Columbia City** 24

Hattie's Hat | **Ballard** 17

Lowell's | **Pike Place** 20

Luna Park Cafe | **W Seattle** 18

Mae's | **Phinney R** 15

Original Pancake | **multi.** 21

Skillet | **Cap Hill** 23

Z Steelhead | **Pike Place** 24

CONTINENTAL

Tosoni's | **Bellevue** 26

CROATIAN

Pogacha | **multi.** 17

CUBAN

Z Paseo | **multi.** 28

DELIS

Bagel Oasis | **Ravenna** 23

Bakeman's | **Dwtn** 22

Buffalo Deli | **Belltown** 27

NEW Dot's Delicatessen | **Fremont** —

FareStart/2100 | **S Seattle** —

Gilbert's/Bagel | **Bellevue** 21

Goldbergs' Deli | **Bellevue** 18

I Love NY Deli | **multi.** 21

Phila. Fevre | **Madison Vly** —

Seatown | **Pike Place** —

NEW Stopsky's Deli | **Mercer Is** —

Tat's Deli | **Pioneer Sq** —

3 Girls Bakery | **Pike Place** 24

DESSERT

Z Bakery Nouveau | **W Seattle** 29

B&O Espresso | **Cap Hill** 20

Belle Epicurean | **multi.** 23

Belle Pastry | **multi.** 24

Z Cafe Besalu | **Ballard** 29

Cheesecake | **multi.** 17

Dilettante | **multi.** 23

Essential Baking Co. | **multi.** 22

Z Gelatiamo | **Dwtn** 27

La Côte | **Madison Vly** 20

Le Fournil French Bakery | **Eastlake** 21

Le Panier | **Pike Place** 24

Macrina | **multi.** 25

Mee Sum | **multi.** 24

Molly Moon Truck | **Location Varies** —

Sweet Iron | **multi.** —

3 Girls Bakery | **Pike Place** 24

ECLECTIC

Beach Cafe | **Kirkland** 19

Black Bottle | **multi.** 22

Chanterelle | **Edmonds** 19

CUISINES

Circa | **W Seattle** 19

Coastal Kitchen | **Cap Hill** 20

☒ Corson Bldg. | **Georgetown** 28

Cyclops | **Belltown** 19

Elemental | **Lake Union** 26

Flying Fish | **S Lake Union** 24

Joey | **multi.** 17

Joule | **Wallingford** 26

Local Vine | **multi.** -

Maple Leaf Grill | **Maple Leaf** 20

Marjorie | **Cap Hill** 25

Phoenecia | **W Seattle** 27

Sand Pt. Grill | **Sand Point** 19

Sip/Wine Bar | **multi.** 19

Sitka & Spruce | **Cap Hill** 26

Sport | **Seattle Ctr** 16

Sunlight Cafe | **Roosevelt** -

Sutra | **Wallingford** 24

Tap House Grill | **multi.** 17

ERITREAN

Dahlak Eritrean | **S Seattle** -

ETHIOPIAN

Assimba | **Cap Hill** 24

Habesha | **Dwtn** 22

EUROPEAN

☒ Cafe Besalu | **Ballard** 29

Carmelita | **Greenwood** 25

Dinette | **Cap Hill** 25

Fonte | **Dwtn** 20

Gallery Café/Frye | **Cap Hill** -

Portalis Wine Bar | **Ballard** -

35th St. Bistro | **Fremont** 22

Tilikum Place | **Belltown** 25

FONDUE

Melting Pot | **multi.** 19

FRENCH

☒ Bakery Nouveau | **W Seattle** 29

Belle Epicurean | **multi.** 23

Belle Pastry | **multi.** 24

Brass. Marg. | **Dwtn** 16

Café Presse | **Cap Hill** 23

Chez Shea/Lounge | **Pike Place** 26

Crepe de France | **Pike Place** 23

☒ Georgian | **Dwtn** 26

La Côte | **Madison Vly** 20

Le Fournil French Bakery | **Eastlake** 21

Le Gourmand | **Ballard** 26

Le Panier | **Pike Place** 24

Luc | **Madison Vly** 25

Lynn's Bistro | **Kirkland** 25

Maximilien | **Pike Place** 23

Portage | **Queen Anne** 25

NEW RN74 | **Dwtn** -

☒ Rover's | **Madison Vly** 28

Saley Crêpes | **Cap Hill** -

611 Supreme | **Cap Hill** 21

FRENCH (BISTRO)

Bastille Café | **Ballard** 19

☒ Boat St. Cafe | **Queen Anne** 27

☒ Cafe Campagne | **Pike Place** 26

Chloé | **Laurelhurst** -

Le Pichet | **Pike Place** 25

NEW Marché | **Pike Place** -

Voilà! Bistrot | **Madison Vly** 21

GASTROPUB

Quinn's Pub | Amer. | **Cap Hill** 24

Spur Gastropub | Amer. | **Belltown** 24

GERMAN

Die BierStube | **Roosevelt** 21

Feierabend | **S Lake Union** 18

GREEK

Costa's | **Univ Dist** 18

Costas Opa | **Fremont** 18

☒ Lola | **Dwtn** 25

Panos Kleftiko | **Queen Anne** 22

Plaka Estiatorio | **Ballard** 27
Santorini Greek | **Kirkland** 29
Taki's Mad Greek | **Ballard** –
Vios Cafe | **multi.** 22
Yanni's | **Phinney R** 26

HAWAIIAN

Kauai Family | **Georgetown** 23
Z Marination | **multi.** 27
'Ohana | **Belltown** 21

HOT DOGS

Dante's Dogs | **Location Varies** 21
Diggity Dog's | **Wallingford** 20
NEW Dot's Delicatessen | **Fremont** –
Matt's Famous Chili Dogs | **S Seattle** 23
Shultzy's | **Univ Dist** 18
Taxi Dogs | **Pike Place** –

ICE CREAM PARLORS

Molly Moon Truck | **Location Varies** –

INDIAN

India Bistro | **multi.** 23
Kabab Hse. | **multi.** 19
Mayuri | **multi.** 23
Moghul Palace | **Bellevue** –
Pabla | **multi.** 22
Roti | **Queen Anne** 21
Shamiana | **Kirkland** 21
Taste of India | **Univ Dist** 22

IRISH

Fadó Irish Pub | **Pioneer Sq** 17
Kells Irish | **Pike Place** 17
Paddy Coynes | **multi.** 16
Wilde Rover | **Kirkland** 16

ITALIAN

(N=Northern; S=Southern)

Abbondanza | **W Seattle** 19
Adriatic Grill | **Tacoma** –
Al Boccalino | **Pioneer Sq** 24
NEW Altura | **Cap Hill** –
Anchovies/Olives | **Cap Hill** 25
Assaggio | N | **Dwtn** 24
NEW Bar del Corso | **Beacon Hill** –
Barolo | **Dwtn** 24
Bisato | **Belltown** 25
Brad's Swingside | **Fremont** 25
Branzino | **Belltown** 25
Buca di Beppo | **multi.** 15
Cafe Bengodi | **Pioneer Sq** –
Z Cafe Juanita | N | **Kirkland** 28
Cafe Lago | **Montlake** 26
Cafe Veloce | **Kirkland** 21
Café Vignole | **S Seattle** –
Z Cantinetta | **multi.** 27
Ciao Bella | **Univ Vill** 23
NEW Cuoco | **S Lake Union** –
Da Pino | **Ravenna** –
Enza | S | **Queen Anne** –
Firenze | N | **Bellevue** 22
Four Swallows | **Bainbridge Is** 26
Frankie's Pizza | **Redmond** 20
Z Gelatiamo | **Dwtn** 27
Grazie | **multi.** 22
How To Cook Wolf | **Queen Anne** 24
Il Bistro | **Pike Place** 23
NEW Il Corvo | **Pike Place** –
Il Fornaio | **Dwtn** 20
Z Il Terrazzo | **Pioneer Sq** 27
La Fontana | S | **Belltown** 23
Z La Medusa | S | **Columbia City** 27
La Rustica | **W Seattle** 24
La Vita É Bella | **Belltown** 22
Luigi's Pizza | **Magnolia** –
Machiavelli | **Cap Hill** 24
Mamma Melina | **Univ Vill** 23
Mioposto | **Mt. Baker** 23
Mondello | **Magnolia** 25

Northlake Tav. | **Univ Dist** 22
Olympia Pizza | **multi.** 19
Osteria La Spiga | **Cap Hill** 23
Palomino | **multi.** 20
Pasta & Co. | **multi.** 22
Pasta Bella | **Ballard** 21
Perché/Pasta | **Green Lk** 24
Pink Door | **Pike Place** 22
Pizzeria Pulcinella | S | **S Seattle** -
Queen Margherita | S | **Magnolia** -
Rist. Italianissimo | N | **Woodinville** 26
Rist. Paradiso | **Kirkland** 20
Romio's | **multi.** 19
Z Salumi | **Pioneer Sq** 27
Salvatore | **Ravenna** 24
Serafina | **Eastlake** 25
Spazzo | **Redmond** 16
Z Spinasse | **Cap Hill** 28
Staple & Fancy | **Ballard** -
Z Steelhead | **Pike Place** 24
Streamliner | **Bainbridge Is** 19
Tavolàta | **Belltown** 25
That's Amore | **Mt. Baker** 24
13 Coins | **multi.** 19
Tropea | **Redmond** 26
Tulio | **Dwtn** 25
Volterra | **Ballard** 25

JAPANESE

(* sushi specialist)

Aoki Grill/Sushi* | **Cap Hill** 20
Benihana | **Dwtn** 19
Blue C Sushi* | **multi.** 16
Boom Noodle | **multi.** 17
Bush Garden* | **Intl Dist** 18
Chiso* | **Fremont** 24
Flo* | **Bellevue** 25
Fort St. George | **Intl Dist** 18
Fuji Sushi* | **Intl Dist** 22
I Love Sushi* | **multi.** 22
Izumi* | **Kirkland** 24
NEW Japonessa Cucina* | **Pike Place** -
Kaname Izakaya | **Intl Dist** -
Kikuya | **Redmond** 19
Z Kisaku Sushi* | **Green Lk** 27
Kushibar | **Belltown** 20
Maneki* | **Intl Dist** 25
Z Mashiko* | **W Seattle** 28
NEW Momiji* | **Cap Hill** -
Moshi Moshi* | **Ballard** 23
Musashi's* | **Wallingford** 23
Z Nishino* | **Madison Pk** 27
Ototo Sushi* | **Queen Anne** 19
Red Fin* | **Dwtn** 21
Rikki Rikki* | **Kirkland** 18
Sam's Sushi* | **multi.** 22
Shiki* | **Queen Anne** 25
Shiku Sushi* | **Ballard** 23
Z Shiro's Sushi* | **Belltown** 27
Sushi Kappo* | **Eastlake** -
Sushiman* | **Issaquah** -
Toyoda Sushi* | **Lake City** 26
Tsukushinbo* | **Intl Dist** -
Umi Sake Hse.* | **Belltown** 25
Wann Izakaya | **Belltown** 20
Wasabi Bistro* | **Belltown** 22

JEWISH

NEW Stopsky's Deli | **Mercer Is** -

KOREAN

Hosoonyi | **Edmonds** 23
Kimchi Bistro | **Cap Hill** 23
Korean Tofu House | **Univ Dist** -
Z Marination | **multi.** 27
Red Lantern | **Intl Dist** -
NEW Revel | **Fremont** -

KOSHER/ KOSHER-STYLE

Bamboo Garden Vegetarian | **Queen Anne** 20

Noah's Bagels | **Univ Vill** 17

LEBANESE

Med. Kitchen | **multi.** 26

MALAYSIAN

Malay Satay | **multi.** 21

MEDITERRANEAN

Andaluca | **Dwtn** 24

Capitol Club | **Cap Hill** 19

Cicchetti | **Eastlake** 23

NEW Golden Beetle | **Ballard** –

Gorgeous George's | **Phinney R** 25

How To Cook Wolf | **Queen Anne** 24

Z La Medusa | **Columbia City** 27

Med. Kitchen | **multi.** 26

Pair | **Ravenna** 26

Poco Wine | **Cap Hill** 19

Primo Grill | **Tacoma** –

Zaina | **multi.** 22

MEXICAN

Agua Verde | **Univ Dist** 23

Azteca | **multi.** 14

Burrito Loco | **Crown Hill** –

Z Cactus | **multi.** 22

Coliman | **Georgetown** –

El Camino | **Fremont** 22

El Camion | **multi.** 28

El Chupacabra | **Greenwood** 16

El Gallito | **Cap Hill** 19

El Mestizo | **Cap Hill** 24

El Puerco Lloron | **Pike Place** 21

El Ranchon Family Mexican | **Magnolia** 22

Galerias | **Cap Hill** 22

Gordito's | **multi.** 21

Jalisco | **multi.** 19

Z La Carta/Mezcaleria | **multi.** 27

La Cocina/Puerco | **Bellevue** 17

NEW La Luna | **Queen Anne** –

Laredos | **Queen Anne** –

Luisa's Mexican Grill | **Greenwood** 23

Malena's Taco | **multi.** 18

Mama's Mex. | **Belltown** 18

Mexico Cantina Y Cocina | **Dwtn** –

NEW Milagro Cantina | **Kirkland** –

Muy Macho | **S Park** –

Ooba's Mex. | **multi.** 24

Peso's | **Queen Anne** 22

NEW Poquitos | **Cap Hill** –

Rancho Bravo | **Cap Hill** 24

Rosita's Mex. | **Green Lk** 17

Saint, The | **Cap Hill** –

Señor Moose | **Ballard** 26

Tacos Guaymas/Cantina | **multi.** 19

Taqueria La Venadita | **Issaquah** –

MOROCCAN

Kasbah | **Ballard** –

Marrakesh | **Belltown** 21

NEW MEXICAN

Santa Fe Cafe | **Phinney R** 20

NOODLE SHOPS

Boom Noodle | **multi.** 17

Henry's Taiwan | **multi.** –

Hue Ky Mi Gia | **multi.** –

Kaname Izakaya | **Intl Dist** –

Krittika Noodles | **Green Lk** –

Mike's Noodle House | **Intl Dist** 23

Pho Bac | **Intl Dist** 24

Pho Thân | **multi.** 22

Tsukushinbo | **Intl Dist** –

PACIFIC NORTHWEST

Allium | **Eastsound** –

Z Anthony's HomePort | **multi.** 21

Anthony's Pier 66 | **Seattle Waterfront** 22
Art of the Table | **Wallingford** 25
Art Rest. | **Dwtn** 23
Z Barking Frog | **Woodinville** 25
Bluff | **Friday Harbor** -
Boka Kitchen | **Dwtn** 20
Brass. Marg. | **Dwtn** 16
Z Canlis | **Lake Union** 27
Chez Shea/Lounge | **Pike Place** 26
Coho Cafe | **multi.** 18
Copperleaf | **SeaTac** -
Cutters | **Pike Place** 22
Z Dahlia Lounge | **Dwtn** 26
Z Etta's | **Pike Place** 25
FareStart | **Dwtn** 23
Four Swallows | **Bainbridge Is** 26
Z Georgian | **Dwtn** 26
Z Herbfarm, The | **Woodinville** 28
Hill's Food & Wine | **Shoreline** 20
Hitchcock | **Bainbridge Is** -
Hunt Club | **First Hill** 22
Inn at Langley | **Langley** 26
Ivar's/Clams | **Seattle Waterfront** 21
Ivar's Salmon | **Lake Union** 21
La Bête | **Cap Hill** -
NEW Local 360 | **Belltown** -
Z Matt's/Mkt. | **Pike Place** 25
Maxwell's Restaurant | **Tacoma** -
Oliver's Twist | **Phinney R** 23
Pearl | **Bellevue** 22
Place Pigalle | **Pike Place** 25
Poco Wine | **Cap Hill** 19
Pogacha | **multi.** 17
Ponti Seafood | **Queen Anne** 24
Portage | **Queen Anne** 25
Purple Café | **multi.** 20
Z Ray's Boathse. | **Shilshole** 24
Ray's Cafe | **Shilshole** 22
Re:Public | **S Lake Union** -
Rose's Bakery | **Eastsound** -
Z Salish Lodge | **Snoqualmie** 23
Sazerac | **Dwtn** 20
Z Six Seven | **Seattle Waterfront** 23
Z SkyCity | **Seattle Ctr** 22
Spring Hill | **W Seattle** 25
St. Clouds | **Madrona** 23
Stumbling Goat | **Greenwood** 23
Taste | **Dwtn** 22
Tin Table | **Cap Hill** 20
Willows Inn | **Lummi Island** -

PACIFIC RIM

Z Wild Ginger | **multi.** 25

PAKISTANI

Kabab Hse. | **multi.** 19
Shamiana | **Kirkland** 21

PAN-LATIN

Azul | **Mill Creek** 22
Mission | **W Seattle** 20
Mojito | **Lake City** 25

PERSIAN

Caspian Grill Persian | **Univ Dist** -

PIZZA

Abbondanza | **W Seattle** 19
Alibi Room | **Pike Place** 21
All-Purpose Pizza | **Leschi** 22
Bambino's Pizzeria | **Belltown** -
NEW Bar del Corso | **Beacon Hill** -
Belltown Pizza | **Belltown** 20
Big Mario's Pizza | **Cap Hill** -
Cafe Bengodi | **Pioneer Sq** -
Cafe Lago | **Montlake** 26
Cafe Veloce | **Kirkland** 21
Ciao Bella | **Univ Vill** 23
Crash Landing | **Ballard** -
Delancey | **Ballard** 26
Delfino's Pizza | **Univ Vill** 23

Flying Squirrel | **multi.** 23
Frankie's Pizza | **Redmond** 20
Kylie's Chicago Pizza | **Fremont** -
La Vita É Bella | **Belltown** 22
Luigi's Pizza | **Magnolia** -
Mioposto | **Mt. Baker** 23
Northlake Tav. | **Univ Dist** 22
Olympia Pizza | **multi.** 19
Pagliacci Pizza | **multi.** 23
Palomino | **multi.** 20
Pegasus Pizza | **W Seattle** 21
Phoenecia | **W Seattle** 27
Piecora's Pizza | **Cap Hill** 21
Pizzeria Pulcinella | **S Seattle** -
Primo Grill | **Tacoma** -
Proletariat Pizza | **White Ctr** -
Queen Margherita | **Magnolia** -
Romio's | **multi.** 19
Z Serious Pie | **multi.** 26
Stellar Pizza | **Georgetown** 22
Tutta Bella | **multi.** 22
Veraci Pizza | **Ballard** 25
Via Tribunali | **multi.** 23
Zeeks Pizza | **multi.** 19

PUB FOOD

Barking Dog | **Ballard** 20
Brouwer's | **Fremont** 22
Buckley's | **multi.** 17
Circa | **W Seattle** 19
Columbia Ale | **Columbia City** 19
DeLuxe B&G | **Cap Hill** 17
Elliott Bay | **multi.** 22
Fadó Irish Pub | **Pioneer Sq** 17
Gordon Biersch | **Dwtn** 15
Hale's Ales | **Fremont** 15
Hilltop Ale Hse. | **Queen Anne** 20
Kells Irish | **Pike Place** 17
Paddy Coynes | **multi.** 16
Pike Pub | **Pike Place** 17
Pyramid Ale | **SODO** 16
Red Door | **Fremont** 16
74th St. Ale | **Phinney R** 21
Two Bells B&G | **Belltown** 22
Wilde Rover | **Kirkland** 16

PUERTO RICAN

La Isla | **Ballard** 21

RUSSIAN

Café Yarmarka | **Pike Place** -
Piroshky Piroshky | **Pike Place** 24

SALVADORAN

Guanaco's | **multi.** 22

SANDWICHES

(See also Delis)

Alki Bakery | **multi.** 21
Baguette Box | **multi.** 24
Z Bakery Nouveau | **W Seattle** 29
Beecher's Cheese | **Pike Place** 25
Belle Epicurean | **multi.** 23
Da Pino | **Ravenna** -
FareStart/2100 | **S Seattle** -
Macrina | **multi.** 25
Other Coast | **multi.** 26
Z Paseo | **multi.** 28
NEW Rub With Love | **Pike Place** -
Z Salumi | **Pioneer Sq** 27
Shultzy's | **Univ Dist** 18
Smarty Pants | **Georgetown** 23
3 Girls Bakery | **multi.** 24

SCANDINAVIAN

Scandinavian Cafe | **Ballard** -

SEAFOOD

Anchovies/Olives | **Cap Hill** 25
Z Anthony's HomePort | **multi.** 21
Anthony's Pier 66 | **Seattle Waterfront** 22

- Z Aqua by El Gaucho | **Seattle Waterfront** 25
- Athenian | **Pike Place** 19
- Beach Cafe | **Kirkland** 19
- Bell St. Diner | **Seattle Waterfront** 23
- Blueacre | **Dwtn** 21
- Bonefish Grill | **Bothell** 21
- Branzino | **Belltown** 25
- Brooklyn Seafood | **Dwtn** 24
- Chandler's Crab | **S Lake Union** 23
- Chinook's | **Magnolia** 21
- Chloé | **Laurelhurst** –
- Coho Cafe | **multi.** 18
- Cutters | **Pike Place** 22
- Dash Pt./Lobster Shop | **Tacoma** 23
- Duke's | **multi.** 19
- Z Elliott's Oyster | **Seattle Waterfront** 24
- Emmett Watson | **Pike Place** 22
- Z Etta's | **Pike Place** 25
- Flying Fish | **S Lake Union** 24
- F.X. McRory's | **Pioneer Sq** 18
- Ho Ho Seafood | **Intl Dist** 20
- Ivar's/Clams | **Seattle Waterfront** 21
- Ivar's Mukilteo | **Mukilteo** 21
- Ivar's Salmon | **Lake Union** 21
- Jack's Fish | **Pike Place** 22
- Lockspot Cafe | **Ballard** 18
- Z Matt's/Mkt. | **Pike Place** 25
- Matts' Rotisserie | **Redmond** 21
- McCormick/Schmick | **multi.** 21
- McCormick's Fish | **Dwtn** 23
- New Star | **Intl Dist** –
- Oyster Bar/Chuckanut | **Bow** 25
- Z Palisade | **Magnolia** 24
- Pike St. Fish | **Cap Hill** 22
- Ponti Seafood | **Queen Anne** 24
- Queen City Grill | **Belltown** 21
- Z Ray's Boathse. | **Shilshole** 24
- Ray's Cafe | **Shilshole** 22
- Salty's | **multi.** 20
- Sea Garden | **Intl Dist** 20
- Z Seastar | **multi.** 25
- Seatown | **Pike Place** –
- Shuckers | **Dwtn** 23
- Sunfish | **W Seattle** 21
- Top Gun | **Bellevue** 22
- Walrus/Carpenter | **Ballard** –

SMALL PLATES

(See also Spanish tapas specialist)

- NEW Bar del Corso | Italian | **Beacon Hill** –
- Bin on Lake | Amer. | **Kirkland** 20
- Bisato | Italian | **Belltown** 25
- Black Bottle | Eclectic | **Belltown** 22
- Boom Noodle | Japanese | **Cap Hill** 17
- Cicchetti | Med. | **Eastlake** 23
- Z Lark | Amer. | **Cap Hill** 27
- Local Vine | Eclectic | **multi.** –
- Oliver's Twist | Pac. NW | **Phinney R** 23
- Pair | Amer. | **Ravenna** 26
- Phoenecia | Eclectic | **W Seattle** 27
- Ponti Seafood | Seafood | **Queen Anne** 24
- Poppy | Amer. | **Cap Hill** 25
- Portalis Wine Bar | Amer./Euro. | **Ballard** –
- Spur Gastropub | Amer. | **Belltown** 24
- Umi Sake Hse. | Japanese | **Belltown** 25

SOUL FOOD

- Island Soul Caribbean | **Columbia City** –
- Kingfish | **Cap Hill** 24
- Where Ya At Matt | **Location Varies** –

SOUTH AMERICAN

(See also Argentinean, Brazilian)

Copacabana | **Pike Place** –

Meza | **Cap Hill** –

SOUTHERN

Catfish Corner | **multi.** 21

Ezell's | **multi.** 23

Kingfish | **Cap Hill** 24

Paragon | **Queen Anne** 19

Sazerac | **Dwtn** 20

NEW Serious Biscuit | **S Lake Union** –

Slim's Last Chance | **Georgetown** 26

SOUTHWESTERN

Z Cactus | **multi.** 22

Santa Fe Cafe | **Phinney R** 20

Z'Tejas | **Bellevue** 18

SPANISH

(* tapas specialist)

Gaudi | **Ravenna** –

Z Harvest Vine* | **Madison Vly** 27

Ocho* | **Ballard** 24

Z Olivar* | **Cap Hill** 26

Tango* | **Cap Hill** 20

STEAKHOUSES

Buenos Aires Grill | **Dwtn** 21

Capital Grille | **Dwtn** 23

Z Daniel's Broiler | **multi.** 24

Z El Gaucho | **multi.** 25

F.X. McRory's | **Pioneer Sq** 18

Z Jak's Grill | **multi.** 24

John Howie | **Bellevue** 25

Melrose Grill | **Renton** 27

Z Metro. Grill | **Dwtn** 26

Morton's | **Dwtn** 25

Outback Steak | **multi.** 15

Ruth's Chris | **multi.** 24

Spencer's Steaks | **SeaTac** –

Szmania's | **Magnolia** 25

TAIWANESE

Facing East | **Bellevue** 26

TEAROOMS

Queen Mary Tea | **Ravenna** 21

THAI

Ayutthaya | **Cap Hill** 20

Bahn Thai | **Queen Anne** 25

Bai Pai Fine | **Ravenna** 25

Bai Tong | **multi.** 24

Buddha Ruksa | **W Seattle** 26

Chantanee | **Bellevue** 25

Galanga Thai | **Tacoma** –

Jhanjay Vegetarian Thai | **multi.** 25

Kaosamai | **multi.** –

Krittika Noodles | **Green Lk** –

Mae Phim Thai | **Dwtn** 23

May | **Wallingford** 26

Noodle Boat | **Issaquah** 26

Racha | **multi.** 20

Thai Curry Simple | **multi.** –

Thai Ginger | **multi.** 22

Thaiku | **Ballard** 22

Thai Siam | **Ballard** –

Thai Tom | **Univ Dist** 25

Thin Pan | **Kirkland** –

Typhoon! | **Redmond** 22

TIBETAN

NEW Ting Momo | **S Lake Union** –

TURKISH

Bistro Turkuaz | **Madrona** 26

Turkish Delight | **Pike Place** –

VEGETARIAN

(* vegan)

Bamboo Garden Vegetarian | **Queen Anne** 20

Cafe Flora | **Madison Pk** 23

CUISINES

Carmelita | **Greenwood** 25

Chaco Canyon* | **multi.** 19

Jhanjay Vegetarian Thai | **multi.** 25

Plum Vegan* | **Cap Hill** 25

Silence-Heart-Nest* | **Fremont** 18

Sunlight Cafe | **Roosevelt** -

Sutra | **Wallingford** 24

VIETNAMESE

NEW Ba Bar | **Cap Hill** -

Z Green Leaf | **Intl Dist** 27

Hue Ky Mi Gia | **multi.** -

Lemongrass | **multi.** 21

Long Provincial | **Dwtn** 21

Monkey Bridge | **Ballard** 21

Monsoon | **multi.** 25

Pho Bac | **Intl Dist** 24

Pho Cyclo | **multi.** 22

Pho Thân | **multi.** 22

Tamarind Tree | **Intl Dist** 25

Thanh Vi | **Univ Dist** 19

Locations

Includes names, cuisines and Food ratings.

Seattle

BALLARD/ SHILSHOLE

☑ Anthony's HomePort | *Pac. NW/Seafood* 21
Azteca | *Mex.* 14
Barking Dog | *Pub* 20
Bastille Café | *French* 19
☑ Cafe Besalu | *Bakery/Euro.* 29
Counter | *Burgers* 21
Crash Landing | *Pizza* –
Delancey | *Pizza* 26
El Camion | *Mex.* 28
Flying Squirrel | *Pizza* 23
NEW Golden Beetle | *Med.* –
Hattie's Hat | *Diner* 17
Hi-Life | *Amer.* 21
India Bistro | *Indian* 23
Jhanjay Vegetarian Thai | *Thai/Veg.* 25
Kasbah | *Moroccan* –
☑ La Carta/Mezcaleria | *Mex.* 27
La Isla | *Puerto Rican* 21
Le Gourmand | *French* 26
Lockspot Cafe | *Amer./Seafood* 18
Louie's | *Chinese* –
Malena's Taco | *Mex.* 18
Monkey Bridge | *Viet.* 21
Moshi Moshi | *Japanese* 23
Ocho | *Spanish* 24
Original Pancake | *Amer.* 21
Other Coast | *Sandwiches* 26
☑ Paseo | *Cuban* 28
Pasta Bella | *Italian* 21
Pho Thân | *Viet.* 22
Plaka Estiatorio | *Greek* 27
Portalis Wine Bar | *Amer./Euro.* –
☑ Ray's Boathse. | *Pac. NW/Seafood* 24
Ray's Cafe | *Pac. NW/Seafood* 22
Red Mill | *Burgers* 24
Sam's Sushi | *Japanese* 22
Scandinavian Cafe | *Scan.* –
Señor Moose | *Mex.* 26
Shiku Sushi | *Japanese* 23
Staple & Fancy | *Italian* –
Taki's Mad Greek | *Greek* –
Thaiku | *Thai* 22
Thai Siam | *Thai* –
3 Girls Bakery | *Bakery* 24
Veraci Pizza | *Pizza* 25
Volterra | *Italian* 25
Walrus/Carpenter | *Amer./Seafood* –

BEACON HILL/ MT. BAKER

NEW Bar del Corso | *Italian* –
Mioposto | *Italian* 23
That's Amore | *Italian* 24

BELLTOWN

Bambino's Pizzeria | *Pizza* –
Belltown Pizza | *Pizza* 20
Bisato | *Italian* 25
Black Bottle | *Eclectic* 22
Branzino | *Italian/Seafood* 25
Buckley's | *Amer.* 17
Buffalo Deli | *Deli* 27
CJ's Eatery | *Diner* 18
NEW Coterie Room | *Amer.* –
Cyclops | *Eclectic* 19
☑ El Gaucho | *Steak* 25
5 Point Café | *Amer.* 18
Frontier Room | *BBQ* 22
Kushibar | *Japanese* 20
La Fontana | *Italian* 23

LOCATIONS

La Vita É Bella | *Italian* 22
NEW Local 360 | *Pac. NW* -
Macrina | *Bakery/Dessert* 25
Mama's Mex. | *Mex.* 18
Marrakesh | *Moroccan* 21
'Ohana | *Hawaiian* 21
Queen City Grill | *Amer.* 21
Z Shiro's Sushi | *Japanese* 27
Spur Gastropub | *Amer.* 24
Tavolàta | *Italian* 25
Tilikum Place | *Euro.* 25
Two Bells B&G | *Pub* 22
Umi Sake Hse. | *Japanese* 25
Uptown Espresso | *Coffee* 19
Wann Izakaya | *Japanese* 20
Wasabi Bistro | *Japanese* 22
Zeeks Pizza | *Pizza* 19

CAPITOL HILL

NEW Altura | *Italian* -
Americana | *Amer.* 20
Anchovies/Olives | *Italian/Seafood* 25
Aoki Grill/Sushi | *Japanese* 20
Assimba | *Ethiopian* 24
Ayutthaya | *Thai* 20
NEW Ba Bar | *Viet.* -
Baguette Box | *Sandwiches* 24
B&O Espresso | *Coffee* 20
Big Mario's Pizza | *Pizza* -
Bleu Bistro | *Amer.* 21
Boom Noodle | *Japanese* 17
Café Presse | *French* 23
Capitol Club | *Med.* 19
Catfish Corner | *Southern* 21
Coastal Kitchen | *Amer./Eclectic* 20
DeLuxe B&G | *Burgers* 17
Dick's Drive-In | *Burgers* 19
Dilettante | *Dessert* 23
Dinette | *Euro.* 25
El Gallito | *Mex.* 19
Elliott Bay Café | *Amer.* 18
El Mestizo | *Mex.* 24
Ezell's | *Amer.* 23
Galerias | *Mex.* 22
Gallery Café/Frye | *Amer./Euro.* -
Glo's | *Amer.* 25
Grill on Broadway | *Amer.* 15
Guanaco's | *Salvadoran* 22
Julia's | *Amer.* 16
Kimchi Bistro | *Korean* 23
Kingfish | *Soul* 24
La Bête | *Pac. NW* -
Z Lark | *Amer.* 27
Lemongrass | *Viet.* 21
Local Vine | *Eclectic* -
Machiavelli | *Italian* 24
Z Marination | *Hawaiian/Korean* 27
Marjorie | *Eclectic* 25
Meza | *S Amer.* -
NEW Momiji | *Japanese* -
Monsoon | *Viet.* 25
Z Olivar | *Spanish* 26
Olympia Pizza | *Greek/Pizza* 19
Osteria La Spiga | *Italian* 23
Other Coast | *Sandwiches* 26
Pagliacci Pizza | *Pizza* 23
Pho Cyclo | *Viet.* 22
Pho Thân | *Viet.* 22
Piecora's Pizza | *Pizza* 21
Pike St. Fish | *Amer./Seafood* 22
Plum Vegan | *Vegan/Veg.* 25
Poco Wine | *Med./Pacific NW* 19
Poppy | *Amer.* 25
NEW Poquitos | *Mex.* -
Quinn's Pub | *Amer.* 24
Rancho Bravo | *Mex.* 24
R&L BBQ | *BBQ* -
Saint, The | *Mex.* -
Saley Crêpes | *French* -

Sitka & Spruce | *Eclectic* 26
611 Supreme | *French* 21
Skillet | *Amer.* 23
Z Spinasse | *Italian* 28
Tacos Guaymas/Cantina | *Mex.* 19
Tango | *Spanish* 20
NEW Terra Plata | *Amer.* –
Thai Curry Simple | *Thai* –
Tin Table | *Pac. NW* 20
Via Tribunali | *Pizza* 23
Vios Cafe | *Greek* 22
Volunteer Pk. Cafe | *Amer.* 25

COLUMBIA CITY/ SEWARD PARK

Columbia Ale | *Pub* 19
Flying Squirrel | *Pizza* 23
Geraldine's | *Amer.* 24
Island Soul Caribbean | *Carib./Soul* –
Jones BBQ | *BBQ* 21
Z La Medusa | *Italian/Med.* 27
Tutta Bella | *Pizza* 22

CROWN HILL

Burrito Loco | *Mex.* –
Dick's Drive-In | *Burgers* 19

DOWNTOWN

Andaluca | *Med.* 24
Art Rest. | *Pac. NW* 23
Assaggio | *Italian* 24
Bakeman's | *Deli* 22
Barolo | *Italian* 24
Belle Epicurean | *Bakery/French* 23
Belle Pastry | *Bakery/Dessert* 24
Benihana | *Japanese* 19
Blueacre | *Seafood* 21
Blue C Sushi | *Japanese* 16
Boka Kitchen | *Pac. NW* 20
Brass. Marg. | *French/Pac. NW* 16
Brooklyn Seafood | *Seafood* 24
Buenos Aires Grill | *Argent.* 21
Capital Grille | *Steak* 23
Cheesecake | *Amer.* 17
Z Dahlia Lounge | *Pac. NW* 26
Dilettante | *Dessert* 23
Dragonfish | *Asian* 19
Earth & Ocean | *Amer.* 22
FareStart | *Pac. NW* 23
Fonte | *Euro.* 20
Z Gelatiamo | *Dessert* 27
Z Georgian | *French/Pac. NW* 26
Gordon Biersch | *Pub* 15
Habesha | *Ethiopian* 22
Icon Grill | *Amer.* 20
Il Fornaio | *Italian* 20
Lecosho | *Amer.* –
Z Lola | *Greek* 25
Long Provincial | *Viet.* 21
Mae Phim Thai | *Thai* 23
McCormick/Schmick | *Seafood* 21
McCormick's Fish | *Seafood* 23
Z Metro. Grill | *Steak* 26
Mexico Cantina Y Cocina | *Mex.* –
Morton's | *Steak* 25
Noah's Bagels | *Bakery* 17
O'Asian | *Chinese* 20
Pabla | *Indian* 22
Palace Kitchen | *Amer.* 25
Palomino | *Italian* 20
P.F. Chang's | *Chinese* 18
Pho Cyclo | *Viet.* 22
Purple Café | *Pac. NW* 20
Red Fin | *Japanese* 21
NEW RN74 | *French* –
Romio's | *Pizza* 19
Ruth's Chris | *Steak* 24
Sazerac | *Pac. NW/Southern* 20
Z Serious Pie | *Pizza* 26
Shuckers | *Seafood* 23
Sip/Wine Bar | *Amer.* 19

- Sweet Iron | *Belgian* –
- Tacos Guaymas/Cantina | *Mex.* 19
- Tap House Grill | *Eclectic* 17
- Taste | *Pac. NW* 22
- Thai Ginger | *Thai* 22
- Tulio | *Italian* 25
- Uptown Espresso | *Coffee* 19
- **Z** Wild Ginger | *Pac. Rim* 25
- Zaina | *Mideast.* 22

EASTLAKE/ LAKE UNION

- Azteca | *Mex.* 14
- **Z** Canlis | *Pac. NW* 27
- Cicchetti | *Med.* 23
- Elemental | *Eclectic* 26
- 14 Carrot Cafe | *Amer.* 20
- Ivar's Salmon | *Pac. NW/Seafood* 21
- Le Fournil French Bakery | *Bakery/French* 21
- Louisa's Café | *Amer.* 16
- Romio's | *Pizza* 19
- Serafina | *Italian* 25
- Sushi Kappo | *Japanese* –

FIRST HILL

- Hunt Club | *Pac. NW* 22

FREMONT/ WALLINGFORD

- Art of the Table | *Pac. NW* 25
- Baguette Box | *Sandwiches* 24
- Blue C Sushi | *Japanese* 16
- Blue Star | *Amer.* 18
- Brad's Swingside | *Italian* 25
- Brouwer's | *Belgian* 22
- **Z** Cantinetta | *Italian* 27
- Chiso | *Japanese* 24
- Costas Opa | *Greek* 18
- Dick's Drive-In | *Burgers* 19
- Diggity Dog's | *Hot Dogs* 20
- Dish | *Amer.* 25
- **NEW** Dot's Delicatessen | *Deli* –
- El Camino | *Mex.* 22
- Essential Baking Co. | *Bakery* 22
- Hale's Ales | *Pub* 15
- Jhanjay Vegetarian Thai | *Thai/Veg.* 25
- Joule | *Eclectic* 26
- Julia's | *Amer.* 16
- Kabul Afghan | *Afghan* 23
- Kaosamai | *Thai* –
- Kylie's Chicago Pizza | *Pizza* –
- May | *Thai* 26
- Musashi's | *Japanese* 23
- Olympia Pizza | *Greek/Pizza* 19
- **Z** Paseo | *Cuban* 28
- Red Door | *Pub* 16
- **NEW** Revel | *Amer./Korean* –
- Silence-Heart-Nest | *Vegan/Veg.* 18
- Sutra | *Eclectic/Veg.* 24
- Tacos Guaymas/Cantina | *Mex.* 19
- 35th St. Bistro | *Euro.* 22
- **Z** Tilth | *Amer.* 28
- Tutta Bella | *Pizza* 22
- **NEW** Uneeda Burger | *Burgers* –
- Uptown Espresso | *Coffee* 19
- Via Tribunali | *Pizza* 23

GEORGETOWN/ SOUTH PARK/ SOUTH SEATTLE

- Alki Bakery | *Bakery* 21
- Café Vignole | *Italian* –
- Coliman | *Mex.* –
- **Z** Corson Bldg. | *Eclectic* 28
- Dahlak Eritrean | *Eritrean* –
- Essential Baking Co. | *Bakery* 22
- Ezell's | *Amer.* 23
- FareStart/2100 | *Deli* –
- Hudson | *Amer.* 19
- Jalisco | *Mex.* 19
- Kauai Family | *Hawaiian* 23
- Matt's Famous Chili Dogs | *Hot Dogs* 23

Muy Macho | *Mex.* | –
Pig Iron BBQ | *BBQ* | 24
Pizzeria Pulcinella | *Pizza* | –
Slim's Last Chance | *Southern* | 26
Smarty Pants | *Sandwiches* | 23
Stellar Pizza | *Pizza* | 22
Via Tribunali | *Pizza* | 23

GREEN LAKE/ GREENWOOD/ PHINNEY RIDGE

Bick's Broadview | *Amer.* | 21
BluWater | *Amer.* | 16
Carmelita | *Euro./Veg.* | 25
Duke's | *Seafood* | 19
El Chupacabra | *Mex.* | 16
Eva | *Amer.* | 26
Fu Man Dumpling | *Chinese* | 24
Gordito's | *Mex.* | 21
Gorgeous George's | *Med.* | 25
Greenlake B&G | *Amer.* | 17
Kabab Hse. | *Pakistani* | 19
Kidd Valley | *Burgers* | 18
Z Kisaku Sushi | *Japanese* | 27
Krittika Noodles | *Noodles/Thai* | –
Luisa's Mexican Grill | *Mex.* | 23
Mae's | *Amer.* | 15
Z Nell's | *Amer.* | 27
Oliver's Twist | *Pac. NW* | 23
Pagliacci Pizza | *Pizza* | 23
Perché/Pasta | *Italian* | 24
Pho Thân | *Viet.* | 22
Red Mill | *Burgers* | 24
Rosita's Mex. | *Mex.* | 17
Santa Fe Cafe | *New Mex.* | 20
74th St. Ale | *Pub* | 21
Stumbling Goat | *Pac. NW* | 23
Tacos Guaymas/Cantina | *Mex.* | 19
Yanni's | *Greek* | 26
Zeeks Pizza | *Pizza* | 19

INTERBAY/ MAGNOLIA

Chinook's | *Seafood* | 21
El Ranchon Family Mexican | *Mex.* | 22
Luigi's Pizza | *Italian* | –
Maggie Bluff's | *Burgers* | 19
Mondello | *Italian* | 25
Pagliacci Pizza | *Pizza* | 23
Z Palisade | *Seafood* | 24
Queen Margherita | *Pizza* | –
Red Mill | *Burgers* | 24
Romio's | *Pizza* | 19
Szmania's | *Steak* | 25
Uptown Espresso | *Coffee* | 19
NEW Wheeler St. Kitchen | *Amer./Pac. NW* | –

INTERNATIONAL DISTRICT

Bush Garden | *Japanese* | 18
Fort St. George | *Japanese* | 18
Fuji Sushi | *Japanese* | 22
Z Green Leaf | *Viet.* | 27
Harbor City BBQ | *Chinese* | –
Henry's Taiwan | *Chinese* | –
Ho Ho Seafood | *Chinese/Seafood* | 20
Honey Court | *Chinese* | 19
Hue Ky Mi Gia | *Chinese/Viet.* | –
Jade Garden | *Chinese* | 22
Kaname Izakaya | *Japanese* | –
Kau Kau BBQ | *Chinese* | 24
Lemongrass | *Viet.* | 21
Malay Satay | *Malaysian* | 21
Maneki | *Japanese* | 25
Mike's Noodle House | *Noodles* | 23
New Star | *Chinese/Seafood* | –
Pacific Café | *Chinese* | –
Phnom Penh | *Cambodian* | –
Pho Bac | *Viet.* | 24
Purple Dot | *Chinese* | 17
Red Lantern | *Asian* | –

LOCATIONS

Sea Garden | *Chinese/Seafood* 20
Shanghai Gdn. | *Chinese* 24
Tai Tung | *Chinese* 23
Tamarind Tree | *Viet.* 25
Thai Curry Simple | *Thai* –
Tsukushinbo | *Japanese* –

LAKE CITY/ NORTHGATE/ NORTH SEATTLE

Azteca | *Mex.* 14
Chiang's Gourmet | *Chinese* 23
Dick's Drive-In | *Burgers* 19
El Camion | *Mex.* 28
Jalisco | *Mex.* 19
Kidd Valley | *Burgers* 18
Mojito | *Pan-Latin* 25
Pagliacci Pizza | *Pizza* 23
Romio's | *Pizza* 19
Saltoro | *Amer.* 20
Toyoda Sushi | *Japanese* 26

LAURELHURST/ SAND POINT

Chloé | *French/Seafood* –
Z Jak's Grill | *Steak* 24
Pagliacci Pizza | *Pizza* 23
Sand Pt. Grill | *Eclectic* 19

LESCHI/MADRONA

All-Purpose Pizza | *Pizza* 22
Bistro Turkuaz | *Turkish* 26
BluWater | *Amer.* 16
Z Daniel's Broiler | *Steak* 24
Hi Spot Cafe | *Amer.* 23
June | *Amer.* –
St. Clouds | *Pac. NW* 23

MADISON PARK/ MADISON VALLEY

Belle Epicurean | *Bakery/French* 23
Bing's Bar & Grill | *Amer.* 16
Z Cactus | *Mex./SW* 22
Cafe Flora | *Veg.* 23
Z Crush | *Amer.* 25
Essential Baking Co. | *Bakery* 22
Z Harvest Vine | *Spanish* 27
La Côte | *Dessert/French* 20
Luc | *Amer./French* 25
NEW Madison Park Conserv. | *Amer.* –
Z Nishino | *Japanese* 27
Phila. Fevre | *Deli* –
Z Rover's | *French* 28
Thai Ginger | *Thai* 22
Voilà! Bistrot | *French* 21

MAPLE LEAF/ ROOSEVELT

Die BierStube | *German* 21
Flying Squirrel | *Pizza* 23
India Bistro | *Indian* 23
Judy Fu's | *Chinese* 20
Maple Leaf Grill | *Eclectic* 20
Sunlight Cafe | *Eclectic/Veg.* –

MONTLAKE

Cafe Lago | *Italian* 26

PIKE PLACE MKT

Alibi Room | *Pizza* 21
Athenian | *Amer./Seafood* 19
Bayou on 1st | *Cajun* –
Beecher's Cheese | *Cheese* 25
Z Cafe Campagne | *French* 26
Café Yarmarka | *Russian* –
Chez Shea/Lounge | *French/Pac. NW* 26
Copacabana | *S Amer.* –
Crepe de France | *French* 23
Crumpet Shop | *Bakery* 24
Cutters | *Pac. NW/Seafood* 22
El Puerco Lloron | *Mex.* 21
Emmett Watson | *Seafood* 22
Z Etta's | *Pac. NW/Seafood* 25
Il Bistro | *Italian* 23

NEW Il Corvo | *Italian* -
I Love NY Deli | *Deli* 21
Jack's Fish | *Seafood* 22
NEW Japonessa Cucina | *Japanese* -
Kells Irish | *Irish* 17
Le Panier | *Bakery/French* 24
Le Pichet | *French* 25
Lowell's | *Amer.* 20
NEW Marché | *French* -
Z Matt's/Mkt. | *Pac. NW/Seafood* 25
Maximilien | *French* 23
Mee Sum | *Chinese/Dessert* 24
Pan Africa Mkt. | *African* -
Pike Pub | *Pub* 17
Pink Door | *Italian* 22
Piroshky Piroshky | *Russian* 24
Place Pigalle | *Pac. NW* 25
NEW Rub With Love | *Amer.* -
Seatown | *Seafood* -
Z Steelhead | *Pac. NW* 24
Taxi Dogs | *Hot Dogs* -
3 Girls Bakery | *Bakery* 24
Turkish Delight | *Turkish* -

PIONEER SQ/SODO

Al Boccalino | *Italian* 24
Cafe Bengodi | *Italian* -
Chuck's Hole In the Wall | *BBQ* -
El Camion | *Mex.* 28
Elliott Bay Café | *Amer.* 18
Fadó Irish Pub | *Irish* 17
F.X. McRory's | *Seafood/Steak* 18
Z Il Terrazzo | *Italian* 27
Jones BBQ | *BBQ* 21
Macrina | *Bakery/Dessert* 25
New Orleans | *Cajun/Creole* 19
Pecos Pit BBQ | *BBQ* 26
Pho Cyclo | *Viet.* 22
Pyramid Ale | *Pub* 16
Z Salumi | *Italian/Sandwiches* 27

Tat's Deli | *Amer.* -
Zaina | *Mideast.* 22

QUEEN ANNE/ SEATTLE CENTER

Bahn Thai | *Thai* 25
Bamboo Garden Vegetarian | *Chinese/Veg.* 20
Betty | *Amer.* 23
Z Boat St. Cafe | *French* 27
Book Bindery | *Amer.* -
Buckley's | *Amer.* 17
Chinoise | *Asian* 20
Crow | *Amer.* 25
Dick's Drive-In | *Burgers* 19
Emmer/Rye | *Amer.* 22
Enza | *Italian* -
5 Spot | *Amer.* 21
Hilltop Ale Hse. | *Pub* 20
How To Cook Wolf | *Italian/Med.* 24
Jalisco | *Mex.* 19
Kidd Valley | *Burgers* 18
NEW La Luna | *Mex.* -
Laredos | *Mex./Tex-Mex* -
NEW Lloyd Martin | *Amer.* -
Macrina | *Bakery/Dessert* 25
Malena's Taco | *Mex.* 18
Melting Pot | *Fondue* 19
Z La Carta/Mezcaleria | *Mex.* 27
Noah's Bagels | *Bakery* 17
Olympia Pizza | *Greek/Pizza* 19
Ototo Sushi | *Japanese* 19
Pagliacci Pizza | *Pizza* 23
Panos Kleftiko | *Greek* 22
Paragon | *Amer.* 19
Peso's | *Mex.* 22
Ponti Seafood | *Seafood* 24
Portage | *French/Pac. NW* 25
Racha | *Thai* 20
Roti | *Indian* 21
Sam's Sushi | *Japanese* 22

Shiki | *Japanese* 25

Z SkyCity | *Pac. NW* 22

Sport | *Eclectic* 16

Ten Mercer | *Amer.* 22

Toulouse | *Cajun/Creole* 23

Uptown China | *Chinese* 22

Uptown Espresso | *Coffee* 19

Via Tribunali | *Pizza* 23

Zeeks Pizza | *Pizza* 19

RAVENNA/WEDGWOOD

Bagel Oasis | *Deli* 23

Bai Pai Fine | *Thai* 25

Black Pearl | *Chinese* 17

Da Pino | *Italian* -

Frank's Oyster | *Amer.* 20

Gaudi | *Spanish* -

Kidd Valley | *Burgers* 18

Pair | *Amer./Med.* 26

Queen Mary Tea | *Tea* 21

Salvatore | *Italian* 24

Vios Cafe | *Greek* 22

Zeeks Pizza | *Pizza* 19

SEATTLE WATERFRONT

Anthony's Pier 66 | *Pac. NW/Seafood* 22

Z Aqua by El Gaucho | *Seafood* 25

Bell St. Diner | *Seafood* 23

Z Elliott's Oyster | *Seafood* 24

Ivar's/Clams | *Seafood* 21

Red Robin | *Burgers* 16

Z Six Seven | *Pac. NW* 23

Uptown Espresso | *Coffee* 19

SOUTH LAKE UNION

NEW Brave Horse | *Amer.* -

Buca di Beppo | *Italian* 15

Chandler's Crab | *Seafood* 23

NEW Cuoco | *Italian* -

Z Daniel's Broiler | *Steak* 24

Duke's | *Seafood* 19

Feierabend | *German* 18

Flying Fish | *Eclectic/Seafood* 24

I Love Sushi | *Japanese* 22

Joey | *Eclectic* 17

Lunchbox Lab | *Burgers* 24

Z Mistral | *Amer.* 26

Paddy Coynes | *Pub* 16

Re:Public | *Pac. NW* -

Z Seastar | *Seafood* 25

NEW Serious Biscuit | *Southern* -

Z Serious Pie | *Pizza* 26

13 Coins | *Italian* 19

NEW Ting Momo | *Tibetan* -

Tutta Bella | *Pizza* 22

Uptown Espresso | *Coffee* 19

UNIVERSITY DISTRICT/ UNIVERSITY VILLAGE

Agua Verde | *Mex.* 23

Azteca | *Mex.* 14

Blue C Sushi | *Japanese* 16

Boom Noodle | *Japanese* 17

Caspian Grill Persian | *Persian* -

Chaco Canyon | *Vegan* 19

Ciao Bella | *Italian* 23

Costa's | *Amer./Greek* 18

Delfino's Pizza | *Pizza* 23

Guanaco's | *Salvadoran* 22

I Love NY Deli | *Deli* 21

Korean Tofu House | *Korean* -

Local Vine -

Mamma Melina | *Italian* 23

Mee Sum | *Chinese/Dessert* 24

Noah's Bagels | *Bakery* 17

Northlake Tav. | *Pizza* 22

Pagliacci Pizza | *Pizza* 23

Pasta & Co. | *Italian* 22

Pho Thân | *Viet.* 22

Shultzy's | *Sandwiches* 18
Sweet Iron | *Belgian* -
Taste of India | *Indian* 22
Tempero/Brasil | *Brazilian* -
Thai Tom | *Thai* 25
Thanh Vi | *Viet.* 19

WEST SEATTLE

Abbondanza | *Pizza* 19
Ⓩ Bakery Nouveau | *Bakery/French* 29
Buddha Ruksa | *Thai* 26
Ⓩ Cactus | *Mex./SW* 22
Chaco Canyon | *Vegan* 19
Circa | *Eclectic* 19
Duke's | *Seafood* 19
Eats Mkt. Café | *Amer.* 20
Elliott Bay | *Pub* 22
Endolyne Joe's | *Amer.* 18
Ⓩ Jak's Grill | *Steak* 24
Jones BBQ | *BBQ* 21
La Rustica | *Italian* 24
Lee's Asian | *Asian* 24
Luna Park Cafe | *Amer.* 18
Ⓩ Mashiko | *Japanese* 28
Mission | *Pan-Latin* 20
Olympia Pizza | *Greek/Pizza* 19
Pegasus Pizza | *Pizza* 21
Phoenecia | *Eclectic* 27
Pho Thân | *Viet.* 22
Salty's | *Seafood* 20
Spring Hill | *Pac. NW* 25
Sunfish | *Seafood* 21
Tacos Guaymas/Cantina | *Mex.* 19
Uptown Espresso | *Coffee* 19
Zeeks Pizza | *Pizza* 19

WHITE CENTER

Proletariat Pizza | *Pizza* -
Tacos Guaymas/Cantina | *Mex.* 19
Zippy's | *Burgers* 23

Eastside

BELLEVUE

Azteca | *Mex.* 14
Bamboo Garden Szechuan | *Chinese* 25
Belle Pastry | *Bakery/Dessert* 24
Bis on Main | *Amer.* 24
Black Bottle | *Eclectic* 22
Blue C Sushi | *Japanese* 16
Boom Noodle | *Japanese* 17
Café Ori | *Chinese* 18
Ⓩ Calcutta Grill | *Amer.* 21
Ⓩ Cantinetta | *Italian* 27
Chantanee | *Thai* 25
Cheesecake | *Amer.* 17
Ⓩ Daniel's Broiler | *Steak* 24
NEW Din Tai Fung | *Chinese* -
Dixie's BBQ | *BBQ* 21
Ⓩ El Gaucho | *Steak* 25
Facing East | *Taiwanese* 26
Firenze | *Italian* 22
Flo | *Japanese* 25
Gilbert's/Bagel | *Deli* 21
Goldbergs' Deli | *Deli* 18
Henry's Taiwan | *Chinese* -
I Love Sushi | *Japanese* 22
Joey | *Eclectic* 17
John Howie | *Steak* 25
Kidd Valley | *Burgers* 18
La Cocina/Puerco | *Mex.* 17
Mayuri | *Indian* 23
McCormick/Schmick | *Seafood* 21
Med. Kitchen | *Lebanese/Med.* 26
Melting Pot | *Fondue* 19
Moghul Palace | *Indian* -
Monsoon | *Viet.* 25
Noble Court | *Chinese* 18
Ooba's Mex. | *Mex.* 24
Outback Steak | *Steak* 15

Paddy Coynes | *Pub* 16

Pagliacci Pizza | *Pizza* 23

Palomino | *Italian* 20

Pasta & Co. | *Italian* 22

Pearl | *Pac. NW* 22

P.F. Chang's | *Chinese* 18

Pho Thân | *Viet.* 22

Pogacha | *Croatian/Pac. NW* 17

Purple Café | *Pac. NW* 20

Red Robin | *Burgers* 16

Ruth's Chris | *Steak* 24

Z Seastar | *Seafood* 25

Spiced | *Chinese* 22

Szechuan Chef | *Chinese* 23

Tap House Grill | *Eclectic* 17

Thai Ginger | *Thai* 22

3 Pigs BBQ | *BBQ* 21

Top Gun | *Chinese/Seafood* 22

Tosoni's | *Continental* 26

Z Wild Ginger | *Pac. Rim* 25

Yea's Wok | *Chinese* -

Zeeks Pizza | *Pizza* 19

Z'Tejas | *SW* 18

ISSAQUAH/ SAMMAMISH

Coho Cafe | *Pac. NW/Seafood* 18

Z Jak's Grill | *Steak* 24

Julia's | *Amer.* 16

Noodle Boat | *Thai* 26

Pogacha | *Croatian/Pac. NW* 17

Red Robin | *Burgers* 16

Z Salish Lodge | *Pacific NW* 23

Shanghai Gdn. | *Chinese* 24

Sip/Wine Bar | *Amer.* 19

Stan's Bar-B-Q | *BBQ* -

Sushiman | *Japanese* -

Taqueria La Venadita | *Mex.* -

Thai Ginger | *Thai* 22

Tutta Bella | *Pizza* 22

Zeeks Pizza | *Pizza* 19

KIRKLAND

Z Anthony's HomePort | *Pac. NW/Seafood* 21

Azteca | *Mex.* 14

Beach Cafe | *Eclectic/Seafood* 19

Bin on Lake | *American* 20

Z Cactus | *Mex./SW* 22

Z Cafe Juanita | *Italian* 28

Cafe Veloce | *Italian* 21

Izumi | *Japanese* 24

Kidd Valley | *Burgers* 18

Lynn's Bistro | *French* 25

Med. Kitchen | *Lebanese/Med.* 26

NEW Milagro Cantina | *Mex.* -

Noah's Bagels | *Bakery* 17

Original Pancake | *Amer.* 21

Outback Steak | *Steak* 15

Purple Café | *Pac. NW* 20

Rikki Rikki | *Japanese* 18

Rist. Paradiso | *Italian* 20

Santorini Greek | *Greek* 29

Shamiana | *Indian/Pakistani* 21

Thin Pan | *Thai* -

Trellis | *Amer.* 22

Wilde Rover | *Pub* 16

Zeeks Pizza | *Pizza* 19

MERCER ISLAND

Bennett's | *Amer.* 18

Noah's Bagels | *Bakery* 17

NEW Stopsky's Deli | *Deli/Jewish* -

REDMOND

Bai Tong | *Thai* 24

Coho Cafe | *Pac. NW/Seafood* 18

Frankie's Pizza | *Italian* 20

Kikuya | *Japanese* 19

Malay Satay | *Malaysian* 21

Matts' Rotisserie | *Amer.* 21

Neville's at the British Pantry | *British* -

Ooba's Mex. | *Mex.* 24
Pho Thân | *Viet.* 22
Pomegranate Bistro | *Amer.* 25
Red Robin | *Burgers* 16
Romio's | *Pizza* 19
Spazzo | *Italian* 16
Spicy Talk Bistro | *Chinese* –
Thai Ginger | *Thai* 22
Tropea | *Italian* 26
Typhoon! | *Thai* 22
Zeeks Pizza | *Pizza* 19

Outlying Areas

BAINBRIDGE ISLAND

Bainbridge BBQ | *BBQ* 17
Cafe Nola | *Amer.* 21
Four Swallows | *Italian/Pac. NW* 26
Hitchcock | *Amer./Pac. NW* –
Streamliner | *Diner/Italian* 19

BOTHELL/KENMORE/MALTBY

Bonefish Grill | *Seafood* 21
Carolina Smoke | *BBQ* –
Grazie | *Italian* 22
Kidd Valley | *Burgers* 18
Maltby Cafe | *Amer.* 22
Mayuri | *Indian* 23
Outback Steak | *Steak* 15
Russell's | *Amer.* 20

BURIEN/DES MOINES/KENT

Alki Bakery | *Bakery* 21
Z Anthony's HomePort | *Pac. NW/Seafood* 21
Azteca | *Mex.* 14
Catfish Corner | *Southern* 21
Dilettante | *Dessert* 23
Duke's | *Seafood* 19
Elliott Bay | *Pub* 22
Ezell's | *Amer.* 23
Hue Ky Mi Gia | *Chinese/Viet.* –
Red Robin | *Burgers* 16
Tin Room Bar | *Amer.* –

EDMONDS/SHORELINE

Z Anthony's HomePort | *Pac. NW/Seafood* 21
Black Pearl | *Chinese* 17
Chanterelle | *Eclectic* 19
Dick's Drive-In | *Burgers* 19
Hill's Food & Wine | *Pac. NW* 20
Hosoonyi | *Korean* 23
Pho Thân | *Viet.* 22

EVERETT/MUKILTEO

Z Anthony's HomePort | *Pac. NW/Seafood* 21
Gordito's | *Mex.* 21
Ivar's Mukilteo | *Seafood* 21
Outback Steak | *Steak* 15
Pho Thân | *Viet.* 22
Red Robin | *Burgers* 16
Romio's | *Pizza* 19
Tacos Guaymas/Cantina | *Mex.* 19

FEDERAL WAY/TACOMA

Adriatic Grill | *Italian* –
Z Anthony's HomePort | *Pac. NW/Seafood* 21
Asado | *Argentinean* –
Azteca | *Mex.* 14
Dash Pt./Lobster Shop | *Seafood* 23
Duke's | *Seafood* 19
Z El Gaucho | *Steak* 25
Galanga Thai | *Thai* –
Indochine | *Asian* 25
NEW Marrow | *Amer.* –
Maxwell's Restaurant | *Pac. NW* –

Melting Pot | *Fondue* 19

Outback Steak | *Steak* 15

Pacific Grill | *Seafood/Steak* 26

Paddy Coynes | *Pub* 16

Pho Thân | *Viet.* 22

Primo Grill | *Med.* –

Tacos Guaymas/Cantina | *Mex.* 19

GIG HARBOR

Z Anthony's HomePort | *Pac. NW/Seafood* 21

Brix 25° | *Amer.* –

LAKE FOREST PARK/ MOUNTLAKE TERR

Honey Bear | *Amer.* 19

Romio's | *Pizza* 19

LYNNWOOD

Blue C Sushi | *Japanese* 16

Buca di Beppo | *Italian* 15

Kabab Hse. | *Indian/Pakistani* 19

P.F. Chang's | *Chinese* 18

Red Robin | *Burgers* 16

Tacos Guaymas/Cantina | *Mex.* 19

MILL CREEK/ SNOHOMISH

Azteca | *Mex.* 14

Azul | *Pan-Latin* 22

NW WASHINGTON

Z Anthony's HomePort | *Pac. NW/Seafood* 21

Oyster Bar/Chuckanut | *Seafood* 25

OLYMPIA

Z Anthony's HomePort | *Pac. NW/Seafood* 21

Outback Steak | *Steak* 15

REDONDO

Salty's | *Seafood* 20

RENTON

Chiang's Gourmet | *Chinese* 23

Ezell's | *Amer.* 23

Kidd Valley | *Burgers* 18

Lemongrass | *Viet.* 21

Melrose Grill | *Steak* 27

SAN JUAN ISLANDS

Allium | *Pac. NW* –

Bluff | *Pac. NW* –

Inn at Ship Bay | *Amer.* –

Rose's Bakery | *Pac. NW* –

Willows Inn | *Pac. NW* –

SEATAC/TUKWILA

Z Anthony's HomePort | *Pac. NW/Seafood* 21

Azteca | *Mex.* 14

Bai Tong | *Thai* 24

Blue C Sushi | *Japanese* 16

Cheesecake | *Amer.* 17

Copperleaf | *Pac. NW* –

Duke's | *Seafood* 19

Grazie | *Italian* 22

Joey | *Eclectic* 17

Outback Steak | *Steak* 15

Pabla | *Indian* 22

Racha | *Thai* 20

Sharp's Roasthse. | *Amer.* –

Spencer's Steaks | *Steak* –

13 Coins | *Italian* 19

WHIDBEY ISLAND

Inn at Langley | *Pac. NW* 26

WOODINVILLE

Z Barking Frog | *Pac. NW* 25

Ezell's | *Amer.* 23

Z Herbfarm, The | *Pac. NW* 28

Ooba's Mex. | *Mex.* 24

Purple Café | *Pac. NW* 20

Racha | *Thai* 20

Red Robin | *Burgers* 16

Rist. Italianissimo | *Italian* 26

Special Features

Listings cover the best in each category and include names, locations and Food ratings. Multi-location restaurants' features may vary by branch.

ADDITIONS

(Properties added since the last edition of the book)

Allium | **Eastsound** –
Altura | **Cap Hill** –
Ba Bar | **Cap Hill** –
Bar del Corso | **Beacon Hill** –
Big Mario's Pizza | **Cap Hill** –
Brave Horse | **S Lake Union** –
Buns | **Location Varies** –
Carolina Smoke | **Bothell** –
Chuck's Hole In the Wall | **Pioneer Sq** –
Copperleaf | **SeaTac** –
Coterie Room | **Belltown** –
Cuoco | **S Lake Union** –
Din Tai Fung | **Bellevue** –
Dot's Delicatessen | **Fremont** –
Golden Beetle | **Ballard** –
Hitchcock | **Bainbridge Is** –
Il Corvo | **Pike Place** –
Inn at Ship Bay | **Eastsound** –
Japonessa Cucina | **Pike Place** –
Korean Tofu House | **Univ Dist** –
Kylie's Chicago Pizza | **Fremont** –
La Luna | **Queen Anne** –
Lloyd Martin | **Queen Anne** –
Local 360 | **Belltown** –
Madison Park Conserv. | **Madison Pk** –
Marché | **Pike Place** –
Marrow | **Tacoma** –
Milagro Cantina | **Kirkland** –
Molly Moon Truck | **Location Varies** –
Momiji | **Cap Hill** –
Poquitos | **Cap Hill** –
Red Lantern | **Intl Dist** –
Revel | **Fremont** –
RN74 | **Dwtn** –
Rub With Love | **Pike Place** –
Serious Biscuit | **S Lake Union** –
Spicy Talk Bistro | **Redmond** –
Stan's Bar-B-Q | **Issaquah** –
Stopsky's Deli | **Mercer Is** –
Tat's Deli | **Pioneer Sq** –
Terra Plata | **Cap Hill** –
Thai Curry Simple | **Intl Dist** –
Ting Momo | **S Lake Union** –
Uneeda Burger | **Fremont** –
Wheeler St. Kitchen | **Magnolia** –
Willows Inn | **Lummi Island** –
Yea's Wok | **Newcastle** –

BREAKFAST

(See also Hotel Dining)

Athenian | **Pike Place** 19
Dish | **Fremont** 25
Elliott Bay Café | **Pioneer Sq** 18
Endolyne Joe's | **W Seattle** 18
5 Point Café | **Belltown** 18
5 Spot | **Queen Anne** 21
14 Carrot Cafe | **Eastlake** 20
Geraldine's | **Columbia City** 24
Glo's | **Cap Hill** 25
Harbor City BBQ | **Intl Dist** –
Hi Spot Cafe | **Madrona** 23
Hudson | **Georgetown** 19
Julia's | **multi.** 16
Macrina | **multi.** 25
Original Pancake | **multi.** 21

BRUNCH

Alki Bakery | **Georgetown** 21
Z Anthony's HomePort | **multi.** 21

Azul | **Mill Creek** 22
B&O Espresso | **Cap Hill** 20
Barking Dog | **Ballard** 20
☒ Barking Frog | **Woodinville** 25
Bastille Café | **Ballard** 19
Bennett's | **Mercer Is** 18
BluWater | **multi.** 16
Boka Kitchen | **Dwtn** 20
Brass. Marg. | **Dwtn** 16
Buckley's | **Seattle Ctr** 17
☒ Cafe Campagne | **Pike Place** 26
Cafe Flora | **Madison Pk** 23
Cafe Nola | **Bainbridge Is** 21
☒ Calcutta Grill | **Newcastle** 21
Chandler's Crab | **S Lake Union** 23
Chanterelle | **Edmonds** 19
Cheesecake | **multi.** 17
Circa | **W Seattle** 19
Coastal Kitchen | **Cap Hill** 20
Coho Cafe | **Issaquah** 18
DeLuxe B&G | **Cap Hill** 17
Dragonfish | **Dwtn** 19
Earth & Ocean | **Dwtn** 22
Eats Mkt. Café | **W Seattle** 20
☒ Etta's | **Pike Place** 25
5 Spot | **Queen Anne** 21
Galerias | **Cap Hill** 22
Geraldine's | **Columbia City** 24
Gordon Biersch | **Dwtn** 15
Grill on Broadway | **Cap Hill** 15
Hale's Ales | **Fremont** 15
Hattie's Hat | **Ballard** 17
Hill's Food & Wine | **Shoreline** 20
Hunt Club | **First Hill** 22
Ivar's/Clams | **Seattle Waterfront** 21
Ivar's Salmon | **Lake Union** 21
Kingfish | **Cap Hill** 24
☒ Lola | **Dwtn** 25
Lynn's Bistro | **Kirkland** 25
Macrina | **multi.** 25
Maximilien | **Pike Place** 23
Mondello | **Magnolia** 25
Monsoon | **multi.** 25
☒ Palisade | **Magnolia** 24
Paragon | **Queen Anne** 19
Pomegranate Bistro | **Redmond** 25
Red Fin | **Dwtn** 21
Salty's | **multi.** 20
Sazerac | **Dwtn** 20
Señor Moose | **Ballard** 26
Serafina | **Eastlake** 25
611 Supreme | **Cap Hill** 21
☒ Six Seven | **Seattle Waterfront** 23
☒ SkyCity | **Seattle Ctr** 22
Smarty Pants | **Georgetown** 23
St. Clouds | **Madrona** 23
☒ Steelhead | **Pike Place** 24
Sunlight Cafe | **Roosevelt** -
That's Amore | **Mt. Baker** 24
13 Coins | **S Lake Union** 19
35th St. Bistro | **Fremont** 22
Tilikum Place | **Belltown** 25
☒ Tilth | **Wallingford** 28
Tulio | **Dwtn** 25
Two Bells B&G | **Belltown** 22
Volterra | **Ballard** 25

BUFFET

(Check availability)

Habesha | **Dwtn** 22
India Bistro | **Ballard** 23
Ivar's Salmon | **Lake Union** 21
Dash Pt./Lobster Shop | **Tacoma** 23
Mayuri | **multi.** 23
Moghul Palace | **Bellevue** -
Pabla | **multi.** 22
☒ Palisade | **Magnolia** 24
Roti | **Queen Anne** 21
Salty's | **multi.** 20

Shamiana | **Kirkland** 21

Z Six Seven | **Seattle Waterfront** 23

Spencer's Steaks | **SeaTac** –

BUSINESS DINING

Andaluca | **Dwtn** 24

Z Aqua by El Gaucho | **Seattle Waterfront** 25

Art Rest. | **Dwtn** 23

Bin on Lake | **Kirkland** 20

Bisato | **Belltown** 25

Blueacre | **Dwtn** 21

Book Bindery | **Queen Anne** –

Branzino | **Belltown** 25

NEW Brave Horse | **S Lake Union** –

Brooklyn Seafood | **Dwtn** 24

Z Calcutta Grill | **Newcastle** 21

Z Canlis | **Lake Union** 27

Capital Grille | **Dwtn** 23

Chantanee | **Bellevue** 25

Copperleaf | **SeaTac** –

Z Corson Bldg. | **Georgetown** 28

NEW Cuoco | **S Lake Union** –

Z Daniel's Broiler | **multi.** 24

NEW Din Tai Fung | **Bellevue** –

Earth & Ocean | **Dwtn** 22

Z El Gaucho | **multi.** 25

Z Elliott's Oyster | **Seattle Waterfront** 24

Z Georgian | **Dwtn** 26

Hitchcock | **Bainbridge Is** –

NEW Japonessa Cucina | **Pike Place** –

John Howie | **Bellevue** 25

Lecosho | **Dwtn** –

Z Lola | **Dwtn** 25

Luc | **Madison Vly** 25

Maxwell's Restaurant | **Tacoma** –

Z Metro. Grill | **Dwtn** 26

NEW Milagro Cantina | **Kirkland** –

Z Mistral | **S Lake Union** 26

Morton's | **Dwtn** 25

Z Nishino | **Madison Pk** 27

Pacific Grill | **Tacoma** 26

Re:Public | **S Lake Union** –

NEW RN74 | **Dwtn** –

Ruth's Chris | **multi.** 24

Z Salish Lodge | **Snoqualmie** 23

Z Seastar | **multi.** 25

Shuckers | **Dwtn** 23

Spencer's Steaks | **SeaTac** –

Sushi Kappo | **Eastlake** –

Tavolàta | **Belltown** 25

Volterra | **Ballard** 25

Z Wild Ginger | **multi.** 25

CATERING

Alki Bakery | **Georgetown** 21

Assimba | **Cap Hill** 24

Baguette Box | **Fremont** 24

Bakeman's | **Dwtn** 22

Z Bakery Nouveau | **W Seattle** 29

Bambino's Pizzeria | **Belltown** –

Beecher's Cheese | **Pike Place** 25

Belle Epicurean | **Dwtn** 23

Belle Pastry | **Bellevue** 24

Bis on Main | **Bellevue** 24

BluWater | **multi.** 16

Z Boat St. Cafe | **Queen Anne** 27

Boom Noodle | **multi.** 17

Buffalo Deli | **Belltown** 27

Z Cactus | **Madison Pk** 22

Z Cantinetta | **Wallingford** 27

Carmelita | **Greenwood** 25

Catfish Corner | **Cap Hill** 21

Chaco Canyon | **Univ Dist** 19

Chandler's Crab | **S Lake Union** 23

Chiso | **Fremont** 24

Z Crush | **Madison Vly** 25

- Ⓩ Dahlia Lounge | **Dwtn** 26
- Ⓩ Daniel's Broiler | **multi.** 24
- Eats Mkt. Café | **W Seattle** 20
- Ⓩ Elliott's Oyster | **Seattle Waterfront** 24
- Emmett Watson | **Pike Place** 22
- Fuji Sushi | **Intl Dist** 22
- Galerias | **Cap Hill** 22
- Gaudi | **Ravenna** –
- Ⓩ Harvest Vine | **Madison Vly** 27
- Il Fornaio | **Dwtn** 20
- I Love Sushi | **multi.** 22
- Ⓩ Il Terrazzo | **Pioneer Sq** 27
- India Bistro | **Ballard** 23
- Indochine | **Tacoma** 25
- Jones BBQ | **multi.** 21
- Kabul Afghan | **Wallingford** 23
- Kasbah | **Ballard** –
- Kauai Family | **Georgetown** 23
- Kau Kau BBQ | **Intl Dist** 24
- Kikuya | **Redmond** 19
- Ⓩ Lark | **Cap Hill** 27
- La Rustica | **W Seattle** 24
- Lee's Asian | **W Seattle** 24
- Lemongrass | **Intl Dist** 21
- Ⓩ Lola | **Dwtn** 25
- Lynn's Bistro | **Kirkland** 25
- Macrina | **multi.** 25
- Malay Satay | **multi.** 21
- Marrakesh | **Belltown** 21
- Mayuri | **Bellevue** 23
- McCormick/Schmick | **Dwtn** 21
- McCormick's Fish | **Dwtn** 23
- Med. Kitchen | **Bellevue** 26
- Ⓩ Metro. Grill | **Dwtn** 26
- Moghul Palace | **Bellevue** –
- Mondello | **Magnolia** 25
- Ⓩ Nell's | **Green Lk** 27
- Ⓩ Nishino | **Madison Pk** 27
- 'Ohana | **Belltown** 21
- Ⓩ Olivar | **Cap Hill** 26
- Palace Kitchen | **Dwtn** 25
- Perché/Pasta | **Green Lk** 24
- Phila. Fevre | **Madison Vly** –
- Pomegranate Bistro | **Redmond** 25
- Primo Grill | **Tacoma** –
- Ⓩ Ray's Boathse. | **Shilshole** 24
- Red Fin | **Dwtn** 21
- Rist. Italianissimo | **Woodinville** 26
- Ⓩ Rover's | **Madison Vly** 28
- Russell's | **Bothell** 20
- Ⓩ Seastar | **Bellevue** 25
- Ⓩ Serious Pie | **Dwtn** 26
- Shanghai Gdn. | **Issaquah** 24
- Shiki | **Queen Anne** 25
- Ⓩ Shiro's Sushi | **Belltown** 27
- Spazzo | **Redmond** 16
- Szmania's | **Magnolia** 25
- Tamarind Tree | **Intl Dist** 25
- Tango | **Cap Hill** 20
- Taste of India | **Univ Dist** 22
- Thai Ginger | **multi.** 22
- That's Amore | **Mt. Baker** 24
- 35th St. Bistro | **Fremont** 22
- Tin Room Bar | **Burien** –
- Typhoon! | **Redmond** 22
- Uptown China | **Queen Anne** 22
- Veraci Pizza | **Ballard** 25
- Volterra | **Ballard** 25
- Ⓩ Wild Ginger | **Dwtn** 25

CELEBRITY CHEFS

William Belickis

- Ⓩ Mistral | **S Lake Union** 26

Seif Chirchi

- Joule | **Wallingford** 26

Don Curtiss

- Volterra | **Ballard** 25

Matthew Dillon

- Z Corson Bldg. | **Georgetown** 28
- Sitka & Spruce | **Cap Hill** 26

Tom Douglas

- NEW Brave Horse | **S Lake Union** –
- NEW Cuoco | **S Lake Union** –
- Z Dahlia Lounge | **Dwtn** 26
- Z Etta's | **Pike Place** 25
- Z Lola | **Dwtn** 25
- Palace Kitchen | **Dwtn** 25
- NEW Rub With Love | **Pike Place** –
- Seatown | **Pike Place** –
- NEW Serious Biscuit | **S Lake Union** –
- Z Serious Pie | **Dwtn** 26
- NEW Ting Momo | **S Lake Union** –

Daisley Gordon

- NEW Marché | **Pike Place** –

Maria Hines

- NEW Golden Beetle | **Ballard** –
- Z Tilth | **Wallingford** 28

Shiro Kashiba

- Z Shiro's Sushi | **Belltown** 27

William Leaman

- Z Bakery Nouveau | **W Seattle** 29

Cormac Mahoney

- NEW Madison Park Conserv. | **Madison Pk** –

Tamara Murphy

- Elliott Bay Café | **multi.** 18
- NEW Terra Plata | **Cap Hill** –

Gordon Naccarato

- Pacific Grill | **Tacoma** 26

Lisa Nakamura

- Allium | **Eastsound** –

Thierry Rautureau

- Luc | **Madison Vly** 25
- Z Rover's | **Madison Vly** 28

Kerry Sear

- Art Rest. | **Dwtn** 23

Holly Smith

- Z Cafe Juanita | **Kirkland** 28

Scott Staples

- NEW Uneeda Burger | **Fremont** –

Ethan Stowell

- Anchovies/Olives | **Cap Hill** 25
- How To Cook Wolf | **Queen Anne** 24
- Staple & Fancy | **Ballard** –
- Tavolàta | **Belltown** 25

Johnathan Sundstrom

- Z Lark | **Cap Hill** 27

Blaine Wetzel

- Willows Inn | **Lummi Island** –

Jason Wilson

- Z Crush | **Madison Vly** 25

Rachel Yang

- Joule | **Wallingford** 26

CHILD-FRIENDLY

(Alternatives to the usual fast-food places; * children's menu available)

- Z Anthony's HomePort* | **multi.** 21
- Anthony's Pier 66* | **Seattle Waterfront** 22
- Beach Cafe* | **Kirkland** 19
- Bell St. Diner* | **Seattle Waterfront** 23
- Carmelita* | **Greenwood** 25
- Catfish Corner* | **Cap Hill** 21
- Chandler's Crab* | **S Lake Union** 23
- Chanterelle* | **Edmonds** 19
- Chiang's Gourmet | **multi.** 23
- Chinook's* | **Magnolia** 21
- Circa* | **W Seattle** 19
- Counter | **Ballard** 21

Earth & Ocean* | **Dwtn** 22

Z Elliott's Oyster* | **Seattle Waterfront** 24

Endolyne Joe's* | **W Seattle** 18

Z Etta's* | **Pike Place** 25

5 Spot* | **Queen Anne** 21

Z Georgian* | **Dwtn** 26

Gordito's* | **Greenwood** 21

I Love NY Deli | **multi.** 21

Maltby Cafe* | **Maltby** 22

Matts' Rotisserie* | **Redmond** 21

McCormick's Fish* | **Dwtn** 23

Original Pancake* | **Kirkland** 21

Pagliacci Pizza* | **Bellevue** 23

Pasta Bella* | **Ballard** 21

Pegasus Pizza* | **W Seattle** 21

Piecora's Pizza* | **Cap Hill** 21

Plum Vegan | **Cap Hill** 25

Ponti Seafood* | **Queen Anne** 24

Primo Grill* | **Tacoma** –

Z Ray's Boathse.* | **Shilshole** 24

Ray's Cafe* | **Shilshole** 22

Salty's* | **multi.** 20

Sand Pt. Grill* | **Sand Point** 19

Santa Fe Cafe* | **Phinney R** 20

Sazerac* | **Dwtn** 20

Z Six Seven* | **Seattle Waterfront** 23

Spencer's Steaks* | **SeaTac** –

Szmania's* | **Magnolia** 25

Tacos Guaymas/Cantina* | **multi.** 19

Tutta Bella* | **Columbia City** 22

Vios Cafe* | **Cap Hill** 22

Z Wild Ginger* | **Dwtn** 25

DANCING

Costas Opa | **Fremont** 18

Galerias | **Cap Hill** 22

Kells Irish | **Pike Place** 17

New Orleans | **Pioneer Sq** 19

'Ohana | **Belltown** 21

DELIVERY/TAKEOUT

(D=delivery, T=takeout)

Agua Verde | T | **Univ Dist** 23

Alki Bakery | T | **Georgetown** 21

All-Purpose Pizza | D | **Leschi** 22

Z Anthony's HomePort | T | **Gig Harbor** 21

Assimba | T | **Cap Hill** 24

Baguette Box | D, T | **multi.** 24

Bainbridge BBQ | D | **Bainbridge Is** 17

Bakeman's | D, T | **Dwtn** 22

Z Bakery Nouveau | T | **W Seattle** 29

Z Barking Frog | T | **Woodinville** 25

Barolo | T | **Dwtn** 24

Bayou on 1st | T | **Pike Place** –

Beach Cafe | T | **Kirkland** 19

Beecher's Cheese | T | **Pike Place** 25

Belle Epicurean | T | **Dwtn** 23

Belle Pastry | T | **Bellevue** 24

Bennett's | T | **Mercer Is** 18

Bis on Main | T | **Bellevue** 24

Black Bottle | T | **Belltown** 22

Black Pearl | D, T | **multi.** 17

BluWater | D, T | **multi.** 16

Buddha Ruksa | T | **W Seattle** 26

Buffalo Deli | D, T | **Belltown** 27

Burrito Loco | T | **Crown Hill** –

Z Cafe Besalu | T | **Ballard** 29

Cafe Flora | T | **Madison Pk** 23

Cafe Veloce | D, T | **Kirkland** 21

Catfish Corner | T | **Cap Hill** 21

Chaco Canyon | T | **Univ Dist** 19

Chanterelle | T | **Edmonds** 19

Chinoise | D, T | **Queen Anne** 20

Chiso | T | **Fremont** 24

CJ's Eatery | T | **Belltown** 18

Copacabana | T | **Pike Place** –

Crumpet Shop | T | **Pike Place** 24

Ƶ Dahlia Lounge | T | **Dwtn** 26
Diggity Dog's | T | **Wallingford** 20
Dixie's BBQ | T | **Bellevue** 21
Eats Mkt. Café | T | **W Seattle** 20
El Camino | T | **Fremont** 22
Elliott Bay | T | **W Seattle** 22
Elliott Bay Café | T | **Pioneer Sq** 18
El Puerco Lloron | T | **Pike Place** 21
Essential Baking Co. | T | **multi.** 22
Ezell's | T | **multi.** 23
FareStart/2100 | T | **S Seattle** –
Flying Fish | T | **S Lake Union** 24
Frontier Room | T | **Belltown** 22
Fuji Sushi | T | **Intl Dist** 22
Galanga Thai | T | **Tacoma** –
Galerias | T | **Cap Hill** 22
Ƶ Gelatiamo | D, T | **Dwtn** 27
Geraldine's | T | **Columbia City** 24
Gilbert's/Bagel | T | **Bellevue** 21
Goldbergs' Deli | T | **Bellevue** 18
Gordito's | T | **Greenwood** 21
Gorgeous George's | T | **Phinney R** 25
Ƶ Green Leaf | T | **Intl Dist** 27
Ƶ Harvest Vine | T | **Madison Vly** 27
Hill's Food & Wine | T | **Shoreline** 20
Ho Ho Seafood | T | **Intl Dist** 20
Honey Bear | T | **Lake Forest Pk** 19
Honey Court | T | **Intl Dist** 19
Il Fornaio | T | **Dwtn** 20
I Love NY Deli | D | **multi.** 21
Indochine | T | **Tacoma** 25
Ivar's/Clams | T | **Seattle Waterfront** 21
Ivar's Mukilteo | T | **Mukilteo** 21
Ivar's Salmon | T | **Lake Union** 21
Jack's Fish | T | **Pike Place** 22
Jade Garden | T | **Intl Dist** 22
Ƶ Jak's Grill | T | **multi.** 24
Jones BBQ | T | **multi.** 21
Judy Fu's | D, T | **Maple Leaf** 20
Kabab Hse. | T | **Greenwood** 19
Kaosamai | D | **Fremont** –
Kasbah | T | **Ballard** –
Kauai Family | T | **Georgetown** 23
Kau Kau BBQ | T | **Intl Dist** 24
Kells Irish | T | **Pike Place** 17
Kikuya | T | **Redmond** 19
Kimchi Bistro | T | **Cap Hill** 23
Kingfish | T | **Cap Hill** 24
Ƶ Kisaku Sushi | T | **Green Lk** 27
Krittika Noodles | T | **Green Lk** –
Ƶ La Carta/Mezcaleria | T | **Ballard** 27
La Vita É Bella | T | **Belltown** 22
Lee's Asian | T | **W Seattle** 24
Le Fournil French Bakery | T | **Eastlake** 21
Le Panier | T | **Pike Place** 24
Louie's | T | **Ballard** –
Louisa's Café | T | **Eastlake** 16
Luigi's Pizza | T | **Magnolia** –
Luisa's Mexican Grill | T | **Greenwood** 23
Machiavelli | T | **Cap Hill** 24
Macrina | T | **multi.** 25
Mae Phim Thai | T | **Dwtn** 23
Malay Satay | D, T | **multi.** 21
Malena's Taco | T | **Queen Anne** 18
Mama's Mex. | T | **Belltown** 18
Matts' Rotisserie | T | **Redmond** 21
Mayuri | T | **Bellevue** 23
Med. Kitchen | T | **Bellevue** 26
Mike's Noodle House | T | **Intl Dist** 23
Mioposto | T | **Mt. Baker** 23
Moghul Palace | T | **Bellevue** –
Mojito | T | **Lake City** 25
Monsoon | T | **Cap Hill** 25
Musashi's | T | **Wallingford** 23

Neville's at the British Pantry | T | **Redmond** –
Nishino | T | **Madison Pk** 27
Noah's Bagels | D, T | **Queen Anne** 17
Noble Court | T | **Bellevue** 18
Northlake Tav. | T | **Univ Dist** 22
O'Asian | T | **Dwtn** 20
Olympia Pizza | D, T | **multi.** 19
Ooba's Mex. | D, T | **multi.** 24
Other Coast | T | **Ballard** 26
Pabla | T | **Dwtn** 22
Pagliacci Pizza | D, T | **multi.** 23
Palace Kitchen | T | **Dwtn** 25
Palomino | D, T | **Dwtn** 20
Pan Africa Mkt. | T | **Pike Place** –
Paseo | T | **Fremont** 28
Pearl | T | **Bellevue** 22
Pecos Pit BBQ | T | **SODO** 26
Pegasus Pizza | T | **W Seattle** 21
Phila. Fevre | T | **Madison Vly** –
Piecora's Pizza | D, T | **Cap Hill** 21
Pig Iron BBQ | T | **S Seattle** 24
Poco Wine | T | **Cap Hill** 19
Pomegranate Bistro | T | **Redmond** 25
Racha | D, T | **multi.** 20
R&L BBQ | T | **Cap Hill** –
Red Fin | T | **Dwtn** 21
Rist. Paradiso | D, T | **Kirkland** 20
Romio's | D | **multi.** 19
Rose's Bakery | T | **Eastsound** –
Salumi | T | **Pioneer Sq** 27
Santorini Greek | T | **Kirkland** 29
Serious Pie | T | **Dwtn** 26
Shamiana | D, T | **Kirkland** 21
Shanghai Gdn. | T | **multi.** 24
Shultzy's | T | **Univ Dist** 18
611 Supreme | T | **Cap Hill** 21
Smarty Pants | T | **Georgetown** 23
Stellar Pizza | T | **Georgetown** 22
Streamliner | T | **Bainbridge Is** 19
Sunfish | T | **W Seattle** 21
Szechuan Chef | T | **Bellevue** 23
Szmania's | T | **Magnolia** 25
Tai Tung | T | **Intl Dist** 23
Taki's Mad Greek | T | **Ballard** –
Taste | T | **Dwtn** 22
Taste of India | T | **Univ Dist** 22
Taxi Dogs | T | **Pike Place** –
Thai Siam | T | **Ballard** –
Thai Tom | T | **Univ Dist** 25
Thanh Vi | T | **Univ Dist** 19
13 Coins | T | **multi.** 19
3 Pigs BBQ | D, T | **Bellevue** 21
Top Gun | T | **Bellevue** 22
Turkish Delight | T | **Pike Place** –
Tutta Bella | T | **multi.** 22
Uptown China | D, T | **Queen Anne** 22
Volunteer Pk. Cafe | T | **Cap Hill** 25
Zaina | T | **Pioneer Sq** 22
Zeeks Pizza | D, T | **multi.** 19

DESSERT SPECIALISTS

Alki Bakery | **multi.** 21
Bakery Nouveau | **W Seattle** 29
B&O Espresso | **Cap Hill** 20
Belle Epicurean | **Dwtn** 23
Belle Pastry | **Bellevue** 24
Cafe Besalu | **Ballard** 29
Cheesecake | **multi.** 17
Dahlia Lounge | **Dwtn** 26
Dilettante | **Dwtn** 23
Earth & Ocean | **Dwtn** 22
Etta's | **Pike Place** 25
Gelatiamo | **Dwtn** 27
Kingfish | **Cap Hill** 24
La Côte | **Madison Vly** 20
Macrina | **multi.** 25
Queen Mary Tea | **Ravenna** 21
Uptown Espresso | **multi.** 19

DINING ALONE

(Other than hotels and places with counter service)

Adriatic Grill | **Tacoma** -
Asado | **Tacoma** -
Baguette Box | **Fremont** 24
Bakeman's | **Dwtn** 22
NEW Bar del Corso | **Beacon Hill** -
Bisato | **Belltown** 25
Blueacre | **Dwtn** 21
Blue C Sushi | **Fremont** 16
Brix 25° | **Gig Harbor** -
Brooklyn Seafood | **Dwtn** 24
☑ Cafe Campagne | **Pike Place** 26
Cafe Flora | **Madison Pk** 23
Chiang's Gourmet | **multi.** 23
Coastal Kitchen | **Cap Hill** 20
Dante's Dogs | **Location Varies** 21
Delancey | **Ballard** 26
El Camion | **multi.** 28
☑ Elliott's Oyster | **Seattle Waterfront** 24
El Mestizo | **Cap Hill** 24
☑ Etta's | **Pike Place** 25
5 Spot | **Queen Anne** 21
Fonte | **Dwtn** 20
14 Carrot Cafe | **Eastlake** 20
Gilbert's/Bagel | **Bellevue** 21
Greenlake B&G | **Green Lk** 17
Guanaco's | **multi.** 22
☑ Harvest Vine | **Madison Vly** 27
Hattie's Hat | **Ballard** 17
Henry's Taiwan | **multi.** -
Hue Ky Mi Gia | **multi.** -
Il Fornaio | **Dwtn** 20
Jones BBQ | **W Seattle** 21
Lemongrass | **multi.** 21
Le Pichet | **Pike Place** 25
Macrina | **multi.** 25
Mae's | **Phinney R** 15
Malay Satay | **multi.** 21
☑ Marination | **Location Varies** 27
☑ Matt's/Mkt. | **Pike Place** 25
☑ Mistral | **S Lake Union** 26
Noodle Boat | **Issaquah** 26
Palace Kitchen | **Dwtn** 25
Proletariat Pizza | **White Ctr** -
☑ Salumi | **Pioneer Sq** 27
Shiku Sushi | **Ballard** 23
Sitka & Spruce | **Cap Hill** 26
Spiced | **Bellevue** 22
St. Clouds | **Madrona** 23
NEW Stopsky's Deli | **Mercer Is** -
Sweet Iron | **multi.** -
Taqueria La Venadita | **Issaquah** -
Tat's Deli | **Pioneer Sq** -
Thai Curry Simple | **Intl Dist** -
Thaiku | **Ballard** 22
Toulouse | **Queen Anne** 23
Two Bells B&G | **Belltown** 22
Volterra | **Ballard** 25
NEW Wheeler St. Kitchen | **Magnolia** -

DRAMATIC INTERIORS

Andaluca | **Dwtn** 24
☑ Aqua by El Gaucho | **Seattle Waterfront** 25
Assaggio | **Dwtn** 24
☑ Barking Frog | **Woodinville** 25
Bastille Café | **Ballard** 19
Brouwer's | **Fremont** 22
Café Presse | **Cap Hill** 23
☑ Canlis | **Lake Union** 27
Capitol Club | **Cap Hill** 19
Cicchetti | **Eastlake** 23
☑ Dahlia Lounge | **Dwtn** 26
☑ Georgian | **Dwtn** 26
☑ Herbfarm, The | **Woodinville** 28
How To Cook Wolf | **Queen Anne** 24

Icon Grill | **Dwtn** 20

Z Lola | **Dwtn** 25

Maximilien | **Pike Place** 23

Z Mistral | **S Lake Union** 26

Z Olivar | **Cap Hill** 26

Z Palisade | **Magnolia** 24

Pearl | **Bellevue** 22

Pink Door | **Pike Place** 22

Shiku Sushi | **Ballard** 23

Z Six Seven | **Seattle Waterfront** 23

Staple & Fancy | **Ballard** -

Toulouse | **Queen Anne** 23

Umi Sake Hse. | **Belltown** 25

Walrus/Carpenter | **Ballard** -

ENTERTAINMENT

(Call for days and times of performances)

Z Aqua by El Gaucho | piano | **Seattle Waterfront** 25

Brad's Swingside | varies | **Fremont** 25

Buenos Aires Grill | tango | **Dwtn** 21

Café Vignole | live music | **S Seattle** -

Capitol Club | DJ | **Cap Hill** 19

Caspian Grill Persian | belly dancing | **Univ Dist** -

Costas Opa | belly dancing | **Fremont** 18

Z Daniel's Broiler | piano | **multi.** 24

Earth & Ocean | DJ | **Dwtn** 22

Z El Gaucho | varies | **multi.** 25

Z Georgian | jazz | **Dwtn** 26

Grazie | jazz | **Bothell** 22

Hunt Club | live music | **First Hill** 22

Z Il Terrazzo | varies | **Pioneer Sq** 27

Jalisco | karaoke | **Queen Anne** 19

Julia's | drag show | **Cap Hill** 16

Kasbah | belly dancing | **Ballard** -

Kells Irish | Irish folk music | **Pike Place** 17

La Fontana | piano | **Belltown** 23

La Vita É Bella | accordion | **Belltown** 22

Le Pichet | varies | **Pike Place** 25

Mama's Mex. | mariachi band | **Belltown** 18

Maple Leaf Grill | varies | **Maple Leaf** 20

Marrakesh | belly dancing | **Belltown** 21

May | DJ/jazz | **Wallingford** 26

New Orleans | blues/jazz | **Pioneer Sq** 19

'Ohana | varies | **Belltown** 21

Paddy Coynes | Irish music | **multi.** 16

Paragon | varies | **Queen Anne** 19

Pink Door | varies | **Pike Place** 22

Pyramid Ale | blues | **SODO** 16

Racha | karaoke | **Seattle Ctr** 20

Serafina | jazz | **Eastlake** 25

Z Six Seven | band/DJ | **Seattle Waterfront** 23

Slim's Last Chance | varies | **Georgetown** 26

St. Clouds | live music | **Madrona** 23

Tacos Guaymas/Cantina | mariachi band | **Green Lk** 19

Taki's Mad Greek | varies | **Ballard** -

Tempero/Brasil | Brazilian music | **Univ Dist** -

Tutta Bella | jazz | **Columbia City** 22

Wasabi Bistro | jazz/Latin | **Belltown** 22

Wilde Rover | bands/trivia | **Kirkland** 16

Yanni's | belly dancing | **Phinney R** 26

FIREPLACES

Z Anthony's HomePort | **multi.** 21
Asado | **Tacoma** -
Bastille Café | **Ballard** 19
Bluff | **Friday Harbor** -
BluWater | **Green Lk** 16
Z Cactus | **W Seattle** 22
Cafe Veloce | **Kirkland** 21
Z Canlis | **Lake Union** 27
Chandler's Crab | **S Lake Union** 23
Coho Cafe | **multi.** 18
Z Daniel's Broiler | **S Lake Union** 24
DeLuxe B&G | **Cap Hill** 17
Duke's | **multi.** 19
El Chupacabra | **Greenwood** 16
Elliott Bay | **W Seattle** 22
Gordito's | **Greenwood** 21
Hilltop Ale Hse. | **Queen Anne** 20
Hunt Club | **First Hill** 22
Il Fornaio | **Dwtn** 20
Inn at Langley | **Langley** 26
Ivar's Mukilteo | **Mukilteo** 21
Joey | **Tukwila** 17
Jones BBQ | **Columbia City** 21
Local Vine | **Cap Hill** -
Louie's | **Ballard** -
Mexico Cantina Y Cocina | **Dwtn** -
Mioposto | **Mt. Baker** 23
Z Mistral | **S Lake Union** 26
Oyster Bar/Chuckanut | **Bow** 25
Paddy Coynes | **multi.** 16
Paragon | **Queen Anne** 19
Pogacha | **multi.** 17
Ponti Seafood | **Queen Anne** 24
Ray's Cafe | **Shilshole** 22
Rist. Italianissimo | **Woodinville** 26
Russell's | **Bothell** 20
Z Salish Lodge | **Snoqualmie** 23
Saltoro | **N Seattle** 20
Salty's | **W Seattle** 20
Sazerac | **Dwtn** 20
Shultzy's | **Univ Dist** 18
Z Six Seven | **Seattle Waterfront** 23
Spazzo | **Redmond** 16
Szmania's | **Magnolia** 25
Wilde Rover | **Kirkland** 16

FOOD TRUCKS

Buns | **Location Varies** -
Dante's Dogs | **Location Varies** 21
El Camion | **multi.** 28
Kaosamai | **Location Varies** -
Z Marination | **Location Varies** 27
Molly Moon Truck | **Location Varies** -
Skillet | **Location Varies** 23
Where Ya At Matt | **Location Varies** -

GAME IN SEASON

Bainbridge BBQ | **Bainbridge Is** 17
Bastille Café | **Ballard** 19
Bis on Main | **Bellevue** 24
Boka Kitchen | **Dwtn** 20
Brad's Swingside | **Fremont** 25
Brix 25° | **Gig Harbor** -
Z Cafe Campagne | **Pike Place** 26
Z Cafe Juanita | **Kirkland** 28
Z Canlis | **Lake Union** 27
Chez Shea/Lounge | **Pike Place** 26
Cicchetti | **Eastlake** 23
Circa | **W Seattle** 19
Copperleaf | **SeaTac** -
Z Corson Bldg. | **Georgetown** 28
Z Crush | **Madison Vly** 25
Z Dahlia Lounge | **Dwtn** 26
Da Pino | **Ravenna** -
Earth & Ocean | **Dwtn** 22
Elemental | **Lake Union** 26
Z El Gaucho | **multi.** 25
Eva | **Green Lk** 26

Four Swallows | **Bainbridge Is** 26
How To Cook Wolf | **Queen Anne** 24
Hunt Club | **First Hill** 22
Il Bistro | **Pike Place** 23
Joule | **Wallingford** 26
June | **Madrona** -
Z Lark | **Cap Hill** 27
Le Gourmand | **Ballard** 26
Z Lola | **Dwtn** 25
Maximilien | **Pike Place** 23
Maxwell's Restaurant | **Tacoma** -
Z Nell's | **Green Lk** 27
Palace Kitchen | **Dwtn** 25
Place Pigalle | **Pike Place** 25
Portage | **Queen Anne** 25
Quinn's Pub | **Cap Hill** 24
Racha | **Tukwila** 20
Re:Public | **S Lake Union** -
Rist. Italianissimo | **Woodinville** 26
Rose's Bakery | **Eastsound** -
Z Rover's | **Madison Vly** 28
Z Salish Lodge | **Snoqualmie** 23
Salvatore | **Ravenna** 24
Serafina | **Eastlake** 25
Z Spinasse | **Cap Hill** 28
Spur Gastropub | **Belltown** 24
Stumbling Goat | **Greenwood** 23
Szmania's | **Magnolia** 25
Tosoni's | **Bellevue** 26
Voilà! Bistrot | **Madison Vly** 21
Volterra | **Ballard** 25

GREEN/LOCAL/ORGANIC

Art of the Table | **Wallingford** 25
NEW Bar del Corso | **Beacon Hill** -
Bastille Café | **Ballard** 19
Bennett's | **Mercer Is** 18
Z Boat St. Cafe | **Queen Anne** 27
Brad's Swingside | **Fremont** 25
Cafe Flora | **Madison Pk** 23
Z Cafe Juanita | **Kirkland** 28
Café Vignole | **S Seattle** -
Z Cantinetta | **multi.** 27
Capitol Club | **Cap Hill** 19
Carmelita | **Greenwood** 25
Chaco Canyon | **Univ Dist** 19
Chez Shea/Lounge | **Pike Place** 26
Copperleaf | **SeaTac** -
Z Crush | **Madison Vly** 25
Cyclops | **Belltown** 19
Dish | **Fremont** 25
NEW Dot's Delicatessen | **Fremont** -
El Camino | **Fremont** 22
Elliott Bay | **multi.** 22
Essential Baking Co. | **multi.** 22
Flying Fish | **S Lake Union** 24
NEW Golden Beetle | **Ballard** -
Z Harvest Vine | **Madison Vly** 27
Z Herbfarm, The | **Woodinville** 28
Hitchcock | **Bainbridge Is** -
How To Cook Wolf | **Queen Anne** 24
Hunt Club | **First Hill** 22
I Love Sushi | **Bellevue** 22
Z La Medusa | **Columbia City** 27
Z Lark | **Cap Hill** 27
Le Gourmand | **Ballard** 26
NEW Local 360 | **Belltown** -
Z Lola | **Dwtn** 25
Lunchbox Lab | **S Lake Union** 24
Macrina | **multi.** 25
Maxwell's Restaurant | **Tacoma** -
Perché/Pasta | **Green Lk** 24
Pike Pub | **Pike Place** 17
Pike St. Fish | **Cap Hill** 22
Plaka Estiatorio | **Ballard** 27
Portage | **Queen Anne** 25
Z Ray's Boathse. | **Shilshole** 24
Rose's Bakery | **Eastsound** -

Z Serious Pie | **Dwtn** 26
Shiku Sushi | **Ballard** 23
Z Spinasse | **Cap Hill** 28
Stumbling Goat | **Greenwood** 23
Sunlight Cafe | **Roosevelt** –
Sutra | **Wallingford** 24
Taste | **Dwtn** 22
Thai Siam | **Ballard** –
Z Tilth | **Wallingford** 28
Trellis | **Kirkland** 22
Volterra | **Ballard** 25
Willows Inn | **Lummi Island** –

HIPSTER HANGOUTS

NEW Altura | **Cap Hill** –
NEW Ba Bar | **Cap Hill** –
Barolo | **Dwtn** 24
Bastille Café | **Ballard** 19
Big Mario's Pizza | **Cap Hill** –
Black Bottle | **Belltown** 22
Bleu Bistro | **Cap Hill** 21
Boom Noodle | **Cap Hill** 17
NEW Brave Horse | **S Lake Union** –
Die BierStube | **Roosevelt** 21
NEW Din Tai Fung | **Bellevue** –
Elemental | **Lake Union** 26
5 Point Café | **Belltown** 18
Flying Squirrel | **multi.** 23
NEW Japonessa Cucina | **Pike Place** –
Joey | **multi.** 17
John Howie | **Bellevue** 25
Kushibar | **Belltown** 20
La Bête | **Cap Hill** –
Le Pichet | **Pike Place** 25
NEW Lloyd Martin | **Queen Anne** –
NEW Local 360 | **Belltown** –
Lunchbox Lab | **S Lake Union** 24
Z Marination | **Cap Hill** 27
Z Matt's/Mkt. | **Pike Place** 25
Mike's Noodle House | **Intl Dist** 23
Z Mistral | **S Lake Union** 26
NEW Momiji | **Cap Hill** –
Moshi Moshi | **Ballard** 23
Ocho | **Ballard** 24
Palace Kitchen | **Dwtn** 25
Paragon | **Queen Anne** 19
Z Paseo | **multi.** 28
Peso's | **Queen Anne** 22
Pike St. Fish | **Cap Hill** 22
NEW Poquitos | **Cap Hill** –
Rancho Bravo | **Cap Hill** 24
Re:Public | **S Lake Union** –
NEW Revel | **Fremont** –
NEW Serious Biscuit | **S Lake Union** –
Z Serious Pie | **multi.** 26
Shiku Sushi | **Ballard** 23
Sitka & Spruce | **Cap Hill** 26
Skillet | **Cap Hill** 23
Spur Gastropub | **Belltown** 24
Toulouse | **Queen Anne** 23
Umi Sake Hse. | **Belltown** 25
Wasabi Bistro | **Belltown** 22
Zippy's | **White Ctr** 23

HISTORIC PLACES

(Year opened; * building)

1890 | Brooklyn Seafood* | **Dwtn** 24
1890 | Essential Baking Co.* | **Wallingford** 22
1900 | Metro. Grill* | **Dwtn** 26
1900 | Plaka Estiatorio* | **Ballard** 27
1900 | Salumi* | **Pioneer Sq** 27
1900 | Wild Ginger* | **Dwtn** 25
1901 | Melrose Grill* | **Renton** 27
1902 | That's Amore* | **Mt. Baker** 24
1903 | Crush* | **Madison Vly** 25

1904 | Maneki | **Intl Dist** 25

1905 | Volunteer Pk. Cafe* | **Cap Hill** 25

1907 | Capital Grille* | **Dwtn** 23

1907 | Dash Pt./Lobster Shop* | **Tacoma** 23

1908 | Tutta Bella* | **Columbia City** 22

1909 | Athenian | **Pike Place** 19

1909 | Hunt Club* | **First Hill** 22

1910 | Corson Bldg.* | **Georgetown** 28

1910 | Re:Public* | **S Lake Union** –

1910 | Tai Tung* | **Intl Dist** 23

1910 | Willows Inn* | **Lummi Island** –

1912 | 3 Girls Bakery | **Pike Place** 24

1916 | Salish Lodge* | **Snoqualmie** 23

1917 | Chez Shea/Lounge* | **Pike Place** 26

1917 | Matt's/Mkt.* | **Pike Place** 25

1920 | Cantinetta* | **Wallingford** 27

1920 | Cyclops* | **Belltown** 19

1920 | Lockspot Cafe | **Ballard** 18

1920 | Salty's* | **W Seattle** 20

1920 | Serafina* | **Eastlake** 25

1920 | Shuckers* | **Dwtn** 23

1924 | Georgian | **Dwtn** 26

1924 | Osteria La Spiga* | **Cap Hill** 23

1926 | Bainbridge BBQ* | **Bainbridge Is** 17

1926 | Shultzy's* | **Univ Dist** 18

1927 | Maxwell's Restaurant* | **Tacoma** –

1927 | Oyster Bar/Chuckanut | **Bow** 25

1929 | 5 Point Café | **Belltown** 18

1929 | Queen City Grill* | **Belltown** 21

1937 | Maltby Cafe* | **Maltby** 22

1938 | Ivar's/Clams | **Seattle Waterfront** 21

1940 | Szmania's* | **Magnolia** 25

1950 | Canlis | **Lake Union** 27

1952 | R&L BBQ | **Cap Hill** –

1953 | Bush Garden | **Intl Dist** 18

1953 | El Gaucho | **Belltown** 25

1954 | Dick's Drive-In | **Wallingford** 19

1954 | Hattie's Hat | **Ballard** 17

1954 | Northlake Tav. | **Univ Dist** 22

1957 | Lowell's | **Pike Place** 20

1961 | SkyCity* | **Seattle Ctr** 22

1962 | DeLuxe B&G | **Cap Hill** 17

HOTEL DINING

Andra, Hotel

Z Lola | **Dwtn** 25

Cedarbrook Lodge

Copperleaf | **SeaTac** –

Edgewater Hotel

Z Six Seven | **Seattle Waterfront** 23

Fairmont Olympic Hotel

Belle Epicurean | **Dwtn** 23

Z Georgian | **Dwtn** 26

Shuckers | **Dwtn** 23

Four Seasons Hotel

Art Rest. | **Dwtn** 23

Friday Harbor House Inn

Bluff | **Friday Harbor** –

Grand Hyatt Hotel

Blue C Sushi | **Dwtn** 16

Ruth's Chris | **Dwtn** 24

Hilton Americas

Spencer's Steaks | **SeaTac** –

Inn at Langley

Inn at Langley | **Langley** 26

Max, Hotel

Red Fin | **Dwtn** 21

Mayflower Park Hotel

Andaluca | **Dwtn** 24

Monaco, Hotel

Sazerac | **Dwtn** 20

1000, Hotel

Boka Kitchen | **Dwtn** 20

Paramount Hotel

Dragonfish | **Dwtn** 19

Salish Lodge & Spa

Z Salish Lodge | **Snoqualmie** 23

Sorrento Hotel

Hunt Club | **First Hill** 22

Vintage Park, Hotel

Tulio | **Dwtn** 25

Warwick Seattle Hotel

Brass. Marg. | **Dwtn** 16

W Hotel

Earth & Ocean | **Dwtn** 22

Willows Lodge

Z Barking Frog | **Woodinville** 25

Woodmark Hotel

Beach Cafe | **Kirkland** 19

Bin on Lake | **Kirkland** 20

LATE DINING

(Weekday closing hour)

Z Aqua by El Gaucho | 12 AM | **Seattle Waterfront** 25

Azul | 12 AM | **Mill Creek** 22

NEW Ba Bar | 2 AM | **Cap Hill** -

B&O Espresso | 12 AM | **Cap Hill** 20

Big Mario's Pizza | varies | **Cap Hill** -

Black Bottle | varies | **multi.** 22

Bleu Bistro | 2 AM | **Cap Hill** 21

BluWater | 1 AM | **multi.** 16

NEW Brave Horse | 12 AM | **S Lake Union** -

Buckley's | 1 AM | **Seattle Ctr** 17

Café Presse | 2 AM | **Cap Hill** 23

Cicchetti | 12 AM | **Eastlake** 23

NEW Coterie Room | 12 AM | **Belltown** -

Dick's Drive-In | 2 AM | **multi.** 19

Dragonfish | 1 AM | **Dwtn** 19

Elemental | 12 AM | **Lake Union** 26

5 Point Café | 24 hrs. | **Belltown** 18

5 Spot | 12 AM | **Queen Anne** 21

Hattie's Hat | 12 AM | **Ballard** 17

Ho Ho Seafood | 1 AM | **Intl Dist** 20

Honey Court | 2 AM | **Intl Dist** 19

Il Bistro | 1 AM | **Pike Place** 23

Jade Garden | 2:30 AM | **Intl Dist** 22

Jalisco | 12 AM | **Queen Anne** 19

Joey | varies | **multi.** 17

Kushibar | 2 AM | **Belltown** 20

La Isla | 2 AM | **Ballard** 21

Laredos | 1 AM | **Queen Anne** -

Le Pichet | 12 AM | **Pike Place** 25

NEW Local 360 | varies | **Belltown** -

Local Vine | 2 AM | **Cap Hill** -

Z Lola | 12 AM | **Dwtn** 25

Long Provincial | varies | **Dwtn** 21

May | 1 AM | **Wallingford** 26

Mission | 2 AM | **W Seattle** 20

Ocho | 11:45 PM | **Ballard** 24

Olympia Pizza | 1 AM | **Cap Hill** 19

Paddy Coynes | varies | **multi.** 16

Palace Kitchen | 1 AM | **Dwtn** 25

Peso's | 1 AM | **Queen Anne** 22

Pike St. Fish | 12 AM | **Cap Hill** 22

Poco Wine | 12 AM | **Cap Hill** 19

NEW Poquitos | 1 AM | **Cap Hill** -

Purple Dot | varies | **Intl Dist** 17

Quinn's Pub | 1 AM | **Cap Hill** 24

Red Door | 2 AM | **Fremont** 16

Sea Garden | 2 AM | **Intl Dist** 20

Serafina | varies | **Eastlake** 25

Sharp's Roasthse. | 12 AM | **SeaTac** -

Shultzy's | varies | **Univ Dist** 18

Skillet | varies | **multi.** 23

Slim's Last Chance | 12 AM | **Georgetown** 26
Smarty Pants | 12 AM | **Georgetown** 23
Tap House Grill | 12 AM | **multi.** 17
Ten Mercer | 12 AM | **Queen Anne** 22
NEW Terra Plata | 1 AM | **Cap Hill** –
13 Coins | 24 hrs. | **multi.** 19
Tin Table | 1 AM | **Cap Hill** 20
Top Gun | 12 AM | **Bellevue** 22
Toulouse | 1 AM | **Queen Anne** 23
Umi Sake Hse. | 1 AM | **Belltown** 25
Via Tribunali | varies | **Cap Hill** 23
Wann Izakaya | 12 AM | **Belltown** 20
Wasabi Bistro | 1 AM | **Belltown** 22
Zeeks Pizza | varies | **Redmond** 19

MEET FOR A DRINK

Adriatic Grill | **Tacoma** –
Alibi Room | **Pike Place** 21
Alki Bakery | **Kent** 21
Americana | **Cap Hill** 20
Anchovies/Olives | **Cap Hill** 25
Z Anthony's HomePort | **multi.** 21
Z Aqua by El Gaucho | **Seattle Waterfront** 25
Art Rest. | **Dwtn** 23
Asado | **Tacoma** –
Azul | **Mill Creek** 22
NEW Bar del Corso | **Beacon Hill** –
Bastille Café | **Ballard** 19
Beach Cafe | **Kirkland** 19
Big Mario's Pizza | **Cap Hill** –
Bin on Lake | **Kirkland** 20
BluWater | **Green Lk** 16
Book Bindery | **Queen Anne** –
NEW Brave Horse | **S Lake Union** –
Brooklyn Seafood | **Dwtn** 24
Z Cactus | **multi.** 22
Capitol Club | **Cap Hill** 19
Chandler's Crab | **S Lake Union** 23
Chantanee | **Bellevue** 25
Columbia Ale | **Columbia City** 19
Crow | **Queen Anne** 25
NEW Cuoco | **S Lake Union** –
Cutters | **Pike Place** 22
Z Daniel's Broiler | **multi.** 24
Dragonfish | **Dwtn** 19
El Camino | **Fremont** 22
Z El Gaucho | **Belltown** 25
Elliott Bay | **multi.** 22
Z Elliott's Oyster | **Seattle Waterfront** 24
Flying Squirrel | **Seward Pk** 23
Fonte | **Dwtn** 20
Four Swallows | **Bainbridge Is** 26
Frontier Room | **Belltown** 22
F.X. McRory's | **Pioneer Sq** 18
Gordon Biersch | **Dwtn** 15
Greenlake B&G | **Green Lk** 17
Hale's Ales | **Fremont** 15
Hilltop Ale Hse. | **Queen Anne** 20
Hudson | **Georgetown** 19
Il Bistro | **Pike Place** 23
Inn at Ship Bay | **Eastsound** –
John Howie | **Bellevue** 25
Kaname Izakaya | **Intl Dist** –
Kells Irish | **Pike Place** 17
NEW La Luna | **Queen Anne** –
Laredos | **Queen Anne** –
Lecosho | **Dwtn** –
NEW Lloyd Martin | **Queen Anne** –
NEW Local 360 | **Belltown** –
Local Vine | **Cap Hill** –
Z Lola | **Dwtn** 25
Long Provincial | **Dwtn** 21
Mama's Mex. | **Belltown** 18
NEW Marché | **Pike Place** –
Maxwell's Restaurant | **Tacoma** –
Z Metro. Grill | **Dwtn** 26

NEW Milagro Cantina | **Kirkland** -

Z Mistral | **S Lake Union** 26

NEW Momiji | **Cap Hill** -

New Orleans | **Pioneer Sq** 19

Ocho | **Ballard** 24

'Ohana | **Belltown** 21

Z Olivar | **Cap Hill** 26

Pacific Grill | **Tacoma** 26

Palace Kitchen | **Dwtn** 25

Peso's | **Queen Anne** 22

Pink Door | **Pike Place** 22

Ray's Cafe | **Shilshole** 22

Red Lantern | **Intl Dist** -

Re:Public | **S Lake Union** -

Ruth's Chris | **multi.** 24

Saint, The | **Cap Hill** -

Sazerac | **Dwtn** 20

Z Serious Pie | **Dwtn** 26

74th St. Ale | **Phinney R** 21

Shiku Sushi | **Ballard** 23

Z Six Seven | **Seattle Waterfront** 23

Slim's Last Chance | **Georgetown** 26

Spur Gastropub | **Belltown** 24

Tango | **Cap Hill** 20

Tavolàta | **Belltown** 25

Tin Table | **Cap Hill** 20

Toulouse | **Queen Anne** 23

Typhoon! | **Redmond** 22

Volterra | **Ballard** 25

Walrus/Carpenter | **Ballard** -

OFFBEAT

Benihana | **Dwtn** 19

Blue C Sushi | **multi.** 16

Buca di Beppo | **multi.** 15

Chaco Canyon | **Univ Dist** 19

Dixie's BBQ | **Bellevue** 21

5 Point Café | **Belltown** 18

5 Spot | **Queen Anne** 21

Luna Park Cafe | **W Seattle** 18

Mae's | **Phinney R** 15

Mama's Mex. | **Belltown** 18

Z Mashiko | **W Seattle** 28

New Orleans | **Pioneer Sq** 19

'Ohana | **Belltown** 21

Pink Door | **Pike Place** 22

Slim's Last Chance | **Georgetown** 26

Zippy's | **White Ctr** 23

OUTDOOR DINING

(G=garden; P=patio; S=sidewalk; T=terrace)

Agua Verde | T | **Univ Dist** 23

Anchovies/Olives | S | **Cap Hill** 25

Z Anthony's HomePort | P, T | **multi.** 21

Anthony's Pier 66 | T | **Seattle Waterfront** 22

Z Aqua by El Gaucho | P | **Seattle Waterfront** 25

Assaggio | P | **Dwtn** 24

B&O Espresso | S | **Cap Hill** 20

Barking Dog | P | **Ballard** 20

Z Barking Frog | P | **Woodinville** 25

Bastille Café | P | **Ballard** 19

Beach Cafe | P | **Kirkland** 19

Z Boat St. Cafe | P | **Queen Anne** 27

Brad's Swingside | T | **Fremont** 25

Brooklyn Seafood | P | **Dwtn** 24

Buffalo Deli | S | **Belltown** 27

Z Cactus | P | **multi.** 22

Z Cafe Besalu | S | **Ballard** 29

Z Cafe Campagne | S | **Pike Place** 26

Z Cafe Juanita | G, P | **Kirkland** 28

Cafe Nola | P | **Bainbridge Is** 21

Carmelita | G | **Greenwood** 25

Chandler's Crab | T | **S Lake Union** 23

Chinoise | S | **Queen Anne** 20

Chinook's | T | **Magnolia** 21

Coastal Kitchen | P | **Cap Hill** 20

SPECIAL FEATURES

- Copacabana | T | **Pike Place** –
- 🅩 Daniel's Broiler | T | **multi.** 24
- Dish | P | **Fremont** 25
- Dragonfish | P | **Dwtn** 19
- El Camino | P | **Fremont** 22
- 🅩 El Gaucho | P | **Bellevue** 25
- 🅩 Elliott's Oyster | T | **Seattle Waterfront** 24
- Emmett Watson | P | **Pike Place** 22
- Firenze | S | **Bellevue** 22
- Flying Fish | P | **S Lake Union** 24
- Galanga Thai | S | **Tacoma** –
- 🅩 Gelatiamo | P | **Dwtn** 27
- Gordito's | P | **Greenwood** 21
- Hunt Club | P | **First Hill** 22
- Il Bistro | T | **Pike Place** 23
- 🅩 Il Terrazzo | P | **Pioneer Sq** 27
- India Bistro | S | **Ballard** 23
- La Fontana | G | **Belltown** 23
- La Rustica | P | **W Seattle** 24
- Le Pichet | S | **Pike Place** 25
- Macrina | S | **multi.** 25
- Maggie Bluff's | P | **Magnolia** 19
- Matt's Famous Chili Dogs | P | **S Seattle** 23
- Matts' Rotisserie | P | **Redmond** 21
- Maximilien | P | **Pike Place** 23
- McCormick's Fish | P | **Dwtn** 23
- 🅩 Nell's | S | **Green Lk** 27
- New Orleans | P | **Pioneer Sq** 19
- Ototo Sushi | P | **Queen Anne** 19
- Oyster Bar/Chuckanut | P | **Bow** 25
- Pagliacci Pizza | P | **multi.** 23
- 🅩 Palisade | T | **Magnolia** 24
- 🅩 Paseo | S | **Fremont** 28
- Pasta & Co. | P, S | **multi.** 22
- Pegasus Pizza | P | **W Seattle** 21
- Pink Door | T | **Pike Place** 22
- Place Pigalle | P | **Pike Place** 25
- Ponti Seafood | P | **Queen Anne** 24
- Purple Café | P | **multi.** 20
- Ray's Cafe | P | **Shilshole** 22
- Red Mill | P | **multi.** 24
- Rist. Italianissimo | P | **Woodinville** 26
- Rist. Paradiso | S | **Kirkland** 20
- Salty's | P, T | **multi.** 20
- Santa Fe Cafe | S | **Phinney R** 20
- Sazerac | P | **Dwtn** 20
- 🅩 Seastar | P | **S Lake Union** 25
- Serafina | P, S | **Eastlake** 25
- Shuckers | P | **Dwtn** 23
- Shultzy's | P | **Univ Dist** 18
- 🅩 Six Seven | T | **Seattle Waterfront** 23
- Slim's Last Chance | S | **Georgetown** 26
- St. Clouds | G, P | **Madrona** 23
- Tacos Guaymas/Cantina | P, S | **multi.** 19
- Tap House Grill | P | **Bellevue** 17
- **NEW** Terra Plata | **Cap Hill** –
- Tulio | P | **Dwtn** 25
- Tutta Bella | S | **multi.** 22
- Two Bells B&G | G | **Belltown** 22
- Typhoon! | P | **Redmond** 22
- Voilà! Bistrot | P | **Madison Vly** 21
- Wasabi Bistro | S | **Belltown** 22
- Zeeks Pizza | P | **multi.** 19

PARKING

(V=valet, *=validated)

- Andaluca | V | **Dwtn** 24
- 🅩 Anthony's HomePort | V | **Kirkland** 21
- Anthony's Pier 66 | V* | **Seattle Waterfront** 22
- 🅩 Aqua by El Gaucho | V* | **Seattle Waterfront** 25
- Art Rest. | V | **Dwtn** 23
- Asado | V | **Tacoma** –

Assaggio | V | **Dwtn** 24
Barolo | V | **Dwtn** 24
Beach Cafe | V* | **Kirkland** 19
Bell St. Diner | V | **Seattle Waterfront** 23
Benihana* | **Dwtn** 19
Bin on Lake | V* | **Kirkland** 20
BluWater | V* | **Green Lk** 16
Boka Kitchen | V | **Dwtn** 20
Brass. Marg. | V | **Dwtn** 16
Brooklyn Seafood | V | **Dwtn** 24
Z Canlis | V | **Lake Union** 27
Capital Grille | V | **Dwtn** 23
Chandler's Crab | V* | **S Lake Union** 23
Chantanee* | **Bellevue** 25
Chez Shea/Lounge | V* | **Pike Place** 26
NEW Coterie Room | V | **Belltown** –
Z Daniel's Broiler | V* | **multi.** 24
NEW Din Tai Fung* | **Bellevue** –
Earth & Ocean | V | **Dwtn** 22
Z El Gaucho | V* | **multi.** 25
Z Elliott's Oyster | V* | **Seattle Waterfront** 24
Frontier Room | V | **Belltown** 22
Z Georgian | V* | **Dwtn** 26
Hunt Club | V | **First Hill** 22
Z Il Terrazzo | V* | **Pioneer Sq** 27
Joey | V* | **multi.** 17
John Howie | V* | **Bellevue** 25
Z Lola | V | **Dwtn** 25
Maximilien* | **Pike Place** 23
McCormick/Schmick | V* | **multi.** 21
Melting Pot | V | **multi.** 19
Z Metro. Grill | V* | **Dwtn** 26
Morton's | V | **Dwtn** 25
O'Asian* | **Dwtn** 20
Pacific Grill | V* | **Tacoma** 26
Paddy Coynes* | **Bellevue** 16
Z Palisade | V | **Magnolia** 24
Palomino* | **Dwtn** 20
Pearl | V | **Bellevue** 22
P.F. Chang's | V | **Bellevue** 18
Pike Pub* | **Pike Place** 17
Pink Door* | **Pike Place** 22
Place Pigalle* | **Pike Place** 25
Ponti Seafood | V | **Queen Anne** 24
Purple Café* | **Dwtn** 20
Pyramid Ale* | **SODO** 16
Rancho Bravo* | **Cap Hill** 24
Z Ray's Boathse. | V | **Shilshole** 24
Ray's Cafe | V | **Shilshole** 22
NEW RN74 | V | **Dwtn** –
Ruth's Chris | V | **Dwtn** 24
Z Salish Lodge | V | **Snoqualmie** 23
Salty's | V | **W Seattle** 20
Sazerac | V | **Dwtn** 20
Z Seastar | V* | **multi.** 25
Shuckers | V | **Dwtn** 23
Z Six Seven | V | **Seattle Waterfront** 23
Z SkyCity | V | **Seattle Ctr** 22
Spencer's Steaks | V | **SeaTac** –
Tap House Grill* | **Bellevue** 17
Ten Mercer | V | **Queen Anne** 22
Trellis | V | **Kirkland** 22
Tulio | V | **Dwtn** 25
Tutta Bella* | **S Lake Union** 22
Z Wild Ginger | V* | **multi.** 25

PEOPLE-WATCHING

Adriatic Grill | **Tacoma** –
Allium | **Eastsound** –
Americana | **Cap Hill** 20
Anchovies/Olives | **Cap Hill** 25
Art of the Table | **Wallingford** 25
Art Rest. | **Dwtn** 23
Asado | **Tacoma** –

Athenian | **Pike Place** 19
NEW Ba Bar | **Cap Hill** –
NEW Bar del Corso | **Beacon Hill** –
Bastille Café | **Ballard** 19
Big Mario's Pizza | **Cap Hill** –
Bin on Lake | **Kirkland** 20
Bisato | **Belltown** 25
Bis on Main | **Bellevue** 24
Black Bottle | **Belltown** 22
Blueacre | **Dwtn** 21
Blue C Sushi | **multi.** 16
BluWater | **Green Lk** 16
Branzino | **Belltown** 25
NEW Brave Horse | **S Lake Union** –
Buddha Ruksa | **W Seattle** 26
Café Presse | **Cap Hill** 23
Café Vignole | **S Seattle** –
Capitol Club | **Cap Hill** 19
Chez Shea/Lounge | **Pike Place** 26
Chiang's Gourmet | **multi.** 23
Cicchetti | **Eastlake** 23
Z Corson Bldg. | **Georgetown** 28
Z Crush | **Madison Vly** 25
NEW Cuoco | **S Lake Union** –
Cutters | **Pike Place** 22
Dick's Drive-In | **multi.** 19
NEW Din Tai Fung | **Bellevue** –
NEW Dot's Delicatessen | **Fremont** –
Elliott Bay Café | **multi.** 18
Emmer/Rye | **Queen Anne** 22
Essential Baking Co. | **multi.** 22
Z Etta's | **Pike Place** 25
Flying Fish | **S Lake Union** 24
Flying Squirrel | **Seward Pk** 23
Frontier Room | **Belltown** 22
Gallery Café/Frye | **Cap Hill** –
Geraldine's | **Columbia City** 24
Gilbert's/Bagel | **Bellevue** 21
Goldbergs' Deli | **Bellevue** 18
NEW Golden Beetle | **Ballard** –
Gorgeous George's | **Phinney R** 25
Grill on Broadway | **Cap Hill** 15
Habesha | **Dwtn** 22
Harbor City BBQ | **Intl Dist** –
How To Cook Wolf | **Queen Anne** 24
Hudson | **Georgetown** 19
Hue Ky Mi Gia | **Intl Dist** –
I Love NY Deli | **Univ Dist** 21
Z Il Terrazzo | **Pioneer Sq** 27
Inn at Ship Bay | **Eastsound** –
Island Soul Caribbean | **Columbia City** –
Jack's Fish | **Pike Place** 22
Jade Garden | **Intl Dist** 22
Joey | **multi.** 17
John Howie | **Bellevue** 25
Joule | **Wallingford** 26
Julia's | **Cap Hill** 16
June | **Madrona** –
Kaname Izakaya | **Intl Dist** –
Kells Irish | **Pike Place** 17
La Bête | **Cap Hill** –
La Côte | **Madison Vly** 20
NEW La Luna | **Queen Anne** –
Laredos | **Queen Anne** –
Lecosho | **Dwtn** –
NEW Lloyd Martin | **Queen Anne** –
NEW Local 360 | **Belltown** –
Local Vine | **Cap Hill** –
Long Provincial | **Dwtn** 21
Luc | **Madison Vly** 25
Machiavelli | **Cap Hill** 24
NEW Madison Park Conserv. | **Madison Pk** –
Mama's Mex. | **Belltown** 18
NEW Marché | **Pike Place** –
Marjorie | **Cap Hill** 25
NEW Marrow | **Tacoma** –

Maxwell's Restaurant | **Tacoma** –

Meza | **Cap Hill** –

NEW Milagro Cantina | **Kirkland** –

Z Mistral | **S Lake Union** 26

NEW Momiji | **Cap Hill** –

Noodle Boat | **Issaquah** 26

Ocho | **Ballard** 24

'Ohana | **Belltown** 21

Z Olivar | **Cap Hill** 26

Osteria La Spiga | **Cap Hill** 23

Ototo Sushi | **Queen Anne** 19

Pacific Grill | **Tacoma** 26

P.F. Chang's | **Bellevue** 18

Phoenecia | **W Seattle** 27

Pike St. Fish | **Cap Hill** 22

Plaka Estiatorio | **Ballard** 27

Purple Café | **multi.** 20

Red Lantern | **Intl Dist** –

Re:Public | **S Lake Union** –

Rikki Rikki | **Kirkland** 18

Ruth's Chris | **Dwtn** 24

Saint, The | **Cap Hill** –

Z Seastar | **multi.** 25

Seatown | **Pike Place** –

NEW Serious Biscuit | **S Lake Union** –

Z Serious Pie | **Dwtn** 26

Shiku Sushi | **Ballard** 23

Sitka & Spruce | **Cap Hill** 26

Slim's Last Chance | **Georgetown** 26

Spiced | **Bellevue** 22

Spicy Talk Bistro | **Redmond** –

Z Spinasse | **Cap Hill** 28

Spring Hill | **W Seattle** 25

Spur Gastropub | **Belltown** 24

Stan's Bar-B-Q | **Issaquah** –

Staple & Fancy | **Ballard** –

Z Steelhead | **Pike Place** 24

NEW Stopsky's Deli | **Mercer Is** –

Taste | **Dwtn** 22

Tat's Deli | **Pioneer Sq** –

Tavolàta | **Belltown** 25

NEW Terra Plata | **Cap Hill** –

Thai Curry Simple | **Intl Dist** –

13 Coins | **multi.** 19

Tilikum Place | **Belltown** 25

Tin Table | **Cap Hill** 20

Toulouse | **Queen Anne** 23

Tsukushinbo | **Intl Dist** –

Umi Sake Hse. | **Belltown** 25

NEW Uneeda Burger | **Fremont** –

Via Tribunali | **multi.** 23

Volterra | **Ballard** 25

Walrus/Carpenter | **Ballard** –

Wasabi Bistro | **Belltown** 22

NEW Wheeler St. Kitchen | **Magnolia** –

Where Ya At Matt | **Location Varies** –

Yea's Wok | **Newcastle** –

POWER SCENES

Art Rest. | **Dwtn** 23

NEW Brave Horse | **S Lake Union** –

Z Calcutta Grill | **Newcastle** 21

Z Canlis | **Lake Union** 27

Z Crush | **Madison Vly** 25

NEW Cuoco | **S Lake Union** –

Z Daniel's Broiler | **multi.** 24

Z El Gaucho | **Belltown** 25

Z Georgian | **Dwtn** 26

Z Il Terrazzo | **Pioneer Sq** 27

John Howie | **Bellevue** 25

Local Vine | **Cap Hill** –

Z Lola | **Dwtn** 25

Luc | **Madison Vly** 25

NEW Madison Park Conserv. | **Madison Pk** –

Z Metro. Grill | **Dwtn** 26

NEW Milagro Cantina | **Kirkland** –

Ƶ Mistral | **S Lake Union** 26
Morton's | **Dwtn** 25
Pacific Grill | **Tacoma** 26
Ƶ Rover's | **Madison Vly** 28
Ruth's Chris | **Dwtn** 24
Ƶ Seastar | **multi.** 25
Ƶ Wild Ginger | **multi.** 25
Ƶ Ray's Boathse. | **Shilshole** 24
Ƶ Rover's | **Madison Vly** 28
Ƶ Salish Lodge | **Snoqualmie** 23
Ƶ Six Seven | **Seattle Waterfront** 23
Ƶ SkyCity | **Seattle Ctr** 22
Umi Sake Hse. | **Belltown** 25
Ƶ Wild Ginger | **Dwtn** 25

PRIVATE ROOMS

(Restaurants charge less at off times; call for capacity)

Al Boccalino | **Pioneer Sq** 24
Ƶ Anthony's HomePort | **multi.** 21
Ƶ Aqua by El Gaucho | **Seattle Waterfront** 25
Art Rest. | **Dwtn** 23
Bick's Broadview | **Greenwood** 21
Bis on Main | **Bellevue** 24
Brad's Swingside | **Fremont** 25
Buenos Aires Grill | **Dwtn** 21
Ƶ Cafe Juanita | **Kirkland** 28
Ƶ Canlis | **Lake Union** 27
Carmelita | **Greenwood** 25
Coastal Kitchen | **Cap Hill** 20
Crow | **Queen Anne** 25
Ƶ Dahlia Lounge | **Dwtn** 26
Ƶ Daniel's Broiler | **multi.** 24
Dash Pt./Lobster Shop | **Tacoma** 23
Ƶ El Gaucho | **multi.** 25
Ƶ Elliott's Oyster | **Seattle Waterfront** 24
Firenze | **Bellevue** 22
Flying Fish | **S Lake Union** 24
Ƶ Georgian | **Dwtn** 26
Ƶ Herbfarm, The | **Woodinville** 28
John Howie | **Bellevue** 25
Maximilien | **Pike Place** 23
Osteria La Spiga | **Cap Hill** 23
Palace Kitchen | **Dwtn** 25
Ƶ Palisade | **Magnolia** 24
Pearl | **Bellevue** 22

QUIET CONVERSATION

Allium | **Eastsound** –
Americana | **Cap Hill** 20
Andaluca | **Dwtn** 24
Art Rest. | **Dwtn** 23
Ƶ Bakery Nouveau | **W Seattle** 29
B&O Espresso | **Cap Hill** 20
Bin on Lake | **Kirkland** 20
Bistro Turkuaz | **Madrona** 26
Ƶ Cafe Campagne | **Pike Place** 26
Ƶ Cafe Juanita | **Kirkland** 28
Café Vignole | **S Seattle** –
Chaco Canyon | **Univ Dist** 19
Chez Shea/Lounge | **Pike Place** 26
Chloé | **Laurelhurst** –
Ciao Bella | **Univ Vill** 23
Ƶ Daniel's Broiler | **multi.** 24
Dinette | **Cap Hill** 25
Earth & Ocean | **Dwtn** 22
Eats Mkt. Café | **W Seattle** 20
Elliott Bay Café | **multi.** 18
Enza | **Queen Anne** –
Essential Baking Co. | **multi.** 22
Eva | **Green Lk** 26
Four Swallows | **Bainbridge Is** 26
Gallery Café/Frye | **Cap Hill** –
Geraldine's | **Columbia City** 24
NEW Golden Beetle | **Ballard** –
Gorgeous George's | **Phinney R** 25
Greenlake B&G | **Green Lk** 17
Hitchcock | **Bainbridge Is** –

Hunt Club | **First Hill** 22

🅩 Il Terrazzo | **Pioneer Sq** 27

Inn at Langley | **Langley** 26

Inn at Ship Bay | **Eastsound** -

Jhanjay Vegetarian Thai | **multi.** 25

John Howie | **Bellevue** 25

Joule | **Wallingford** 26

La Côte | **Madison Vly** 20

Long Provincial | **Dwtn** 21

Lynn's Bistro | **Kirkland** 25

NEW Marché | **Pike Place** -

🅩 Nell's | **Green Lk** 27

Noodle Boat | **Issaquah** 26

Pacific Grill | **Tacoma** 26

Pair | **Ravenna** 26

Pearl | **Bellevue** 22

Portage | **Queen Anne** 25

Primo Grill | **Tacoma** -

🅩 Rover's | **Madison Vly** 28

Russell's | **Bothell** 20

Saltoro | **N Seattle** 20

611 Supreme | **Cap Hill** 21

Spring Hill | **W Seattle** 25

Spur Gastropub | **Belltown** 24

Tavolàta | **Belltown** 25

Tilikum Place | **Belltown** 25

NEW Wheeler St. Kitchen | **Magnolia** -

RAW BARS

🅩 Anthony's HomePort | **multi.** 21

Anthony's Pier 66 | **Seattle Waterfront** 22

🅩 Aqua by El Gaucho | **Seattle Waterfront** 25

Blueacre | **Dwtn** 21

Brooklyn Seafood | **Dwtn** 24

Chaco Canyon | **W Seattle** 19

Chinook's | **Magnolia** 21

Cutters | **Pike Place** 22

🅩 Elliott's Oyster | **Seattle Waterfront** 24

Emmett Watson | **Pike Place** 22

F.X. McRory's | **Pioneer Sq** 18

Matts' Rotisserie | **Redmond** 21

Monsoon | **Bellevue** 25

🅩 Seastar | **multi.** 25

Shuckers | **Dwtn** 23

Sushi Kappo | **Eastlake** -

Walrus/Carpenter | **Ballard** -

ROMANTIC PLACES

Allium | **Eastsound** -

Art Rest. | **Dwtn** 23

Bin on Lake | **Kirkland** 20

Bis on Main | **Bellevue** 24

Bistro Turkuaz | **Madrona** 26

🅩 Boat St. Cafe | **Queen Anne** 27

Book Bindery | **Queen Anne** -

🅩 Cafe Campagne | **Pike Place** 26

🅩 Cafe Juanita | **Kirkland** 28

🅩 Canlis | **Lake Union** 27

🅩 Cantinetta | **multi.** 27

Capitol Club | **Cap Hill** 19

Chez Shea/Lounge | **Pike Place** 26

Chloé | **Laurelhurst** -

Ciao Bella | **Univ Vill** 23

Copperleaf | **SeaTac** -

Four Swallows | **Bainbridge Is** 26

🅩 Harvest Vine | **Madison Vly** 27

🅩 Herbfarm, The | **Woodinville** 28

Hitchcock | **Bainbridge Is** -

Hunt Club | **First Hill** 22

Il Bistro | **Pike Place** 23

Inn at Ship Bay | **Eastsound** -

John Howie | **Bellevue** 25

Joule | **Wallingford** 26

June | **Madrona** -

Kasbah | **Ballard** -

La Côte | **Madison Vly** 20

La Fontana | **Belltown** 23

Z Lark | **Cap Hill** 27

La Rustica | **W Seattle** 24

Le Gourmand | **Ballard** 26

Long Provincial | **Dwtn** 21

NEW Madison Park Conserv. | **Madison Pk** –

NEW Marché | **Pike Place** –

Maximilien | **Pike Place** 23

Oliver's Twist | **Phinney R** 23

Pacific Grill | **Tacoma** 26

Pair | **Ravenna** 26

Pink Door | **Pike Place** 22

Place Pigalle | **Pike Place** 25

Portage | **Queen Anne** 25

Z Rover's | **Madison Vly** 28

Z Salish Lodge | **Snoqualmie** 23

Saltoro | **N Seattle** 20

Serafina | **Eastlake** 25

Szmania's | **Magnolia** 25

Tavolàta | **Belltown** 25

35th St. Bistro | **Fremont** 22

Voilà! Bistrot | **Madison Vly** 21

Volterra | **Ballard** 25

Willows Inn | **Lummi Island** –

SENIOR APPEAL

Alki Bakery | **Kent** 21

Allium | **Eastsound** –

Z Anthony's HomePort | **multi.** 21

Z Bakery Nouveau | **W Seattle** 29

Belle Pastry | **Dwtn** 24

Café Vignole | **S Seattle** –

Z Calcutta Grill | **Newcastle** 21

Carolina Smoke | **Bothell** –

Chanterelle | **Edmonds** 19

Chinook's | **Magnolia** 21

Chuck's Hole In the Wall | **Pioneer Sq** –

Copperleaf | **SeaTac** –

NEW Cuoco | **S Lake Union** –

Dante's Dogs | **Location Varies** 21

Dash Pt./Lobster Shop | **Tacoma** 23

Eats Mkt. Café | **W Seattle** 20

Elliott Bay Café | **multi.** 18

Essential Baking Co. | **multi.** 22

Four Swallows | **Bainbridge Is** 26

Gallery Café/Frye | **Cap Hill** –

Z Georgian | **Dwtn** 26

Geraldine's | **Columbia City** 24

Goldbergs' Deli | **Bellevue** 18

Gorgeous George's | **Phinney R** 25

Hitchcock | **Bainbridge Is** –

Hue Ky Mi Gia | **multi.** –

Hunt Club | **First Hill** 22

Inn at Ship Bay | **Eastsound** –

Ivar's/Clams | **Seattle Waterfront** 21

Ivar's Mukilteo | **Mukilteo** 21

Ivar's Salmon | **Lake Union** 21

La Côte | **Madison Vly** 20

NEW La Luna | **Queen Anne** –

Laredos | **Queen Anne** –

Maneki | **Intl Dist** 25

Maxwell's Restaurant | **Tacoma** –

McCormick/Schmick | **Dwtn** 21

Northlake Tav. | **Univ Dist** 22

Pacific Grill | **Tacoma** 26

Z Palisade | **Magnolia** 24

Queen Margherita | **Magnolia** –

Queen Mary Tea | **Ravenna** 21

Z Ray's Boathse. | **Shilshole** 24

Red Lantern | **Intl Dist** –

Russell's | **Bothell** 20

Z Salish Lodge | **Snoqualmie** 23

Saltoro | **N Seattle** 20

NEW Serious Biscuit | **S Lake Union** –

Slim's Last Chance | **Georgetown** 26

Stan's Bar-B-Q | **Issaquah** –

NEW Stopsky's Deli | **Mercer Is** –

Taste | **Dwtn** 22

Tat's Deli | **Pioneer Sq** –

13 Coins | **multi.** 19

NEW Uneeda Burger | **Fremont** –

NEW Wheeler St. Kitchen | **Magnolia** –

Willows Inn | **Lummi Island** –

Yea's Wok | **Newcastle** –

SINGLES SCENES

Art Rest. | **Dwtn** 23

Barolo | **Dwtn** 24

Big Mario's Pizza | **Cap Hill** –

Black Bottle | **Belltown** 22

Brouwer's | **Fremont** 22

Capitol Club | **Cap Hill** 19

Z Daniel's Broiler | **multi.** 24

Z El Gaucho | **Belltown** 25

Fadó Irish Pub | **Pioneer Sq** 17

F.X. McRory's | **Pioneer Sq** 18

Gordon Biersch | **Dwtn** 15

Hale's Ales | **Fremont** 15

Hattie's Hat | **Ballard** 17

Il Bistro | **Pike Place** 23

Joey | **multi.** 17

Kells Irish | **Pike Place** 17

La Isla | **Ballard** 21

Laredos | **Queen Anne** –

Le Pichet | **Pike Place** 25

Z Lola | **Dwtn** 25

Mama's Mex. | **Belltown** 18

Z Metro. Grill | **Dwtn** 26

New Orleans | **Pioneer Sq** 19

'Ohana | **Belltown** 21

Palace Kitchen | **Dwtn** 25

Paragon | **Queen Anne** 19

Pearl | **Bellevue** 22

Peso's | **Queen Anne** 22

Purple Café | **multi.** 20

Pyramid Ale | **SODO** 16

Ruth's Chris | **multi.** 24

Salty's | **multi.** 20

Shiku Sushi | **Ballard** 23

Two Bells B&G | **Belltown** 22

Wasabi Bistro | **Belltown** 22

Wilde Rover | **Kirkland** 16

Z Wild Ginger | **multi.** 25

THEME RESTAURANTS

Benihana | **Dwtn** 19

Buca di Beppo | **multi.** 15

Cafe Veloce | **Kirkland** 21

Luna Park Cafe | **W Seattle** 18

Wilde Rover | **Kirkland** 16

TRENDY

Allium | **Eastsound** –

Anchovies/Olives | **Cap Hill** 25

Art Rest. | **Dwtn** 23

NEW Ba Bar | **Cap Hill** –

Baguette Box | **multi.** 24

Bastille Café | **Ballard** 19

Big Mario's Pizza | **Cap Hill** –

Bin on Lake | **Kirkland** 20

Bisato | **Belltown** 25

Black Bottle | **Belltown** 22

Blueacre | **Dwtn** 21

Blue C Sushi | **multi.** 16

Boka Kitchen | **Dwtn** 20

Book Bindery | **Queen Anne** –

Branzino | **Belltown** 25

Z Cactus | **Kirkland** 22

Café Presse | **Cap Hill** 23

Z Cantinetta | **multi.** 27

Capitol Club | **Cap Hill** 19

Chiso | **Fremont** 24

Cicchetti | **Eastlake** 23

Copperleaf | **SeaTac** –

Z Corson Bldg. | **Georgetown** 28

Crow | **Queen Anne** 25

Z Crush | **Madison Vly** 25

NEW Cuoco | **S Lake Union** –

Dante's Dogs | **Location Varies** 21

Delancey | **Ballard** 26

Dinette | **Cap Hill** 25

NEW Din Tai Fung | **Bellevue** –

NEW Dot's Delicatessen | **Fremont** –

Earth & Ocean | **Dwtn** 22

Elemental | **Lake Union** 26

Elliott Bay Café | **multi.** 18

Emmer/Rye | **Queen Anne** 22

Eva | **Green Lk** 26

Flying Squirrel | **Seward Pk** 23

Fonte | **Dwtn** 20

Fort St. George | **Intl Dist** 18

Frontier Room | **Belltown** 22

Z Harvest Vine | **Madison Vly** 27

Hitchcock | **Bainbridge Is** –

How To Cook Wolf | **Queen Anne** 24

Hue Ky Mi Gia | **multi.** –

Inn at Ship Bay | **Eastsound** –

Z Jak's Grill | **W Seattle** 24

NEW Japonessa Cucina | **Pike Place** –

Joey | **multi.** 17

Joule | **Wallingford** 26

June | **Madrona** –

La Bête | **Cap Hill** –

Z La Carta/Mezcaleria | **Ballard** 27

NEW La Luna | **Queen Anne** –

Z Lark | **Cap Hill** 27

Lecosho | **Dwtn** –

Le Pichet | **Pike Place** 25

NEW Lloyd Martin | **Queen Anne** –

NEW Local 360 | **Belltown** –

Local Vine | **Cap Hill** –

Z Lola | **Dwtn** 25

Luc | **Madison Vly** 25

NEW Madison Park Conserv. | **Madison Pk** –

NEW Marché | **Pike Place** –

Z Marination | **Location Varies** 27

Marjorie | **Cap Hill** 25

NEW Marrow | **Tacoma** –

Z Matt's/Mkt. | **Pike Place** 25

NEW Milagro Cantina | **Kirkland** –

Z Mistral | **S Lake Union** 26

Molly Moon Truck | **Location Varies** –

NEW Momiji | **Cap Hill** –

Moshi Moshi | **Ballard** 23

Ocho | **Ballard** 24

Z Olivar | **Cap Hill** 26

Oliver's Twist | **Phinney R** 23

Osteria La Spiga | **Cap Hill** 23

Pacific Grill | **Tacoma** 26

Palace Kitchen | **Dwtn** 25

Pearl | **Bellevue** 22

Phoenecia | **W Seattle** 27

Pike St. Fish | **Cap Hill** 22

Purple Café | **multi.** 20

Purple Dot | **Intl Dist** 17

Red Fin | **Dwtn** 21

Re:Public | **S Lake Union** –

Saint, The | **Cap Hill** –

Z Salumi | **Pioneer Sq** 27

Seatown | **Pike Place** –

NEW Serious Biscuit | **S Lake Union** –

Z Serious Pie | **Dwtn** 26

Shiku Sushi | **Ballard** 23

Sitka & Spruce | **Cap Hill** 26

Slim's Last Chance | **Georgetown** 26

Z Spinasse | **Cap Hill** 28

Spring Hill | **W Seattle** 25

Spur Gastropub | **Belltown** 24

Staple & Fancy | **Ballard** –

Sushi Kappo | **Eastlake** -
Sutra | **Wallingford** 24
Taste | **Dwtn** 22
Tavolàta | **Belltown** 25
NEW Terra Plata | **Cap Hill** -
Z Tilth | **Wallingford** 28
Toulouse | **Queen Anne** 23
Umi Sake Hse. | **Belltown** 25
NEW Uneeda Burger | **Fremont** -
Via Tribunali | **multi.** 23
Volterra | **Ballard** 25
Walrus/Carpenter | **Ballard** -
NEW Wheeler St. Kitchen | **Magnolia** -
Where Ya At Matt | **Location Varies** -

VIEWS

Agua Verde | **Univ Dist** 23
Allium | **Eastsound** -
Z Anthony's HomePort | **multi.** 21
Anthony's Pier 66 | **Seattle Waterfront** 22
Z Aqua by El Gaucho | **Seattle Waterfront** 25
Art Rest. | **Dwtn** 23
Athenian | **Pike Place** 19
Azteca | **Ballard** 14
Beach Cafe | **Kirkland** 19
Belle Epicurean | **Madison Pk** 23
Bell St. Diner | **Seattle Waterfront** 23
Bin on Lake | **Kirkland** 20
Bluff | **Friday Harbor** -
BluWater | **multi.** 16
Book Bindery | **Queen Anne** -
Z Cactus | **multi.** 22
Z Calcutta Grill | **Newcastle** 21
Z Canlis | **Lake Union** 27
Chandler's Crab | **S Lake Union** 23
Chez Shea/Lounge | **Pike Place** 26
Chinook's | **Magnolia** 21
Cutters | **Pike Place** 22
Z Daniel's Broiler | **multi.** 24
Dash Pt./Lobster Shop | **Tacoma** 23
Z Elliott's Oyster | **Seattle Waterfront** 24
I Love Sushi | **S Lake Union** 22
Inn at Ship Bay | **Eastsound** -
Ivar's/Clams | **Seattle Waterfront** 21
Ivar's Salmon | **Lake Union** 21
Joey | **S Lake Union** 17
Kells Irish | **Pike Place** 17
NEW Local 360 | **Belltown** -
Lowell's | **Pike Place** 20
Maggie Bluff's | **Magnolia** 19
NEW Marché | **Pike Place** -
Maximilien | **Pike Place** 23
Z Nell's | **Green Lk** 27
Oyster Bar/Chuckanut | **Bow** 25
Palace Kitchen | **Dwtn** 25
Z Palisade | **Magnolia** 24
Pink Door | **Pike Place** 22
Place Pigalle | **Pike Place** 25
Ponti Seafood | **Queen Anne** 24
Z Ray's Boathse. | **Shilshole** 24
Ray's Cafe | **Shilshole** 22
Red Door | **Fremont** 16
Red Robin | **Issaquah** 16
Rose's Bakery | **Eastsound** -
Z Salish Lodge | **Snoqualmie** 23
Salty's | **multi.** 20
Seatown | **Pike Place** -
Z Six Seven | **Seattle Waterfront** 23
Z SkyCity | **Seattle Ctr** 22
Sunfish | **W Seattle** 21
Sushi Kappo | **Eastlake** -
Tacos Guaymas/Cantina | **Green Lk** 19
That's Amore | **Mt. Baker** 24
3 Girls Bakery | **Pike Place** 24

Turkish Delight | **Pike Place** –

Willows Inn | **Lummi Island** –

VISITORS ON EXPENSE ACCOUNT

Allium | **Eastsound** –

Z Barking Frog | **Woodinville** 25

Bin on Lake | **Kirkland** 20

Z Canlis | **Lake Union** 27

Chandler's Crab | **S Lake Union** 23

Copperleaf | **SeaTac** –

Z Corson Bldg. | **Georgetown** 28

Z Crush | **Madison Vly** 25

Z Dahlia Lounge | **Dwtn** 26

Z Daniel's Broiler | **multi.** 24

Z El Gaucho | **Belltown** 25

Z Georgian | **Dwtn** 26

Z Herbfarm, The | **Woodinville** 28

Hunt Club | **First Hill** 22

Inn at Ship Bay | **Eastsound** –

Joule | **Wallingford** 26

Local Vine | **Cap Hill** –

Maxwell's Restaurant | **Tacoma** –

Z Metro. Grill | **Dwtn** 26

Morton's | **Dwtn** 25

Z Ray's Boathse. | **Shilshole** 24

Z Rover's | **Madison Vly** 28

Ruth's Chris | **Dwtn** 24

Z Salish Lodge | **Snoqualmie** 23

Z Seastar | **multi.** 25

Volterra | **Ballard** 25

Willows Inn | **Lummi Island** –

WATERSIDE

Agua Verde | **Univ Dist** 23

Z Anthony's HomePort | **multi.** 21

Anthony's Pier 66 | **Seattle Waterfront** 22

Z Aqua by El Gaucho | **Seattle Waterfront** 25

Beach Cafe | **Kirkland** 19

Bell St. Diner | **Seattle Waterfront** 23

Bin on Lake | **Kirkland** 20

Bluff | **Friday Harbor** –

BluWater | **multi.** 16

Z Cactus | **W Seattle** 22

Chandler's Crab | **S Lake Union** 23

Chinook's | **Magnolia** 21

Z Daniel's Broiler | **multi.** 24

Dash Pt./Lobster Shop | **Tacoma** 23

Duke's | **multi.** 19

Z Elliott's Oyster | **Seattle Waterfront** 24

I Love Sushi | **S Lake Union** 22

Inn at Ship Bay | **Eastsound** –

Ivar's/Clams | **Seattle Waterfront** 21

Ivar's Mukilteo | **Mukilteo** 21

Ivar's Salmon | **Lake Union** 21

NEW Madison Park Conserv. | **Madison Pk** –

Maggie Bluff's | **Magnolia** 19

Oyster Bar/Chuckanut | **Bow** 25

Z Palisade | **Magnolia** 24

Ponti Seafood | **Queen Anne** 24

Z Ray's Boathse. | **Shilshole** 24

Ray's Cafe | **Shilshole** 22

Red Robin | **Issaquah** 16

Salty's | **multi.** 20

Z Six Seven | **Seattle Waterfront** 23

WINNING WINE LISTS

Alki Bakery | **Kent** 21

Allium | **Eastsound** –

Anchovies/Olives | **Cap Hill** 25

Z Anthony's HomePort | **multi.** 21

Anthony's Pier 66 | **Seattle Waterfront** 22

Art Rest. | **Dwtn** 23

Z Barking Frog | **Woodinville** 25

Barolo | **Dwtn** 24

Bin on Lake | **Kirkland** 20

Bis on Main | **Bellevue** 24

Brad's Swingside | **Fremont** 25

Brass. Marg. | **Dwtn** 16

Z Cafe Campagne | **Pike Place** 26

Z Cafe Juanita | **Kirkland** 28

Z Canlis | **Lake Union** 27

Chez Shea/Lounge | **Pike Place** 26

Copperleaf | **SeaTac** –

Z Corson Bldg. | **Georgetown** 28

Z Crush | **Madison Vly** 25

NEW Cuoco | **S Lake Union** –

Z Dahlia Lounge | **Dwtn** 26

Z Daniel's Broiler | **multi.** 24

Earth & Ocean | **Dwtn** 22

Elemental | **Lake Union** 26

Eva | **Green Lk** 26

Flying Fish | **S Lake Union** 24

Four Swallows | **Bainbridge Is** 26

Z Georgian | **Dwtn** 26

Grazie | **multi.** 22

Z Harvest Vine | **Madison Vly** 27

Z Herbfarm, The | **Woodinville** 28

Hill's Food & Wine | **Shoreline** 20

Hunt Club | **First Hill** 22

Il Bistro | **Pike Place** 23

Inn at Ship Bay | **Eastsound** –

Le Gourmand | **Ballard** 26

Le Pichet | **Pike Place** 25

Local Vine | **Cap Hill** –

Z Lola | **Dwtn** 25

Mamma Melina | **Univ Vill** 23

NEW Marché | **Pike Place** –

Z Metro. Grill | **Dwtn** 26

Monsoon | **Cap Hill** 25

Morton's | **Dwtn** 25

Z Nell's | **Green Lk** 27

Osteria La Spiga | **Cap Hill** 23

Poco Wine | **Cap Hill** 19

Portalis Wine Bar | **Ballard** –

Purple Café | **multi.** 20

Queen City Grill | **Belltown** 21

Z Ray's Boathse. | **Shilshole** 24

Z Rover's | **Madison Vly** 28

Russell's | **Bothell** 20

Ruth's Chris | **Dwtn** 24

Z Salish Lodge | **Snoqualmie** 23

Z Seastar | **Bellevue** 25

Tango | **Cap Hill** 20

Tavolàta | **Belltown** 25

Voilà! Bistrot | **Madison Vly** 21

Volterra | **Ballard** 25

Z Wild Ginger | **multi.** 25

Willows Inn | **Lummi Island** –

WORTH A TRIP

Bainbridge Island

- Four Swallows 26
- Hitchcock –

Bow

- Oyster Bar/Chuckanut 25

Eastsound

- Allium –
- Inn at Ship Bay –

Langley, Whidbey Island

- Inn at Langley 26

Lummi Island

- Willows Inn –

Snoqualmie

- Z Salish Lodge 23

Tacoma

- Pacific Grill 26

Woodinville

- Z Herbfarm, The 28

Wine Vintage Chart

This chart is based on a 30-point scale. The ratings (by U. of South Carolina law professor **Howard Stravitz**) reflect vintage quality and the wine's readiness to drink. A dash means the wine is past its peak or too young to rate. Loire ratings are for dry whites.

Whites	95	96	97	98	99	00	01	02	03	04	05	06	07	08	09	10
France:																
Alsace	24	23	23	25	23	25	26	22	21	22	23	21	26	26	23	26
Burgundy	27	26	22	21	24	24	23	27	23	26	26	25	26	25	25	-
Loire Valley	-	-	-	-	-	-	-	25	20	22	27	23	24	24	24	25
Champagne	26	27	24	25	25	25	21	26	21	-	-	-	-	-	-	-
Sauternes	21	23	25	23	24	24	29	24	26	21	26	25	27	24	27	-
California:																
Chardonnay	-	-	-	-	22	21	24	25	22	26	29	24	27	23	27	-
Sauvignon Blanc	-	-	-	-	-	-	-	-	-	25	24	27	25	24	25	-
Austria:																
Grüner V./Riesl.	22	-	25	22	26	22	23	25	25	24	23	26	25	24	25	-
Germany:	22	26	22	25	24	-	29	25	26	27	28	26	26	26	26	-

Reds	95	96	97	98	99	00	01	02	03	04	05	06	07	08	09	
France:																
Bordeaux	25	25	24	25	24	29	26	24	26	25	28	24	24	25	27	-
Burgundy	26	27	25	24	27	22	23	25	25	23	28	24	24	25	27	-
Rhône	26	22	23	27	26	27	26	-	26	25	27	25	26	23	27	-
Beaujolais	-	-	-	-	-	-	-	-	-	-	27	25	24	23	28	25
California:																
Cab./Merlot	27	24	28	23	25	-	27	26	25	24	26	24	27	26	25	-
Pinot Noir	-	-	-	-	-	-	26	25	24	25	26	24	27	24	26	-
Zinfandel	-	-	-	-	-	-	25	24	26	24	23	21	26	23	25	-
Oregon:																
Pinot Noir	-	-	-	-	-	-	-	26	24	25	24	25	24	27	24	-
Italy:																
Tuscany	25	24	29	24	27	24	27	-	24	27	25	26	25	24	-	-
Piedmont	21	27	26	25	26	28	27	-	24	27	26	26	27	26	-	-
Spain:																
Rioja	26	24	25	22	25	24	28	-	23	27	26	24	24	25	26	-
Ribera del Duero/ Priorat	25	26	24	25	25	24	27	-	24	27	26	24	25	27	-	-
Australia:																
Shiraz/Cab.	23	25	24	26	24	24	26	26	25	25	26	21	23	26	24	-
Chile:	-	-	-	-	24	22	25	23	24	24	27	25	24	26	24	-
Argentina:																
Malbec	-	-	-	-	-	-	-	-	-	25	26	27	26	26	25	-

ZAGAT

Seattle Transit Map

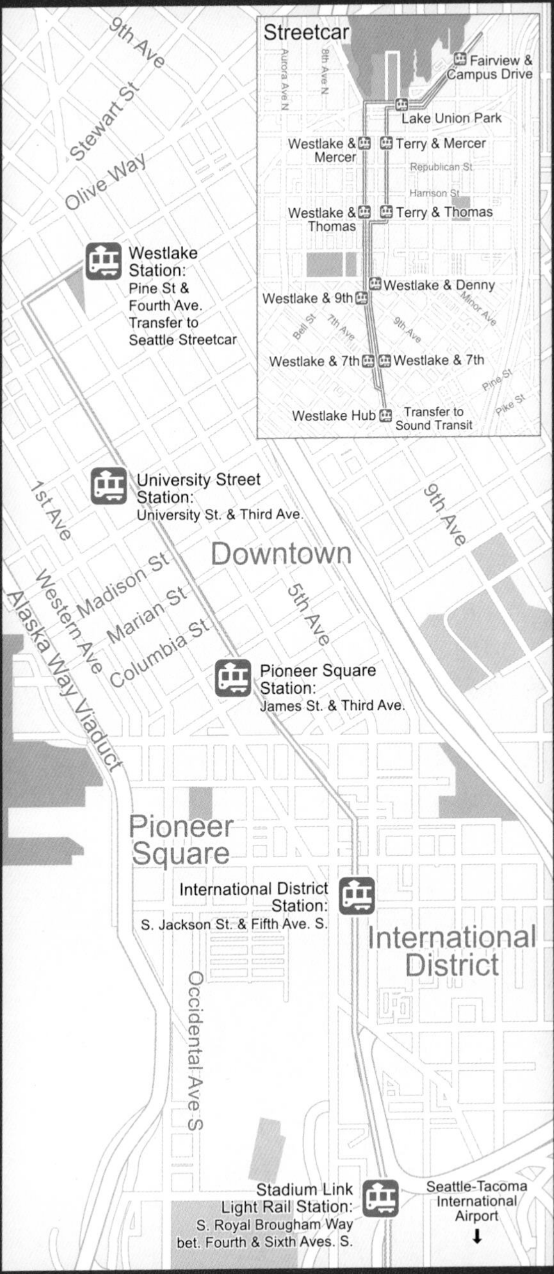

Streetcar
Aurora Ave N
8th Ave N
Fairview & Campus Drive
Lake Union Park
Westlake & Mercer
Terry & Mercer
Republican St
Harrison St
Westlake & Thomas
Terry & Thomas
Westlake & Denny
Minor Ave
Westlake & 9th
Bell St
7th Ave
9th Ave
Westlake & 7th
Westlake & 7th
Pine St
Pike St
Westlake Hub
Transfer to Sound Transit
9th Ave
Stewart St
Olive Way
Westlake Station:
Pine St & Fourth Ave.
Transfer to Seattle Streetcar
University Street Station:
University St. & Third Ave.
1st Ave
9th Ave
Downtown
Madison St
Marian St
Columbia St
5th Ave
Western Ave
Alaska Way Viaduct
Pioneer Square Station:
James St. & Third Ave.
Pioneer Square
International District Station:
S. Jackson St. & Fifth Ave. S.
International District
Occidental Ave S
Stadium Link Light Rail Station:
S. Royal Brougham Way bet. Fourth & Sixth Aves. S.
Seattle-Tacoma International Airport

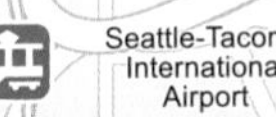

Seattle's Most Popular Restaurants

Map coordinates follow each name. Sections A-G show downtown Seattle (see adjacent map). Sections H-N show Bellevue and outlying regions (see reverse side of map).

1. Wild Ginger (E-2)
2. Dahlia Lounge (D-1)
3. Canlis (K-3)
4. Cafe Juanita (I-5)
5. Rover's (B-6)
6. Metropolitan Grill (F-2)
7. Cafe Campagne (E-1)
8. Etta's (E-1)
9. Ray's Boathouse (J-1)
10. Serious Pie (B-2, D-1)
11. Bakery Nouveau (N-2)
12. Anthony's HomePort† (J-1)
13. Il Terrazzo Carmine (G-2)
14. Herbfarm (H-7)
15. Matt's in the Market (E-2)
16. El Gaucho† (D-1)
17. Seastar (C-2, L-5)
18. Tilth (J-3)
19. Lola (D-2)
20. Barking Frog (H-6)
21. Lark* (E-4)
22. Jak's Grill† (J-4)
23. Salumi (G-3)
24. Daniel's Broiler† (B-2)
25. Elliott's Oyster (F-1)
26. Crush (C-6)
27. Steelhead Diner (E-1)
28. Cactus† (K-4)
29. Purple Café† (E-2)
30. Ruth's Chris (D-2, L-5)
31. 13 Coins (C-2, N-3)
32. Flying Fish (C-2)
33. Palace Kitchen (D-2)
34. McCormick/Schmick (F-2, L-5)
35. Nishino* (A-7)
36. Le Pichet (E-1)
37. Poppy (B-4)
38. La Carta/Mezcal (J-2, K-2)
39. Harvest Vine (B-6)

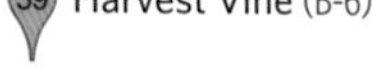

40. Monsoon (B-5, L-5)

*Indicates tie with above

† Indicates multiple branches

N 155th St
NE 145th St
523
5
522
N 130th St
NE 125th St
Lake City
Northgate
522
35th Ave NE
Sand Point Way NE
5th Ave NE
Lake City Way NE
NE 95th St
99
N 85th St
Pontiac Bay
15th Ave NE
12th Ave NE
35th Ave NE
40th Ave NE
Warren G Maguson Park
5
18
22
Wolf Bay
University District
Stone Way N
Union Bay
520
Evergreen Point Floating Bridge
28
Madison Park
5
24th Ave E
15th Ave E
Capitol Hill
Aurora Ave N
South Lake Union
Lake Washington
Denny Way
Broadway
12th Ave
23rd Ave
34th Ave
E Cherry St
Seattle
S Jackson St
Int'l Dist.
90
90
Interstate 90 Express
Alaskan Way Viaduct
1st Avenue South
5
23rd Ave S
Beacon Ave S
Mercer
Airport Way S
50th Ave S
31
15th Ave S
Wilson
S Orcas St

5
6
7
20
14
Woodinville
202
NE 132nd St
4
NE 124th St
NE 124th St
NE 116th St
nita Bay
124th Ave NE
132nd Ave NE
Willows Rd NE
NE 104th St
202
Kirkland
NE 95th St
NE 90th St
908
Redmond
908
Moss Bay
6th St S
202
520
Lakeview Dr
108th Ave NE
148th Ave NE
Marymoor Park
140th Ave NE
Bridle Trails State Park
Bel-Red Rd
520
520
520
92nd Ave NE
100th Ave
405
30
34
1
Bel Red Rd
Northup Way
116th Ave NE
40
17
NE 8th St
148th Ave NE
Bellevue
Main St
140th Ave SE
156th Ave SE
Weowna Beach Park
148th Ave SE
Mercer Slough Nature Park
90
90
sland
90
164th Ave SE
Map data ©2011 Google, Sanborn
6
7